Selected awards won by *Frasier* from its debut in 1993 through the 1998-1999 season:

- Unprecedented five consecutive Emmy Awards for Outstanding Comedy Series

- Unprecedented three consecutive Television Critics Association Awards and three consecutive BANFF Television Festival Rockie Awards, a feat never accomplished in the seventeen-year history of that television festival

- Four consecutive Viewers for Quality Television (VQT) Awards

- Emmy Award for Outstanding Writing in a Comedy Series for "The Good Son"

- Awards from the Golden Globe, the Humanitas Prize, the Peabody

- Series star Kelsey Grammer has won three Emmy Awards for Outstanding Lead Actor in a Comedy Series, and David Hyde Pierce as Dr. Niles Crane has won two Emmy Awards for Outstanding Supporting Actor in a Comedy Series

THE

FRASIER™

SCRIPTS

THE FRASIER™ SCRIPTS

Created by
David Angell/Peter Casey/David Lee

Introduction by
Christopher Lloyd

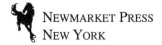
NEWMARKET PRESS
NEW YORK

10   9   8   7   6   5   4   3   2   1

Library of Congress Cataloging-in-Publication Data

The Frasier scripts/created by David Angell/Peter Casey/David Lee: introduction by Christopher Lloyd.
       p. cm.
     ISBN 1-55704-403-1 (pb)
     1. Frasier (Television program)
  PN1992.77.F72F73   1999
  791.45'72--dc21   99–28512
                                         CIP

QUANTITY PURCHASES
Companies, professional groups, clubs, and other organizations may qualify for special terms when ordering quantities of this title. For information, write Special Sales, Newmarket Press, 18 East 48th Street, New York, NY 10017, call (212) 832-3575, or fax (212) 832-3629.

Designed by Timothy Shaner for Night & Day Design

Manufactured in the United States of America.

Contents

Introduction

Twenty-four Wednesdays every year, about sixty people gather in a conference room at Paramount Studios in Hollywood. Among these sixty are an affable, rambunctious five. These are the cast of *Frasier*. Also among them are an ashen, nail-biting ten. This is the writing staff of *Frasier*.

The occasion is the "table reading." This is the first reading aloud of that week's *Frasier* script by the cast. The episode won't be shot until the following Tuesday, after five days of rehearsal and rewriting, a honing process that can result in the script being overhauled entirely (hence the nail biting and ashening of faces). But the table reading sets the tone for the week and also marks that time when the script ceases to be merely words on a page and becomes a living thing, a play.

As at most such births, a range of emotions is on display: fear, joy, laughter, tears. And not all the babies are beautiful. Some are flabby, or misshapen, or just too long. But every now and then there's one that's just right. Certainly that was the case with the fifteen shows in this volume.

Something about each one – whether it was the particular story we were telling, or the way we were telling it – just struck a nerve with everyone. So with this book you have the ability to imagine yourself at those fifteen charmed table readings. You simply need to summon the glorious baritone of Kelsey Grammer, the flinty counterpoint of David Hyde Pierce, the rasp of John Mahoney, the airy lilt of Jane Leeves, and the smoky twang of Peri Gilpin and you've got all the tools you need.

Frasier has, in its way, been charmed since the start. "The Good Son," the pilot script for the show, had a lot to do with that. The table reading for that show was in fact the first time all five cast members had been in the same room together and so there was a natural trepidation about what sort of chemistry there would be. But by the time Kelsey Grammer and David Hyde Pierce had played their first scene together (and since we are talking about chemistry, I will even be scientific enough to pinpoint the exact moment; it's when Frasier says: "When was the last time you had an unexpressed thought?" to which Niles responds: "I'm having one now"), there was little doubt that these two would be brilliant together.

In fact all the actors worked brilliantly together, and not just in the comedic scenes. Toward the end of the second act Martin (John Mahoney) and Frasier finally have the confrontation that has been brewing since the start and it's a long, angry, mean, and very true-sounding fight. That doesn't happen in sitcoms very often. It happens in pilot scripts even less, the thinking presumably being that if you are trying to get an audience to like these people, perhaps having them say harsh hurtful things to each other for a *long* time isn't the best way to do that. But the scene played beautifully, and it taught us as writers that we never had to shy away from a dramatic scene – these actors would make such scenes compelling, even in the framework of a comedy. I think what the scene ultimately taught the audience was that this was a program which promised not just to be funny, but also perhaps to be poignant and true.

One hundred and fifty episodes later we are still trying to deliver on that promise: to be funny, first, but also to be true to these characters, to explore their wants and needs in ways that occasionally achieve something like poignancy. The other scripts in this book represent various approaches we've taken to that end. There's flat-out farce ("The Matchmaker," "The Ski Lodge") and old-fashioned romantic comedy ("Mixed Doubles"). There's also swashbuckling ("An Affair To Forget"), dancing ("Moon Dance"), parody ("Slow Tango in South Seattle"), and something akin to a silent movie ("Three Valentines"). It has always been a point of pride at *Frasier* that we can write – or perhaps more properly, that the vast talent of our actors allows us to write – in a broad range of styles and this book should demonstrate that. Many of these scripts have won individual awards for writing and all have been instrumental in *Frasier*'s winning the Emmy Award for best comedy an unprecedented five years consecutively.

It should be noted that while each of these scripts is credited to an individual or team of writers, each was in fact was contributed to greatly by the entire *Frasier* writing staff. That's our system: we figure out the stories together, and we polish the scripts together. It's a sometimes-rancorous process. Ten people swinging hammers at the same piece of bronze trying to make a beautiful sculpture will almost surely result in some hurt fingers. But something about our process may be uniquely suited to the creation of *Frasier*, for *Frasier* is, at its root, the story of a family, a family which struggles—collaborates clumsily—but which in the end survives, one might even say thrives. We enjoyed writing these scripts and we hope you enjoy reading them.

Christopher Lloyd
Executive Producer of *Frasier*

The cast at the beginning of season six: Dan Butler (Bulldog Brisco), Peri Gilpin (Roz Doyle), John Mahoney (Martin Crane), Kelsey Grammer (Frasier Crane) and Moose (Eddie), David Hyde Pierce (Niles Crane), and Jane Leeves (Daphne Moon).

The real star of the show. (At least he thinks he is.)

The Cast

Frasier Crane . . . . Kelsey Grammer
Martin Crane . . . . John Mahoney
Niles Crane . . . . David Hyde Pierce
Daphne Moon . . . . Jane Leeves
Roz Doyle . . . . Peri Gilpin
Bulldog Brisco . . . . Dan Butler
Eddie . . . . Moose

Additional Cast Members

The Good Son
Russell (v.o.) . . . . Griffin Dunne
Waitress . . . . Gina Ravarra
Deliveryman . . . . Cleto Augusto
Claire (v.o.) . . . . Linda Hamilton

Call Me Irresponsible
Hank (v.o.) . . . . Eddie Van Halen
Marco (v.o.) . . . . Bruno Kirby
Catherine . . . . Amanda Donohoe

A Midwinter Night's Dream
Eric . . . . Dean Erickson

Slow Tango in South Seattle
Steven (v.o.) . . . . James Spader
Thomas Jay Fallow . . . . John O'Hurley
Amber Edwards . . . . Susan Brown
Gil Chesterton . . . . Edward Hibbert
Mrs. Warner . . . . Myra Carter
Clarice . . . . Constance Towers
Man . . . . David Sederholm

The Matchmaker

Tom O'Connor . . . . Eric Lutes

An Affair to Forget

Gretchen (v.o.) . . . . Glenne Headley
Marta . . . . Irene Olga Lopez
Gunnar . . . . Brian Cousins

Moon Dance

Lacey Lloyd . . . . Christine McGraw
Andrew Lloyd . . . . Hank Stratton
Conductor . . . . Michael G. Hawkins
Claire Barnes . . . . Nancy Stafford

The Two Mrs. Cranes

Gil Chesterton . . . . Edward Hibbert
Clive . . . . Scott Atkinson

Mixed Doubles

Adelle . . . . Allison MacKie
Rodney . . . . Kevin Farrell

Ham Radio

Gil Chesterton . . . . Edward Hibbert
Ian . . . . Jack Betts
Mel White . . . . Richard Easton
Noel Shempsky . . . . Patrick Kerry
Maxine . . . . Hope Allen

Perspectives on Christmas

Masseur . . . . Albert Macklin
Albert . . . . Conrad Janis
Doris . . . . Brooks Almy
Jane . . . . Marilyn O'Connor
Woman . . . . Jennifer Williams
Man . . . . Mark Capri
Sally . . . . Jamie Alexis
Billy . . . . J. B. Gaynor
Vic . . . . Zachary McLemore

Room Service

Lilith . . . . Bebe Neuwirth
Waiter . . . . John Ducey
Betsy (v.o.) . . . . Hale Berry

The Ski Lodge

Annie . . . . Cynthia Lamontagne
Guy James . . . . Patrick Stuart
Connie . . . . Lisa Robinson

Three Valentines

Cassandra Stone . . . . Virginia Madsen
Violinist . . . . Peter Waldman
Mario . . . . Armando Molina
Maître d' . . . . Dan Kern
Waiter . . . . Lawrence Lowe

Season One

The Good Son

Call Me Irresponsible

A Midwinter Night's Dream

The Good Son

Episode #60181-098

Created and Written by
David Angell/Peter Casey/David Lee

Directed by
James Burrows

Frasier in his new home, the KACL Radio Studio . . .

. . . and Martin in his – his beloved BarcaLounger in Frasier's flat.

ACT ONE

Scene A

A black screen. In white letters appears "The Job."

Man #1 (V.O.)
I'm a long-time listener, first-time caller. My problem began when I . . .

FADE IN:
MONTAGE – (V.O.'S) – DAY/1
INT. CAB – DAY
A cabbie is listening to his radio.

Woman #1 (V.O.)
I don't know him anymore. It's like living with a stranger. Take yesterday . . .

CROSS FADE TO:
INT. KITCHEN – DAY
A messy kitchen, a frazzled housewife, and a screaming infant in a highchair. The radio is on.

Woman #1 (V.O.)
At least I thought I had a normal childhood. Aw, hell, who knows what's normal anymore. I . . .

CROSS FADE TO:
EXT. PARK – DAY
A man jogs in the park. He's listening to his walkman.

Woman #2 (V.O.) *(blubbering)*
I'm sorry, I thought I had this under control. I, I, I . . . Give me a minute.

The jogger rolls his eyes.

CROSS FADE TO:
EXT. NEWSSTAND – DAY
A newsstand, featuring a portable radio next to the cash register. A coat hangar is used as an antenna.

Woman #3 (V.O.) *(thick Middle Eastern accent)*
I tell him, "I'm a human being. I'm a human being. You can't treat me like a dog." You've got to help me, Dr. Crane.

CROSS FADE TO:

Scene B

INT. RADIO STUDIO – DAY – DAY/1

Frasier, Roz, Russell (v.o.)

KACL – a typical radio studio: two rooms separated by a glass partition and a door. On one side, **Frasier Crane** *is seated at a desk with a multiline phone and microphone. He is wearing headphones. On the other side of the glass is his call screener,* **Roz Doyle***. Another glass partition in the studio looks out into the hallway. The lights are low. Frasier is in the middle of answering a caller.*

> **Frasier** *(firmly, with concern)*
> Listen to yourself, Bob. You follow her to work. You eavesdrop on her calls. You open her mail. The minute you started doing those things, the relationship was over. Thank you for your call.

He punches a button on the console.

> **Frasier** *(cont'd)*
> Roz, do we have time for one more?

Roz *speaks into the microphone in the booth in a soothing radio voice.*

> **Roz**
> Yes, Dr. Crane. On line four we have Russell from Kirkland. He feels like he's caught in a rut.

Frasier *pushes a button on the phone.*

> **Frasier**
> This is Dr. Frasier Crane. I'm listening.

> **Russell** (v.o.)
> Well, I've been feeling, sort of, you know, depressed lately.

> **Frasier**
> For how long?

> **Russell** (v.o.)
> Oh, the last seven or eight years.

> **Frasier**
> Go on.

> **Russell** (v.o.)
> I don't know, my life's not going anywhere. It's not that it's bad. It's just the same old apartment, the same old job, the same old people, day after day. Sometimes I just . . .

Roz *signals from the booth that time is running short and* **Frasier** *has to wrap this up.*

> **Frasier**
> Russell, we're nearing the end of our hour. Let me see if I can cut to

the chase by using myself as an example. Six months ago I was living in Boston. My wife had left me, which was very painful, then she came back, which was excruciating. I thought I could look past her indiscretion but I was only kidding myself. On top of that, my practice had grown stagnant and my social life consisted of hanging around a bar night after night. Suddenly I realized I was clinging to a life that wasn't working anymore. I knew I had to do something, anything. So I put an end to the marriage and moved back here to my hometown of Seattle. Go Seahawks! I took action, Russell and you can too. Move, change, do something. If it's a mistake, do something else. Will you do that, Russell? Will you? Russell? *(turning to Roz)* I think we lost him.

Roz
No, we cut to the news about thirty seconds ago.

Frasier *takes off his headset, gets up, and heads into* **Roz**'s *control room.*

Frasier
Oh, for crying out loud. I finally bare my soul to all of Seattle and they're listening to "Chopper Dave's Rush-Hour Roundup"? At least the rest of the show was good. *(then)* It was a good show, wasn't it?

Roz
Here. *(hands him a slip of paper)* Your brother called.

Frasier
You know, in the trade, we call that avoidance. Don't change the subject. What did you think?

She points to her console.

Roz
Did I ever show you what this button does?

Frasier
I'm not a piece of Lalique. I can handle criticism. How was I today?

Roz
Let's see. You dropped two commercials, you left a total of twenty-eight seconds of dead air, you scrambled the station's call letters, you spilled yogurt on the control board, and you kept referring to Jerry with the identity crisis as "Jeff."

Frasier *(pause)*
You say my brother called.

CUT TO:

Scene C
A black screen. In white letters appears "The Brother."

Niles (V.O.)

So I said to the gardener, "Yoshi, I do not need a Zen garden in my backyard.

FADE IN:

EXT. SEATTLE STREET – DAY – DAY/1 – 2ND UNIT

Niles (V.O.)

A city bus is stopped, picking up passengers. On the side of the bus is a large advertisement. On it is **Frasier's** *smiling face and the words "Dr. Frasier Crane. He listens. KACL – 780 am." The bus pulls away to reveal "Cafe Nervosa," one of Seattle's popular coffee houses.*

Niles (V.O.) *(cont'd)*

If I want to rake gravel every ten minutes to maintain my inner harmony, I'll move to Yokohama."

CUT TO:

INT. COFFEE HOUSE – CONTINUOUS – DAY/1

Niles, Frasier, Waitress, Extras

Frasier *and his brother,* **Dr. Niles Crane**, *stand at the counter.* **Frasier** *has his nose in a menu.*

Niles *(cont'd)*

Well, this offends him so he starts pulling up Maris's prized camellias by the handful. I couldn't stand for that, so I marched right into the morning room and locked the door until he cooled down. Tell me you would have handled it differently, Frasier.

After a beat, **Frasier** *looks up.*

Frasier

Oh, I'm sorry, Niles, I didn't realize you'd stopped talking.

Niles

You haven't heard a word I said.

Frasier

Niles, you're a psychiatrist. You know what it's like to listen to people prattling on endlessly about their mundane lives.

Niles

Touché. And on that subject, I heard your show today.

Frasier

And?

Niles

You know what I think about pop psychiatry.

Frasier

Yes, yes, I know what you think about everything. When was the last time you had an unexpressed thought?

Niles

I'm having one now.

They both chuckle good-naturedly. A **Waitress** *approaches.*

Waitress

You guys ready?

Frasier *(to waitress)*

Two cafe latte supremos.

Niles *moves to a chair and begins to dust it off with a handkerchief. He offers it to* **Frasier**.

Frasier *(cont'd)*

No, thank you.

Niles

So, Frasier, how are you doing on your own?

Frasier

I'm fine. I love my new life. I love the solitude. I miss Frederick like the dickens, of course. He's quite a boy. He's playing goalie on the pee wee soccer team now. He's a chip off the old block.

Niles

You hated sports.

Frasier

And so does he, but the fresh air's good for him.

They both laugh at this.

Niles

This has been fun, Frasier, but we have a problem. That's why I thought we should talk.

Frasier

Is it Dad?

Niles

I'm afraid so. One of his old buddies from the police force called this morning. He went over to see him. Found him on the bathroom floor.

Frasier

Oh my God.

Niles

No, it's okay, he's fine.

Frasier

What? His hip again?

Niles nods.

Niles

Frasier, I don't think he can live alone anymore.

Frasier

What can we do?

Niles

Well, I know this isn't going to be anyone's favorite solution, but I took the liberty of checking out a few convalescent homes for him.

He reaches into his briefcase and takes out a pile of pamphlets.

Frasier

A home? He's still a young man.

Niles

Well, you certainly can't take care of him. You're just getting your new life together.

Frasier

Absolutely. Besides, we've never been sympatico. I remember a car trip as a child. We drove from Seattle to Spokane and the only thing he said to me was, "I think we've got a problem with your brother, Frasier."

Niles

Yes, well, and, of course, I can't take care of him.

Frasier

Yes, of course, of course. *(beat)* Why?

Niles

Dad doesn't get along with Maris.

Frasier

Who does?

Niles

I thought you liked my Maris.

Frasier

I do. I like her from a distance. You know, the way you like the sun. Maris is like the sun . . . except without the warmth.

Niles

Well then, I guess we're agreed on what to do with Dad.

Niles *picks up a pamphlet from the table.*

Niles *(cont'd) (reading)*

"Golden Acres. We care so you don't have to."

Frasier

It says that?

Niles

It might as well.

Frasier *(resigned)*

Alright, I'll make up the guest room.

Niles

You're a good son, Frasier.

Frasier

Oh God, I am, aren't I?

Frasier *buries his head in his hands as* **Niles** *comforts him. The* **Waitress** *brings them their coffee.*

Waitress

Two cafe supremos. Anything to eat?

Frasier

No. I've lost my appetite.

Niles

I'll have a large piece of cheesecake.

CUT TO:

Scene D

A black screen. In white letters appears "The Father."

FADE IN:

INT. FRASIER'S LIVING ROOM – DAY – DAY/2

Frasier, Niles, Martin, Deliveryman

It's a smart, clean, meticulously decorated condo. The furnishings lean toward the contemporary, with well chosen pieces of art and sculpture. Center is a view of the Seattle skyline. There is a knock at the door. **Frasier,** *at the piano, goes to the door. He steels himself and opens the door.* **Niles** *is standing there with a few suitcases in his hand.*

Niles

We finally made it.

Niles *enters followed by their father,* **Martin**, *using a walker.*

Frasier
Ah, Dad, welcome to your new home. You look great.

Martin
Don't B.S. me. I do not look great. I spent Monday on the bathroom floor. You can still see the tile marks on my face.

Niles *(sotto to Frasier)*
Gives you some idea about the ride over in the car.

Frasier *claps his hands and rubs them together, trying to lighten the moment.*

Frasier
Well, here we are. Now, Dad, rest assured the refrigerator is stocked with your favorite beer, Ballantines, and we've got plenty of hot links and coleslaw. I even rented a Charles Bronson movie for later.

Martin
You can cut the "Welcome to Camp Crane" speech. We all know why I'm here. Your old man can't be trusted to be alone for ten minutes without falling on his ass, and Frasier got stuck with me. Isn't that right?

Frasier *and* **Niles** *look at each other.*

Frasier/Niles
No, no, no.

Frasier *(cont'd)*
I want you here. It will give us an opportunity to get reacquainted.

Martin
That implies we were acquainted at one point.

Niles
Listen, why don't I take Dad's things into his new "bachelor quarters" so you two scoundrels can plan some hijinx?

Niles *exits with the bags down the hallway to the bedroom.*

Martin
I think that wife of his is making him nutso.

Frasier
Yes, we Crane boys sure know how to marry, don't we? *(Then)* Dad, let me get you a beer.

Frasier *crosses to the kitchen.* **Martin** *looks around the room.*

Frasier *(cont'd)*

So, do you like what I've done with the place? Every piece was carefully chosen. The lamp, Corbu. The chair by Eames. This sofa is an exact replica of the one Coco Chanel had in her Paris atelier.

Martin

Nothing matches.

Frasier

It's a style of decorating. It's called eclectic. The theory behind it is, if you have great pieces of furniture, it doesn't matter if they match. They'll go together.

Martin

It's your money.

Martin *walks over to the window and gazes at the skyline.*

SFX: the doorbell rings.

Frasier

Great view, isn't it? *(indicating)* That's the Space Needle over there.

Martin

Thank you for pointing that out. Being born and raised here, I never would have known that.

As **Niles** *reenters from the other room,* **Frasier** *crosses to the door and opens it. It's a* **Deliveryman**.

Deliveryman

Delivery for Martin Crane.

Martin

In here.

Deliveryman

Coming through.

Frasier *steps back. The* **Deliveryman** *brings in a Barcalounger.*

Frasier

Excuse me, excuse me. Wait a minute.

Deliveryman

Where do you want it?

Martin

Where's the TV?

Niles *(indicating)*

In that credenza.

Martin
Point it at that thing.

Deliveryman
What about this chair?

Niles
Here. Let me get it out of the way.

Niles *picks up the chair and moves it. The* **Deliveryman** *replaces it with* **Martin**'s *Barcalounger.*

Frasier
Careful. That's a Wassily. *(re: lounger)* Dad, Dad, as dear as I'm sure this piece is to you, I don't think it quite goes with anything here.

Martin
I know. It's eclectic.

Martin *pays the* **Deliveryman**. *He exits.*

Frasier
Niles, help me out here.

Martin
Sit in it, Frasier, it's really comfortable.

Frasier *grabs* **Niles** *by the shirt and pulls him aside.*

Frasier
I see what you're doing. You're agreeing with the old man because you're afraid he might ask to live with you and Maris.

Niles *(re: shirt)*
Please, Frasier, you're scrunching my Tommy Hilfiger.

Frasier
Listen, you little twit . . .

Martin
You're going to have to run an extension cord over here so I can plug in the vibrating part.

Frasier *(beaten)*
Yes, yes, that will be the crowning touch.

Niles
Now that you two are settled in, I've got to run. I'm late for my dysfunctional family seminar.

As he heads for the door:

Niles *(cont'd)*

Dad, have you mentioned Eddie yet?

Frasier *turns to* **Martin**.

Frasier *(panicked)*

Eddie?

Niles

Ta ta.

Niles *exits.*

Frasier

Oh, Dad, no. Not Eddie.

Martin

He's my best friend. Hand me my beer.

Frasier

But he's weird. He gives me the creeps. All he does is stare at me.

Martin

It's your imagination.

Frasier

No, Dad, no. I'm sorry, but I'm putting my foot down. Eddie's *not* moving in here.

Cut to:

Scene E

A black screen. In white letters appears the word, "Eddie."

Cross fade to:

INT. FRASIER'S LIVING ROOM – NIGHT – NIGHT/2

Martin, Frasier, Eddie

Martin *is sitting in his Barcalounger watching the Charles Bronson movie. We pan over to* **Frasier** *on his Coco couch. We continue the pan. Sitting next to* **Frasier** *is* **Eddie***, a small long-haired Jack Russell terrier.* **Eddie** *stares at* **Frasier**.

Fade out.

End of Act One

ACT TWO

Scene H

FADE IN:
INT. COFFEE HOUSE – DAY – DAY/3
Niles, Frasier, Extras
Niles *is there,* **Frasier** *rushes in.*

Frasier

Oh, Niles, there you are. Sorry I'm late. Just as I was leaving, Dad decided to fix lunch by the glow of a small kitchen fire. *(beat)* I tell you, this last week with Dad has been a living hell. When I'm there, I feel like my territory is being violated and when I'm away, I worry about what he's up to. My nerves are completely shot. I've got to do something to calm down. *(to Waitress)* Double espresso, please. *(to Niles)* You don't still have the brochures from those rest homes, do you?

Niles

Of course I do. You're forgetting Maris is five years older than I am. But do you really think that's necessary?

Frasier

I don't have a life anymore. Tuesday I gave up my tickets to the theater. Wednesday, it was the symphony.

Niles

That reminds me, weren't you going to the opera on Friday?

Frasier *takes two tickets out of his pocket.*

Frasier

Yes. Here.

Niles

Thank you. *(looking at tickets)* Die Fledermaus. Oh, well, they're free.

Frasier

Isn't there any way you and Maris . . .?

Niles

Funny you should mention that. Maris and I were just discussing this. We think we should do more to share the responsibility.

Frasier

You mean you'd take him?

Niles

Oh, dear God, no. But we'd be willing to help you pay for a home care worker.

Frasier

A what?

Niles

You know, someone who cooks, and cleans, and can help Dad with his physical therapy.

Frasier

Look, the last thing I need is someone else under foot.

Niles

No, no, someone part-time. That's the beauty of it. They'll only be there when you're not.

Frasier

These angels exist?

Niles

I know of an agency. Let me arrange to have them send a few over to meet you.

Frasier

Niles, I don't know how to thank you. I feel the overwhelming urge to hug you.

Niles

Remember what Mom always said. A handshake is as good as a hug.

Frasier

Wise woman.

They shake hands.

CUT TO:

Scene J

A black screen. In white letters appears "The Health Care Worker."

FADE IN:

MONTAGE

INT. HALLWAY OF FRASIER'S BUILDING – DAY – DAY/4

Frasier, Extras

A quick sequence of **Frasier** *bidding farewell to a number of applicants with pleasantries such as "Thank you very much," "You'll be hearing from us," "It's been a pleasure."*

RESET TO:

INT. HALLWAY – MOMENTS LATER – DAY/4

Frasier, Extras

Another applicant. She appears robust, kind, neatly dressed: the epitome of competence.

Frasier

I've never been more impressed with any human being in my entire life. It has truly been an honor to meet you.

Frasier *closes the door.*

Frasier *(cont'd)* (O.S.) *(blowing up)*:

Now what was wrong with that one?!!

The woman reacts and walks away.

RESET TO:

INT. FRASIER'S LIVING ROOM – DAY – DAY/4

Frasier, Martin, Eddie, Daphne

Martin

She was casing the joint.

Frasier

Casing the joint? She spent two years with Mother Teresa.

Martin

Well, if I were Mother Teresa, I'd check my jewelry box.

SFX: the doorbell rings.

Frasier

This is the last one. Can you at least try to keep an open mind?

Martin

I hate this whole stinking idea.

Frasier

There, was that so difficult?

Frasier opens the door to reveal **Daphne Moon***, an English working class woman in her mid- to late twenties. At this moment, she is reaching into her blouse and adjusting her bra.*

Daphne

Oh hello. Caught me with my hand in the biscuit tin. *(extending her hand)* I'm Daphne. Daphne Moon.

Frasier *(they shake)*

Frasier Crane. Won't you come in?

Daphne

Thank you.

She enters.

Frasier

This is my father, Martin Crane. Dad, this is Daphne Moon.

They exchange greetings.

Daphne *(re: Eddie)*

And who would this be?

Frasier

That is Eddie.

Martin

I call him Eddie Spaghetti.

Daphne

Oh, he likes pasta?

Martin

No, he has worms.

Frasier

Uh, have a seat, Miss Moon.

Daphne

Daphne. Thank you. *(re: Barcalounger)* Oh, will you look at that.
What a comfy chair. Like I always say, start with a good piece and
replace the rest *(indicating Frasier's furniture)* when you can afford it.

She smiles at **Frasier**. *So does* **Martin**.

Frasier

Uh, yes, well, um, Miss Moon, tell us a little about yourself.

Daphne

Well, I'm originally from Manchester, England.

Frasier

Oh really. Did you hear that, Dad?

Martin

I'm three feet away. There's nothing wrong with my hearing.

Daphne

I've only been in the U.S. for a few months but I have quite an
extensive background in home care and physical therapy, as you can
see from my résumé. I also . . .

She looks at **Martin**.

Daphne *(cont'd)*
You were a policeman, weren't you?

Martin
Yeah. How did you know?

Daphne
I must confess, I'm a bit psychic. Nothing big. Just little things I sense about people. It's not like I can pick the lottery. If I could, I wouldn't be talking to the likes of you two, now would I?

She laughs. **Martin** *finds that amusing.*

Frasier
Perhaps I should describe the duties around here. You would be responsible for . . .

Daphne *(to Frasier)*
Wait a minute, I'm getting something on you. You're a florist.

Frasier
No, I'm a psychiatrist.

Daphne
Well, it comes and goes. Usually it's strongest during my time of the month. Oh, I guess I let out a little secret there, didn't I?

Frasier
It's safe with us. *(checking watch)* Well, I think we've learned everything we need to know about you. And a dash extra. Thank you very much. We'll be in touch.

Daphne *(to Martin)*
You must be very proud of your son the psychiatrist.

Martin
Sons. Two sons. Two shrinks. They took after their mother, rest her soul. She was one too. It was quite a household. I couldn't scratch myself without being analyzed.

Daphne
We Brits don't believe much in psychiatry. I mean, isn't that what friends are for?

Frasier
That's very quaint.

Daphne *(to Eddie)*
You're a dog, aren't you?

Frasier

Well, we'll be calling you, Miss Moon.

Martin

Why wait? You're hired.

Daphne

Oh wonderful!

Frasier

Excuse me. Aren't we getting ahead of ourselves, here? I think we should discuss this. Privately.

Daphne

Oh, of course you should. I completely understand. I'll just pop into the loo. You do have one, don't you?

Frasier *(indicating)*

Yes.

Daphne

I love America.

Daphne *exits.*

Frasier

Dad, what do you think you're doing?

Martin

You wanted me to pick one . . . I picked one.

Frasier

But she's a kook. I don't like her.

Martin

What does it matter? She's only going to be here when you're not.

Frasier

Then what's my problem? *(calling)* Daphne.

Daphne *reenters.*

Frasier *(cont'd)*

You've been retained.

Daphne

Oh, wonderful. I had a premonition I would.

Frasier

Quelle surprise.

Daphne

I'll move my things in tomorrow.

Frasier

Wait a minute. Move in? There must be some misunderstanding. This isn't a live-in position.

Daphne

Oh dear. The lady at the agency said . . .

Frasier

Well, the lady at the agency was wrong. This is a part-time position. I'm afraid this just won't work out.

Frasier *starts to usher her out.*

Martin

Wait a minute, Frasier. I want to talk about this.

Frasier

Dad, there's nothing to discuss.

Daphne

You two need to talk. I'll pop back in here and enjoy some more of your African erotic art.

Daphne *heads for the bathroom.*

Martin

Check out the one over the towel rack. You gotta be young to try that.

Frasier

Perhaps it's best if you leave.

Daphne

Well, all right.

Frasier

We'll contact you. If not by telephone, then through the toaster.

She exits.

Frasier

I'm not having another person living in this house.

Martin

Give me one good reason why.

Frasier

Well, for one thing there's no room for her.

Martin

What about the room across the hall from mine?

Frasier

My study?! You expect me to give up my study? Where I read, where I do my most profound thinking?

Martin

Use the can like the rest of the world. *(then)* You'll adjust.

Frasier

I don't want to adjust. I've done enough adjusting. I'm in a new city, I have a new job, I'm freshly divorced, I'm separated from my little boy, which by itself would make me nuts, and now my father and his dog are living with me. I think that's enough on my plate. The whole idea of getting someone in here was to help ease my burden, not to add to it.

Martin

Did you hear that, Eddie? We're a burden.

Frasier

Dad, you're twisting my words. I meant burden in its most positive sense.

Martin

Oh, as in "Gee what a lovely burden"?

Frasier

Something like that, yes.

Martin

Hey, you're not the only one getting screwed here. Two years ago I'm sailing toward retirement and some punk robbing a convenience store puts a bullet in my hip. Next thing you know, I'm trading my golf clubs in for one of these. *(He holds up the walker)* I had a lot of plans too, you know, and this may come as a shock, Sonny Boy, but one of them wasn't living with you.

Frasier

I'm just trying to do the right thing here, trying to be the good son.

Martin

Oh, don't worry, after I'm gone, you can live guilt-free knowing that you've done right by your papa.

Frasier

That's what you think this is all about, guilt?

Martin

Isn't it?

Frasier

Of course it is! But the point is, I did it. I took you in. And I've got news for you . . . I wanted to do it. Because you're my father. And you know how you repay me? Ever since you moved in here, it's been a snide comment about this or a smart little put-down about that. Well, I've done my best to make a new home for you here and once, just once, would it have killed you to say thank you? One lousy thank you?

There's a pause.

Martin
C'mon, Eddie. It's past your dinner time.

He and **Eddie** *exit to the kitchen.* **Frasier** *angrily exits, slamming the door behind him.*

Cut to:

Scene K

A black screen. In white letters appears "Lupe Velez."

Fade in:
INT. RADIO STUDIO – LATER THAT DAY – DAY/4
Frasier, Roz, Martin (v.o.), **Claire** (v.o.)
Frasier *comes blasting in to his booth.*

Frasier
They have got to move the bathroom closer to the studio!

He flings himself into the chair and puts on his headphones. **Roz** *points to him. He speaks into the microphone.*

Frasier *(cont'd)*
I'll be right back after these messages.

He punches a button on the console.

Frasier *(cont'd) (to Roz, irritated)*
Can't I just put that on tape?

Roz
Who stole the seat off your bicycle?

Frasier
Oh, sorry, it's this thing with my father and this person he wants to hire. . . . I thought I was starting my life over with a clean slate. I had this picture of the way things were going to be and then, I don't know . . .

Roz
Ever heard of Lupe Velez?

Frasier
Who?

Roz

Lupe Velez. The movie star in the thirties. The Mexican Spitfire.
Her career hit the skids so she decided to take one final stab at
immortality. She figured if she couldn't be remembered for her
movies, she'd be remembered for the way she died. And all Lupe
wanted was to be remembered. So she plans this lavish suicide.
Flowers, candles, silk sheets, white satin gown, full hair and make-
up, the works. She takes an overdose of pills, lays on the bed and
imagines how beautiful she's going to look on the front page of
tomorrow's newspaper. Unfortunately, the pills didn't set well with
the enchilada combo plate she sadly chose as her last meal. She
stumbles toward the bathroom, trips and falls head first into the toilet.
And that's how they found her.

Frasier

Is there a reason you're telling me this?

Roz

Yeah. Even though things may not happen like we planned, they can
work out anyway.

Frasier

Remind me again how it worked for Lupe, last seen with her head in
the toilet?

Roz

All she wanted was to be remembered. *(beat)* Will you ever forget
that story?

Roz *goes back into her booth, looks at the clock, and points at* **Frasier**.

Frasier

Welcome back. Roz, who's our next caller?

Roz

We have Martin on line one. He's having a problem with his son.

Frasier

Hello, Martin. This is Dr. Frasier Crane. I'm listening.

Martin (V.O.)

I'm a first-time caller.

Frasier *stiffens.*

Frasier

Welcome to the program. How can I help you?

Martin (V.O.)
I just moved in with my son and, uh, it ain't working. There's a lot of tension between us.

Frasier
I can imagine. Why do you think that's so?

Martin (V.O.)
I guess maybe I didn't see he had a nice new life planned out for himself and I kind of got in the way.

Frasier
You know these things are a two-way street. Perhaps your son wasn't sensitive enough to see how your life was changing.

Martin (V.O.)
You got that right. I've been telling him that ever since I got there.

Frasier
I'm sure he appreciated your candor.

Martin (V.O.)
But maybe sometimes I've got to learn to keep my trap shut.

Frasier
That's good advice for us all. Anything else?

Martin (V.O.)
I'm worried my son doesn't know that I really appreciate what he's done for me.

Frasier
Why don't you tell him?

Martin (V.O.)
You know how it is with fathers and sons. We always have a hard time saying that stuff.

Frasier
Well, if it helps, I suspect your son already knows how you feel.

There is a pause.

Frasier *(cont'd)*
Is that all?

Martin (V.O.)
I guess that's it. Thank you, Dr. Crane.

Frasier
My pleasure, Martin.

Martin (v.o.)
Did you hear what I said? I said, thank you.

Frasier
Yes, I heard.

Martin *hangs up.* **Frasier** *just sits there without saying anything.* **Roz** *interrupts.*

Roz
Uh, Dr. Crane? We have Claire on line four. She's having trouble getting over a breakup.

Frasier
Hello, Claire. I'm listening.

Claire (v.o.)
I'm, uh, well, I'm a mess. Eight months ago, my boyfriend and I broke up and I can't get over it. The pain isn't going away. It's almost like I'm in mourning.

Frasier
Claire, you are in mourning. But you're not mourning the loss of your boyfriend . . .

As Frasier continues the call, we:

CROSS FADE TO:

Scene L

INT. FRASIER'S LIVING ROOM – LATER THAT NIGHT – NIGHT/4
Frasier, Martin, Eddie, Daphne
We pan across the apartment to see **Frasier** *and his new "family" watching TV.* **Martin** *is sitting in his Barcalounger.* **Eddie, Frasier,** *and* **Daphne** *are sitting on the couch.*

Frasier (v.o.)
You're mourning what you thought your life was going to be. Let it go. Things don't always happen how you plan. It's not necessarily bad. It doesn't mean things won't work out anyway.

Eddie *puts one paw on* **Frasier***'s leg.*

Frasier *(cont'd)* (v.o.)
Have you ever heard of Lupe Velez?

FADE OUT.

End of Act Two

Daphne prepares Eddie for the Crane household Christmas photograph.

Frasier shares M&M's and sympathy with Catherine (guest star Amanda Donohoe).

Call Me Irresponsible

Episode #40571-006

Written by
Anne Flett-Giordano & Chuck Ranberg

Created by
David Angell/Peter Casey/David Lee

Directed by
James Burrows

ACT ONE

Scene A

A black screen. In white letters appears "If You Speak, They Will Listen."

FADE IN:

INT. RADIO STUDIO – DAY – DAY/1

Frasier, Roz, Hank (V.O.), **Marco** (V.O.)

Frasier *is on the air.*

Frasier

The time is four twenty-five and this is Dr. Frasier Crane. Roz, who's our next caller?

Roz

We have Hank on line three. He's having trouble with his neighbor.

Frasier

Go ahead, Hank. I'm listening.

There's a pause.

Hank (V.O.)

Am I on?

Frasier

Yes. I'm listening. *(pause)* Hank, are you there?

Hank (V.O.)

Am I on?

Frasier

Yes. Turn down your radio and just speak into the phone.

Hank (V.O.)

Hello?

Frasier

Stop trying to hear yourself. We're on a seven second delay.

Hank (V.O.)

Can you hear me?

Frasier *(disconnects call)*

Oh for crying out loud. People, would you please turn off your stupid radios?

He sees **Roz** *shaking her head.*

Frasier *(cont'd)*

I mean, just those of you calling in. Who else have we got, Roz?

Roz

On line two we have Marco. He's having relationship problems.

Frasier

Hello, Marco. I'm listening.

Marco (V.O.)

Well I . . . I started seeing this woman two years ago. I think it was two years ago . . . It was right around Thanksgiving . . . Yeah, the leaves on the trees were changing . . .

Frasier

Close enough. What's your problem?

Marco (V.O.)

It's not really my problem, it's more like her problem. Lately, she keeps pressing me for a commitment.

Frasier

Well, what's holding you back?

Marco (V.O.)

I don't know. I just . . . I guess I just want to keep my options open. You know, in case somebody better comes along?

Frasier

Somebody better comes along? Somebody better comes along? Marco, Marco, Marco! Do you hear yourself?

Marco (V.O.)

No, I turned my radio off after you blasted that other guy.

Frasier

I suggest you give your motives a thorough examination, and if you can't make a commitment, then you owe it to both of you to break it off.

Marco (V.O.)

Yeah?

Frasier

Yeah. Thank you for your call. *(disconnects the call, continues)* What's with guys like that anyway? Roz, you've been around the block a few times. You ever meet anyone like Marco?

Roz

They're all Marcos. You can't swing a dead cat without hitting a Marco.

Frasier

Come on now, if they were all Marcos no one would be having a relationship.

Roz

Well I'm not, my sister's not, none of my friends are. I think we may have entered the Marco Decade.

Frasier

What do you think, Seattle? Are there any non-Marcos out there? Or is Roz just destined to live a life of hopeless, loveless spinsterhood? Back after this.

Frasier *hits a button on his panel.* **Roz** *takes off her headphones.*

Roz *(sarcastic)*

Gee, and to think I was this close to calling in sick today.

AS WE:

FADE OUT.

Scene B

A black screen. In white letters appears "'Twas Two Months Before Christmas . . ."

FADE IN:

INT. FRASIER'S LIVING ROOM – THAT NIGHT – NIGHT/1

Martin, Daphne, Frasier, Eddie

SPFX: fire in fireplace

Daphne *is adjusting a camera on a tripod, aiming it toward the fireplace. There are three human-sized stockings and one little* **Eddie** *stocking hung above the fireplace.* **Martin** *is putting the finishing touches on an artificial Christmas tree.*

Martin

This feels weird. It isn't even Halloween yet. Do we really have to do this?

Daphne

If we're going to have a picture for the Christmas card, we've got to make it look like Christmas.

Martin

I don't see why we can't do what my wife and I used to do: Put Frasier and Niles in matching sweaters and sit them on the hood of the car.

Daphne

Well, this year we're going to be a little more artistic, all right?

Martin

Where the hell is Frasier anyway? I could use a little help.

Daphne

He's still napping. It's good for him. You know, my grandfather used to nap every afternoon. He lived to be ninety-three.

Martin

Really?

Daphne

He'd lie there on the sofa and you couldn't wake him for the world. Grammy would say, "He might as well be a dead man." Then, of course, one day we couldn't wake him because he really was a dead man. Poor Grammy. For weeks she kept insisting, "He's napping, he's napping."

Martin *puts the last ornament on the tree.*

Martin

Okay, I'm going to plug her in.

Martin *plugs the tree in and it lights up. They both stand back and admire their work.*

Daphne

Oh, that's lovely. *(singing)* "Deck the halls with boughs of holly . . ."

Martin *joins in.*

Martin/Daphne

". . . Fa la la la la la la la la. 'Tis the season to be jolly. Fa la la la la la la la la . . ."

As **Daphne** *and* **Martin** *continue singing,* **Frasier** *enters, taking in the scene. Disoriented, he looks at his watch, then feels his face.*

Frasier

Exactly how long have I been asleep?

Martin

Oh good, you're up. Now we can get this picture taken.

Frasier

What picture?

Daphne

Our Christmas card picture. We told you about it last week, remember?

Frasier

Well, can we at least wait a few minutes? I'm still kind of puffy.

Daphne

Oh, you look fine. Now, the theme this year is "Santa's Workshop."
Everybody put on your little elf hats.

Daphne *and* **Martin** *put their elf hats on.*

Frasier

I am not putting that on my head. I am a respected professional.

Martin

But if you don't, it'll look stupid.

Frasier

Oh, I think that ship has already sailed.

Martin

Put the hat on, Frasier.

Frasier

Don't tell me what to do.

Martin

I am telling you. Put the hat on.

Frasier

No! You can't make me.

Daphne

Boys, boys, please don't fight. Are you forgetting what day it is?

Frasier

It's October twenty-first.

Martin

Could we just get the picture taken, please?

Daphne *finishes setting up the camera.*

Daphne

All right, I've got it all set. Thirty seconds, gents.

Martin *and* **Frasier** *start to pose.* **Daphne** *joins them.*

Daphne *(cont'd)*

Wait, something's missing. Where's Eddie?

Martin

He's in the bathroom having a drink. *(calling)* Eddie!

Eddie *trots in. He's wearing reindeer antlers and bells around his neck. He gets into the picture just as the camera flashes.*

SPFX: camera flash

Frasier

I can always hope there's a postal strike.

As we:

FADE OUT.

Scene C

A black screen. In white letters appears "M&M's and Sympathy."

FADE IN:

INT. RADIO STUDIO – NEXT DAY – DAY/2

Frasier, Roz, Catherine

Frasier *is on the air.*

Frasier

Well, that's it for today's show. This is Dr. Frasier Crane. Now go out there and make it a great day, Seattle.

Frasier *takes off his headset.* **Roz** *enters his booth, carrying an 8 x 10 glossy.*

Roz

There's a fan in the hall who wants your autograph.

Frasier

All right, give it here. I'll sign it.

Roz *hands* **Frasier** *the picture. He looks through the glass and sees* **Catherine**, *a very attractive woman. She sees him looking and smiles sweetly.*

Frasier *(cont'd)*

Is that her?

Roz

Uh-huh.

Frasier

Well, maybe I better handle this in person.

Frasier *takes an 8 x 10 glossy and exits to the hall.*

RESET TO:

INT. STUDIO HALLWAY – CONTINUOUS – DAY/2

Frasier, Catherine

Frasier *(cont'd)*

Hello. My producer said you'd like my autograph. How should I make this out?

Catherine
You disgust me! You parasitic fraud!

Frasier
Well, that's different from the usual "best regards."

Frasier *starts to walk away.* **Catherine** *pulls him back by his arm.*

Catherine
Oh, no, Mister. You're going to listen to me. For once you're going to face the consequences of what happens after you hang up on your callers.

Frasier
What consequences? What are you talking about?

Catherine
I'm Marco's girlfriend. Or should I say ex-girlfriend, thanks to you.

Frasier
Marco? You mean "Marco-who-didn't-want-to-commit" Marco?

Catherine
You damn radio shrinks. You couldn't just tell him to take a little more time. That kind of advice doesn't get big ratings. "Break up with her, get on with your life and ruin hers." Now that's entertainment!

Frasier
Now hold on one minute. I don't hand out advice lightly. Marco clearly stated he wanted to keep his options open.

Catherine
Oh, bull. Marco would never say that.

Frasier
You're right. To be exact he said he was only staying with you until someone better came along.

Catherine
He told you that?

Frasier
He told most of Seattle that.

This hits **Catherine** *hard.*

Frasier *(cont'd)*
I'm sorry I had to tell you, but at least now you know the truth.

Catherine *turns her back to* **Frasier**. **Frasier** *heads back to the studio. He hears her start to cry softly.*

> **Frasier** (*cont'd*)

Oh no, no. Please don't cry.

Catherine *cries harder.* **Frasier** *puts a folder over his mike.*

> **Frasier** (*cont'd*)

You're in a place of business.

> **Catherine**

Boy, I can really pick 'em, can't I?

> **Frasier**

Hey, don't go there. This is not your fault. You're an attractive woman. A tad overemotional perhaps.

Catherine *starts to cry even harder. She turns her back to him.*

> **Frasier** (*cont'd*)

But some men like that.

Frasier *awkwardly tries to comfort her, not knowing whether to offer his handkerchief, put his arm around her, or pat her on the shoulder.*

> **Frasier** (*cont'd*)

Ssh . . . It's okay . . . It's okay . . .

A technician enters the booth.

> **Frasier** (*cont'd*)

Hey, Stan. How're you doing? Nice job on the promos.

Catherine *is still sobbing.*

> **Frasier** (*cont'd*) (*to Catherine*)

Would you like to maybe sit down?

She shakes her head.

> **Frasier** (*cont'd*)

How about a glass of water?

She shakes her head again. **Frasier** *looks around desperately and spots the candy machine.*

> **Frasier** (*cont'd*)

M&M's?

Catherine *looks up and dabs her eyes.*

> **Catherine**

Plain or peanut?

> **Frasier**

Whichever you like?

Catherine *(sniffles)*

Peanut.

Frasier *exits to the candy machine. She follows him out. During the following,* **Frasier** *puts some change into the machine and gets the M&M's.*

Catherine *(cont'd)*

I guess I should've seen this coming. Marco practically had a coronary when I brought over a toothbrush to keep at his apartment.

He hands her the M&M's and they sit down on chairs next to the candy machine.

Catherine

Thanks. *(offering candy)* You want one?

Frasier

No, thanks. *(then)* If he was that resistant, why did you stay with him?

Catherine

I just wanted it to work. I had so much invested in it.

Frasier

But that's no reason to settle for someone who isn't madly in love with you.

Catherine

Right now, I'm not sure if there are any men out there who are actually capable of falling madly in love.

Frasier

Of course there are. On the most basic level, men and women are the same. We both need to love and be loved, to have someone we feel we matter to, and who matters to us. To make a commitment to another human being is the ultimate expression of our humanity.

Catherine *(touched)*

Wow. Your wife is really lucky.

Frasier

I'm sure she'd agree with you, especially now that our marriage is over.

Catherine

Oh God, I'm sorry.

Frasier

It practically destroyed me. Even now . . . To this day . . . Well . . . Maybe I will have one of those M&M's.

Frasier *helps himself from her bag.*

Catherine
Hey, you like the yellow ones too.

Frasier
Yeah, people try to tell you they're all the same.

Catherine
Why are relationships always so hard? And so fattening?

Frasier
They aren't always. In med school, I heard of a documented case of a couple that met, got along, and lived happily ever after.

Amused, **Catherine** *chuckles.*

Catherine
I don't mind the happily ever after part. It's the dating part. If I have to tell one more stranger the story of my life over northern Italian cuisine, I'm going to choke on a breadstick.

Frasier
I know. I've often felt it would save a lot of energy if we could just exchange résumés over appetizers.

Catherine
Half the time I'm ready to exchange good-byes over appetizers.

Frasier
At least you don't get stuck with the bill.

Catherine
You haven't dated much lately, have you?

Frasier
No. I've grown quite used to eating alone.

Catherine
I always turn on the TV so it at least feels like there's someone else in the room.

Frasier
Is that what you'll be doing tonight?

Catherine
Unless I just keep eating M&M's, which is a distinct possibility.

Frasier
Look . . . I know this is a little unusual, but we seem to be having a rather nice conversation and, well . . . There's a little place around the corner that has pretty good food, not a breadstick in sight . . .

(quickly) Forgive me, that was terribly presumptuous. I don't even know your name and here I am . . .

Catherine

It's Catherine. And I'd love to. Just give me a minute to fix my make-up.

Frasier

Oh, sure, sure.

He watches her exit down the hallway, then:

Frasier *(cont'd)*

Yes!

He hits the candy machine. Candy comes out.

Frasier *(cont'd)*

All right! Milk Duds!

AS WE:

FADE OUT.

End of Act One

ACT TWO

Scene D

FADE IN:

INT. CAFE NERVOSA – DAY – DAY/3

Frasier, Catherine, Niles

It's several days later. **Frasier** *is at a table with* **Catherine**. *They are holding hands, examining each other's fingers.*

Frasier

Soft and supple, yet strong, right down to the beautiful almond-shaped nails.

Frasier *pulls his hand away and admires it.*

Frasier *(cont'd)*

You really like the way my hand looks?

Catherine

Uh-huh. What do you see in my hands?

Frasier

My future and my last chance at happiness.

Catherine *snorts and can't help but laugh.*

Frasier *(cont'd)*

That was a bit much, wasn't it?

Catherine

Yeah, a bit. It looked like the people at the next table were about to stone us with bran muffins.

Catherine *gets up to leave.*

Catherine *(cont'd)*

I've got to go. I'm late for work.

Frasier

Wait, wait. We haven't decided what we're doing tonight. Shall we dine at Antonio's? Le Cigare Volant?

Catherine

We've gone out the last three nights. Why don't we just stay in?

Frasier

What a wonderful idea. I'll send Dad and Daphne to a movie and I'll cook for you. Be at my house, eight o'clock.

Catherine

I won't be able to get there till eight-thirty. I have to stop off and change.

Frasier

No, no don't ever change. I like you just the way you are.

The people at the tables next to them groan.

Frasier *(cont'd) (turning)*

I know, I know. I'm a little out of practice, okay?

Catherine

See you tonight.

Catherine *gives* **Frasier** *a kiss and starts out.* **Niles** *enters and passes* **Catherine**, *who exits. He crosses over to* **Frasier's** *table signaling the waiter for a coffee.*

Niles

I'll dispense with the usual adolescent teasing and come straight to the point. Who was that babe-o-rama?

Frasier

Niles, don't try to be hip. You remind me of Bob Hope when he dresses up as the Fonz. Her name is Catherine.

Niles

She's very fetching.

Frasier

She's more than that. She's smart, funny, she's a successful architect, and she has no idea how beautiful she really is.

Niles

So how long have you known her?

Frasier

Three days.

Niles

Have you two . . .?

Frasier

No, as if it's any of your business.

A beat.

Niles

But you . . .?

Frasier

Yes, soon.

Another beat.

Niles

We are talking about . . .

Frasier

Of course we are!

A beat.

Niles

Sex, right?

Frasier

Yes!

Niles

So, how did you two meet?

The waiter approaches and sets down a coffee for **Niles**.

Frasier

It was just one of those crazy things. She came to the station to chew me out.

Niles

You're kidding.

Frasier

No, a couple of days earlier, her boyfriend called in to my show and I told him to break up with her.

Niles *stops sipping his coffee and inhales sharply.*

Frasier *(cont'd)*

I hope that sound means you burned your tongue.

Niles

Frasier, where are your ethics? You can't date someone who's involved with one of your patients.

Frasier

I'm not. Marco's not a patient. He's a caller. There's a big difference. Besides, I spoke to him before I even met Catherine.

Niles

Ah, rationalization. The last refuge of an unsound argument.

Frasier

Damn it, Niles! I'm not rationalizing. There's no problem here.

Niles

Well, as long as your conscience is clear. I'm not sure if mine would be.

Frasier

Frankly, I don't care about your conscience. I don't need your approval. I don't need you to like it. I don't need you for anything.

Frasier *starts to exit.*

Frasier *(cont'd) (an afterthought)*

Oh, by the way, my car is in the shop and I need you to give me a ride home from work.

Niles

No problem.

As Frasier exits, we:
Fade out.

Scene E

A black screen. In white letters appears "He's Baaack."

Fade in:
INT. RADIO STUDIO – NIGHT – NIGHT/3
Roz, Frasier, Marco (V.O.)
Roz *is in her booth.* **Frasier** *enters his booth, takes his seat, and puts on his headset.*

Roz

Ten seconds and I have news for you. Marco's on line two.

Frasier

Marco?

Roz

You know, the guy you got out of the way so you could get his girlfriend for yourself? And I thought this was going to be a dull day. Five seconds.

Frasier

I don't want to talk to him. I'm not talking to him. There's no way I'm talking to him.

Roz

. . . Three . . . two . . .

Roz *gives* **Frasier** *the "you're on" sign.*

Frasier

And we're back. Roz, who do we have on the line?

Roz

Marco.

Frasier

Hello, Marco.

Marco (V.O.)

Hi, Dr. Crane. I spoke to you the other day and I took your advice and broke up with my girlfriend.

CUT TO:

INT. NILES'S CAR – NIGHT – NIGHT/3

Niles

While he's driving, **Niles** *is punching various buttons on his radio. When he hears* **Frasier's** *voice, he turns up the volume. (During the following, we'll intercut between* **Niles's** *car and the radio station.)*

Frasier

Well, what can I say but, "Bravo, Marco." Roz, who's our next caller?

Marco (V.O.)

Wait, wait, wait. The problem is she's already dating someone else. It really makes me nuts, the thought of her with another guy. It makes me want to pound him.

Frasier

What makes you think she's dating someone else?

Marco (V.O.)

Well, the other night I couldn't get her on the phone, so I drove by her place and saw her parked outside talking to some guy in a black BMW.

Frasier

Did you, uh, get a good look at the guy?

Marco (V.O.)

No, it was too dark.

Frasier

Oh, thank God.

Marco (V.O.)

Why?

Frasier

Well, I'd hate to see you do something rash.

Marco (V.O.)

I think I made a big mistake, Doc. Do you think I should ask her to take me back?

Frasier

No! What I mean is . . . no! You don't want your ex-girlfriend, you just don't want anyone else to have her. Isn't that true?

Marco (V.O.)

I don't know.

Frasier

Marco, you're not thinking straight now. I am. So let me do your thinking for you. Stop spying on your ex-girlfriend and get on with your life. In fact, you might even think about moving to a new city and starting over.

Frasier *hits a button on his console.*

Frasier *(cont'd)*

We'll be right back after this commercial break.

Frasier *takes off his headphones and pushes back from the console, spent.* **Roz** *is staring at him through the glass.*

Frasier *(cont'd)*

What?!

AS WE:

FADE OUT.

Scene H

A black screen. In white letters appears "Stop! In the Name of Love."

FADE IN:

INT. NILES'S CAR – NIGHT – NIGHT/3

Frasier, Niles

Niles *is parked at the curb. The car door opens and* **Frasier** *gets in.*

Frasier

Thanks for picking me up.

Niles *starts the car and pulls out into traffic.*

Niles

No problem, Frasier. It's only a few miles out of my way . . . At rush hour. But I don't mind, really. It gave me a chance to listen to your show.

Frasier

I see.

Niles

I just have one question for you. Can you honestly tell me that the advice you gave Marco was based on his best interest and not on yours?

Frasier

No, I can't, Niles. And you know what else? I don't care. I'm in love and I don't care. Catherine's mine now. I'm in and Marco's out!

Niles

You're insane.

Frasier

Perhaps. But you just went through a stop sign.

Niles *hits the brakes. They lunge forward in their seats.*

Frasier *(cont'd)*

Not now . . . we're in the middle of the intersection.

Niles *gives it the gas.*

Frasier *(cont'd)*

I haven't felt this way in ages. There's an excitement about this. I feel tingly, Niles.

Niles

Tingly?

Frasier

That's right . . . tingly. I'm tingling all over. My senses are alive.

He rolls down the car window.

Frasier *(cont'd) (yelling out)*
Do you hear that, Seattle? I'm tingly! *(a beat, reacting)* Hey, same to
you, buddy!

Niles
This goes against everything you stand for. This is not you.

Frasier
I know. That's what makes it so remarkable. Through my entire
career as a psychiatrist, if I would so much as approach a breach in
ethics it would make me queasy. I would actually get a sick feeling in
the pit of my stomach, but this time . . .

Niles
Tingly?

Frasier
Bingo. Hey Niles, I've got an idea.

Niles
What?

Frasier
Next stop light, Chinese fire drill.

Niles
I'm warning you, Frasier. I'll mace you if I have to.

AS WE:
FADE OUT.

Scene J

FADE IN:
INT. FRASIER'S LIVING ROOM – LATER THAT NIGHT – NIGHT/3
Catherine, Frasier, Eddie
Frasier *and* **Catherine** *are seated at the dining room table. They have just
finished their meal.* **Frasier** *pours the last bit of wine into* **Catherine's** *glass.
The lights are low and soft music is playing in the background.*

Catherine
That was the most delicious salmon Marseilles I ever tasted.

Frasier
Then you should try my "salmon chanted evening."

Catherine
Tell me you didn't say that.

Frasier

It was the Lafitte talking. "Lafitte don't fail me now."

Catherine

Stop, stop.

Frasier *rises, takes his and* **Catherine's** *dishes and silverware, and exits to the kitchen.* **Catherine** *follows him and leans against the island.*

Catherine *(cont'd)*

Have you ever made love in the kitchen?

Frasier *drops the plates into the sink.*

Frasier

Well, the dishes are done.

Frasier *quickly moves to* **Catherine** *and they go into a passionate embrace. While kissing, their bodies intertwine, he bends her back onto the island and her leg wraps around his flank. This goes on for a few beats until* **Frasier's** *passionate moaning sounds become queasy moaning sounds. He pushes* **Catherine** *away.*

Catherine

What's the matter?

Frasier

I'm sorry. I'm feeling a little queasy. Maybe I'm just not a kitchen person.

Frasier *exits into the living room.* **Catherine** *follows.* **Frasier** *takes a few deep breaths.*

Catherine

Maybe you're just too warm.

She unbuttons **Frasier's** *shirt.*

Frasier

Yeah, yeah, that's it. You look much too warm too.

Frasier *starts unbuttoning* **Catherine's** *shirt. They continue to unbutton, embrace, and kiss, moving across the room until they fall onto the sofa. Once again,* **Frasier** *starts making "queasing" noises.*

Catherine

I'm sorry. Was I kneeling on you?

Frasier *crosses to the balcony.*

Frasier

No, I think I just need a little fresh air. Are you feeling okay?

Catherine

I'm fine.

Frasier

Damn. It wasn't the fish.

Catherine

Well, there is a bug going around.

Frasier

No, it's not a bug.

Catherine

Then what is it?

A long beat, then:

Frasier

It's us. It's when we kiss and touch. I get queasy. It used to be tingly, now it's queasy.

Catherine

Are you saying that the thought of making love to me makes you sick to your stomach?

Frasier

Yes. But don't take it personally.

Catherine

Gee, why would I do that?

She rises.

Frasier

It's not you. It's me. Every time I come close to breaching my ethics, I get sick.

Catherine

When did you breach your ethics?

Frasier

Marco called my show today. He wanted to get back together with you. I told him not to.

Catherine

So?

Frasier

So I have a feeling I told him that not because it was best for him, but because it was best for me.

Catherine

Who cares?

Frasier

Any psychiatrist worth his salt cares. That's why we don't get personally involved with our patients, or their girlfriends.

Catherine

Are you saying you want to break up with me?

Frasier

I don't want to. I have to. If I don't I'll throw up on your shoes.

Catherine

I don't believe this is happening. How can this be so easy for you?

Frasier

Easy? This is killing me. Don't you think I'd like to pick you up right now, carry you over to that Eames Classic and show you why it's the best engineered chair in the world?

Catherine

Then why don't you?

Frasier

I told you. I can't.

Catherine

And nothing will change your mind?

Frasier

I'm sorry.

Catherine

Well thanks a lot, Dr. Crane.

She crosses to get her coat.

Catherine *(cont'd)*

First, you screw up things with Marco and now you're dumping me. And to think, I was going to have sex with you. *(twisting the knife)* And it was going to be hot, like you've never had before. I'm talking steamy, sweat dripping down your back, neighbors pounding on the walls kind of sex. But hey, you won't be alone tonight. You've got your ethics.

Catherine *crosses to the door, then turns to* **Frasier**.

Catherine *(cont'd)*

By the way, the fish was dry.

She exits.

Frasier *(calling after her)*
That was a cheap shot!

Frasier *crosses to the window and sits in the Eames Classic, looking out at the Seattle skyline.* **Eddie** *enters and jumps up on the footstool. He stares at* **Frasier***.*

Frasier *(cont'd)*
I envy you, Eddie. The biggest questions you ever face are "Who's going to feed me?" and "Who's going to walk me?" I won't have that kind of joy for another forty years . . .

As FRASIER CONTINUES TO STARE AT THE SKYLINE, WE:
FADE OUT.

End of Act Two

Scene K

END CREDITS
FADE IN:
INT. FRASIER'S LIVING ROOM – NIGHT – NIGHT/1
Frasier, Martin, Daphne, Eddie
Over the end credits we see a series of rejected photos from the Christmas card shoot.

FADE OUT.

End of Show

Daphne meets "Eric the Red."

A dark and stormy night . . .

A Midwinter Night's Dream

Episode #40571-015

Written by
Anne Flett-Giordano & Chuck Ranberg

Created by
David Angell/Peter Casey/David Lee

Directed by
David Lee

ACT ONE

Scene A

FADE IN:

INT. CAFE NERVOSA – DAY – DAY/1

Niles, Frasier, Eric, Daphne

Frasier *and* **Niles** *are at a table giving their order to the long-haired waiter,* **Eric**.

Niles

Double cappuccino, half-caf, nonfat milk, with enough foam to be aesthetically pleasing, but not so much that it would leave a mustache.

Eric

Cinnamon or chocolate on that?

Niles *(to Frasier)*

They always make this so complicated. *(then, to Eric)* Cinnamon.

Eric *(to Frasier)*

And you?

Frasier

Let's see, I think I'm in the mood for . . .

Daphne *enters the cafe.* **Niles** *instantly perks.*

Niles

Oh look, it's Daphne. Daphne!

Upon her approach, **Frasier** *and* **Niles** *start to rise.*

Daphne

Hello, I thought I might run into you here. Sit, sit. I just stopped in for a bag of beans. We're running low at home.

Frasier

I'll have . . .

Eric *(to Daphne)*

Can I get you something?

Daphne

Two pounds of . . .

Eric/Daphne

. . . the Kenya blend.

Daphne

You remembered.

Eric
Hard to forget.

Frasier
Excuse me. You never got my order.

Eric *(ignoring Frasier)*
Most people find that blend too intense.

Daphne
Not me. I like something that holds its body on my tongue.

Niles *knocks over the sugar.*

Frasier *(to Eric)*
Uh, we seem to have spilled something here.

Eric *tosses* **Frasier** *a towel.*

Eric *(to Daphne)*
I don't suppose you'd be interested in something robust, if it didn't come on too strong?

Daphne
If it was a little bit sweet I might take a liking to it.

As **Frasier** *cleans off the table,* **Niles** *grabs the towel from him and wipes his brow.*

Eric
Would you like to step over to the counter and try my special blend?

Daphne
I'd love to.

They cross to the counter.

Frasier *(calling out after them)*
Nothing for me, thanks.

Niles
Frasier, that man is hitting on our Daphne. I don't know how she stands it.

At the counter, **Daphne** *and* **Eric** *laugh.*

Frasier
Yes, she's a brave little soul.

Niles
Look at him, he's running his dirty little eyes all over her.

Frasier
Apropos of nothing, Niles, how are things with you and Maris?

Niles

You're not implying that my concern for Daphne's welfare is anything less than pure, are you?

Frasier

I don't know. You tell me.

Niles

You know, that's your great shortcoming. You're always distrustful. You're always suspicious. Sometimes you just have to have faith that people are . . . *(noticing Eric and Daphne)* What the hell is he doing now?!

Frasier

I believe he's bagging her beans.

Niles *(alarmed)*

What?! *(then, realizing)* Oh, yes. Well, of course.

Daphne *crosses by their table on the way out. She's all aglow.*

Daphne

Eric over there is taking me to a club to hear his band tonight. I realize it's not my regular night off but I'll switch it with Saturday, if it's all right with you. Isn't he cute? I already have a nickname for him: Eric the Red. It fancies him, doesn't it? He looks a bit like a Viking. Ta.

Daphne *starts to exit, then stops.*

Daphne *(cont'd)*

Oh, look at me. I almost forgot my beans. Earth to Daphne.

Daphne *takes her bag of coffee and exits, giggling merrily.*

Frasier *(calling after her)*

Why don't you just take the night off.

Niles *is beside himself.*

Niles

How could she like him? The man has community college written all over him.

Frasier

Niles, what is going on here? This infatuation with Daphne is getting way out of hand.

Niles

You mean it's noticeable?

Frasier

Painfully. Speaking as your older brother, I have to tell you it's getting embarrassing. I didn't think much about it when it was a simple flirtation, but now I'm wondering if it isn't symptomatic of something going on with you and Maris.

Niles *is silent.*

Frasier *(cont'd)*

Well is it?

Niles

Oh, I can't lie to you, Frasier. Truth is, Maris and I are in a bit of a rut. We seem to have lapsed into this gray, numbing blandness.

Frasier

But that's nothing to be worried about. That's a fairly common thing after, what, fifteen years of marriage?

Niles

Nine.

Frasier *(astonished)*

Really. *(then)* Maybe you just need to find a way to spice things up.

Niles

You mean boudoir-wise?

Frasier

Well, for starters.

Niles

Like how?

Frasier

Well, I'm sure you and Maris could . . . you could . . . Well, it's you and Maris, so . . . I'm stumped.

AS WE:

FADE OUT.

Scene B

FADE IN:

INT. RADIO STUDIO – DAY – DAY/1

Roz, Frasier

Roz *is in her booth as* **Frasier** *arrives for work.*

Frasier

Hey Roz, how are you?

Roz

Do you really want to know how I am or are you just making conversation? Because if you really want to know how I am, I'll tell you.

Frasier

I was just making conversation. Actually, I need your advice.

Roz

On what?

Frasier

A subject in which you're quite well versed: sex.

Roz

How can I help you?

Frasier

This isn't about me. This is advice for a friend.

Roz

Uh-huh.

Frasier

No really. What do you do when the romance starts to go out of a relationship?

Roz

I get dressed and go home.

Frasier

Let's pretend you were actually capable of a long-term relationship. What would you do to keep things cooking?

Roz

Well, once I had a boyfriend take me out to a bar and we pretended we were strangers picking each other up. That was kind of hot.

Frasier

So you used fantasy and role playing.

Roz

Yeah, it was so much fun we tried it again. Only that time he got so into it he went home with someone else.

Frasier

Sorry.

Roz

Oh hell, she was gorgeous. One more drink and I would've gone home with her. My point is, women need to see the men they make love to as exciting, romantic figures. If you want to keep this woman interested, try creating a fantasy for an evening. Personally, I think you'd make a wonderful fireman.

Frasier
I told you we're not talking about me.

Roz
Yeah, right. Trust me. You'd look adorable with a big red hat and an axe. Almost showtime, Sparky.

Frasier *crosses into his booth.*

Frasier
Roz, I'm telling you it's not me. But if it were, I'll have you know that Frasier Crane would not have to rely on costumes and props to keep a woman trembling on the threshold of ecstasy. Although I do recall one steamy night when my ex-wife and I played a rousing little game of escaped convict and the warden's daughter.

Roz *points to the on-air sign. It's lit up.* **Frasier** *reacts.*

Frasier *(cont'd) (over intercom)*
How long have I been on?

Roz
Long enough.

Frasier
Celebrity voice of Dr. Frasier Crane impersonated.

As we:
Fade out.

Scene C

A black screen. In white letters appears "Ahoy Matey!"

Fade in:
INT. FRASIER'S LIVING ROOM – NIGHT – NIGHT/2
Frasier, Niles, Martin, Daphne, Eric
It's the middle of the night. The room is dark and empty.

Sfx: doorbell. More doorbell. Frantic doorbell.

Frasier *enters, tying his robe. He flicks on the lights as he crosses to the door and checks through the peephole.*

Frasier
Niles?!

He opens the door to **Niles***, who enters wearing a raincoat. He is very agitated.*

Niles

I'm sorry, Frasier, but the most horrible thing has happened. Maris
kicked me out.

Frasier

Why? What for?

Niles *takes off his raincoat to reveal a pirate costume – ruffled shirt, striped pantaloons, and a plastic sword tied on his sash.*

Frasier *(cont'd)*

Oh dear.

Martin *enters in his robe.*

Martin

What's going on out here? Niles?

Niles

Hello, Dad.

Martin *looks at him for a long beat, then turns back.*

Martin

Never mind, I don't want to know.

Niles

Dad, wait, there's a perfectly reasonable explanation for the way I'm
dressed. I was trying to create a romantic fantasy for Maris by
dressing up as the dashing pirate, Jean Lafitte.

Martin *(to Frasier)*

Why is he telling me? I said I don't want to know.

Niles

I'm just trying to explain.

Frasier

Fine, but keep in mind I reserve the right to yell "stop" at any time.

Niles

My plan was to leave a treasure map downstairs for Maris, with clues
that would lead her to my whereabouts, then hide in the linen closet
and wait for her to find me.

Martin

Dressed like that?

Niles *takes the eyepatch out of his pocket.*

Niles

Actually, at the time I was only wearing my eye patch. Though, technically, is it still an eye patch when you're wearing it on your . . .

Frasier

Stop!

Martin

Go on, Niles. *(to Frasier)* Sorry. I'm hooked.

Niles

There I was, lying in wait, with my little plastic sword clenched in my teeth, when suddenly the closet door was thrown open and I found myself face to face with the upstairs maid. She began screaming what I gather were some very unflattering things in idiomatic Guatemalan, when Maris stumbled upon the scene and completely misconstrued it. The next thing I knew she ordered me out of the house. I barely had time to grab my pantaloons and buckle my swash.

A beat, then **Martin** *bursts into laughter.*

Niles *(cont'd)*

Dad . . . Dad, it's not funny.

A beat. Then **Martin** *tries to suppress his laughter.*

Martin

Where'd you come up with this stupid idea?

Niles

Frasier.

Frasier

All I suggested was some sexual role playing. You're the one who came up with the Pirates of the Caribbean.

Niles *(collapsing on sofa)*

Oh, I've really bungled this one, haven't I?

Martin

Ah, come on. These things happen. You can stay with us tonight. Tomorrow morning you and Maris will sort things out.

Niles

What if we don't? What will I do then?

Frasier

Well I'm sure they can always use an extra busboy at the Jolly Roger. *(laughs, then)* Sorry, just trying to lighten the mood. I'll go get you a robe and some blankets.

Frasier *exits down the hallway.*

Niles

I'll never be able to face the maid again.

Martin

I don't think it's your face she'll remember. *(laughs again)* Sorry. Aw, come on, Niles. Everybody has embarrassing stories to tell. Did I ever tell you about the time I got locked out in the backyard in my underwear?

Niles

Only every Thanksgiving.

Martin

Well, don't worry. I won't be telling that story this year.

Frasier *reenters with pillows and blankets.*

Frasier

Here we go. Canadian goose-down pillows, Egyptian cotton sheets, and a vicuna throw, in case you get chilly during the night.

Niles

How perfect.

Martin

I still say a couple of years in the service would have done you two a world of good. Good night.

Martin *exits down the hallway.*

Niles

You know, Maris and I have had our disagreements, but it's never been this serious. I feel terrible having her mad at me. It's times like this when I kind of wish I could cry.

Frasier

Don't be embarrassed on my account.

Niles

No, it's not that. I'm just not someone who cries. It's not in my nature. When Maris's Uncle Lyle died, I had to shut my hand in the car door just to make a decent showing at the funeral.

Frasier

You're a complex little pirate, aren't you? Well, good night.

Frasier *turns off the light as he exits.* **Niles** *crawls under the blanket and tries to get comfortable. He can't. After a beat, he pulls a plastic hook out from under the covers and drops it on the floor. Suddenly the door opens,* *revealing* **Daphne** *and* **Eric**. *They linger in the doorway, backlit from outside.* **Niles** *scrunches up so as not to be seen.*

Daphne
Thank you again, Eric. I had a wonderful time.

Eric
Me too.

They kiss. **Niles** *tries to peek over the back of the sofa.*

Daphne
Well, good night.

Eric
Good night.

They kiss again. **Niles** *is dying.*

Daphne
I'd say goodnight again, but I'm starting to get a bit weak in the knees.

Eric
I'll call you.

They kiss again. **Eric** *exits.* **Daphne** *shuts the door, sighs, and exits to her room.* **Niles** *begins to cry like a baby, as we:*

FADE OUT.

Scene D

FADE IN:
INT. FRASIER'S LIVING ROOM – DAY – DAY/3
Daphne, Martin, Frasier, Niles
Frasier, **Martin**, *and* **Daphne** *are finishing breakfast.*

Daphne
. . . And he actually composed a song for me. Oh, I don't want to put a curse on it by talking about it too much. I know we've only had a few dates, but already I'm exhibiting the three signs of a woman in love: I can't stop thinking about him, I can't eat, and I bought myself all new underwear.

Daphne *exits to the kitchen.*

Martin
We've got to get her a girlfriend to talk to.

Niles *enters from the hallway in a bathrobe.*

Niles

Well, I just got off the phone with Maris. She went to Arizona for the weekend.

Frasier

Why?

Niles

She said she was so shattered by the experience she had to fly to her favorite spa and contemplate the future of our marriage from a mud bath.

Daphne

It'll probably be good for Mrs. Crane. Eric thinks the earth is very grounding.

Niles

Eric, Eric, Eric! Must everything be about Eric?! *(catches himself)* I'm sorry. I'm so upset I don't know what I'm saying.

Frasier

I suggest when Maris returns you two should invest some time in some intensive couples therapy. There's a Reichian workshop that I can . . .

Martin

Blah, blah, blah, blah. Look, all Maris needs is to know that you love her. Buy her some flowers, fix her a romantic dinner when she comes home. That's guaranteed to make any woman forgive you.

Niles

You really think that will work?

Martin

If it didn't, you wouldn't be here.

Niles

Well, I'd be willing to give it a try, but it's impossible. Our cook walked out in sympathy with Maris.

Daphne

I could help you prepare something. I have a late date with Eric . . . *(off Niles's look)* . . . a. My elderly aunt, Erica. But I could come over early and have everything ready by the time Mrs. Crane arrives.

Niles

You would do that for me?

Daphne

Of course.

Niles

Well, thank you, Daphne.

Daphne

What do you think Mrs. Crane would like for dinner?

Niles

Well, you have free rein. Just bear in mind that she can't have shellfish, poultry, red meat, saturated fats, nitrates, wheat, starch, sulfites, MSG, or dairy. *(beat)* Did I say nuts?

Frasier

Oh, I think that's implied.

As WE:

FADE OUT.

Scene E

A black screen. In white letters appears "It Was a Dark and Stormy Night." Beat. Then: "No, Really."

SFX: thunder

FADE IN:

INT. NILES'S CONSERVATORY – NIGHT – NIGHT/4

Niles, Daphne

SPFX: rain and trees blowing in the wind

It is a tall, Victorian-style room with huge conservatory windows overlooking the woods. Think Toad Hall. A stone wall features a roaring fireplace, in front of which is a small sofa and a coffee table set for a romantic dinner. There is a grand piano, and tall palms and leafy indoor plants are everywhere. Rain falls hard against the windows and the trees outside blow in the wind. **Niles***, in a smoking jacket, enters with a damp and shivering* **Daphne***.*

Niles

Here Daphne, come warm yourself by the fire. How did you get so wet?

Daphne

One of your trees blew down in your driveway. I had to walk the last hundred yards. *(a beat)* I must say, you have a beautiful home.

Niles

Thank you. Actually, it was Maris's family home. When I was a mere intern I used to drive through these hills dreaming of the life I would someday lead, and then one afternoon there was Maris, looking so

helpless, banging at the electric gates with her little fists and
a tire iron.

Daphne

They'd locked her in?

Niles

No, no, that was much later. This time she was coming home from
the antique mart with a rare bell jar once owned by Sylvia Plath,
when the gates failed to open. Naturally I stopped to offer my
assistance, and as our hands touched there was a sudden spark of
electricity. Then as if by magic, the gates parted before us, and we
took it as a sign.

Daphne

You knew you were meant to be together.

Niles

Yes. We were married just three short years later.

Daphne *picks up an ornate clock.*

Daphne

Oh, look at this. It's beautiful.

Niles

It's a glockenspiel. We bought it on our honeymoon in Zurich. I
brought it down from the attic to remind Maris of better times. It used
to play beautiful music, but it doesn't anymore. How's that for irony?
(then) Well, why don't we get you some dry clothes so you can get
dinner started and we can get you home in time for your date?

Niles *starts to exit.* **Daphne** *begins softly weeping.*

Niles *(cont'd)*

Daphne, what is it?

Daphne

Nothing.

Niles

No, it's definitely something. I'm a psychiatrist, I can read the signs.

Daphne

I'm sorry. I didn't want to spoil your reunion with Mrs. Crane, but . . .
(sobs) Eric broke up with me.

Niles

He did?

Daphne

Yes. He said he couldn't commit to me and his music at the same time. He had to stay focused. I know it was an excuse. I've heard his music. He must have another girl.

She starts to cry. **Niles** *tentatively puts a comforting arm around* **Daphne**. *This is probably as close as they've ever been, and he can't but appreciate it.*

Niles

He's a fool, Daphne. If he can't appreciate you, you're better off without him.

Daphne

Right now I'm not so sure, but thank you, Dr. Crane.

She rests her head on his shoulder.

SFX: telephone rings

Niles *(picks it up; into phone)*

Niles Crane . . . Oh Maris!

Niles *leaps to his feet.*

Niles *(cont'd)*

Where are you? . . . What do you mean you can't come home? . . . Yes, I know it's a bad storm . . .

Niles *looks at* **Daphne**, *all backlit from the fire and glistening from the rain. He doubts he's strong enough to resist.*

Niles *(cont'd) (into phone)*

. . . but I really think you should come home, Maris.

SPFX: another flash of lightning

SFX: more thunder

Niles *(cont'd) (into phone)*

Of course I sound excited, I am excited! . . . *(covering)* To have you home again. No, of course I don't want you to come home if it's not safe. *(resigned)* All right, I understand. See you tomorrow then. Yes, yes, ditto.

Niles *hangs up and turns to* **Daphne**.

Niles *(cont'd) (nervously)*

Looks like it's just the two of us.

Daphne

You mean Mrs. Crane won't be coming?

SPFX: another huge flash of lightning

SFX: a big thunderclap

LIGHT CUE: lights go out

The room is lit only by the fireplace.

Daphne *(cont'd)*
Oh my, there goes the electricity. What do we do now?

SPFX: flash of lightning

WITH A FLASH OF LIGHTNING, WE SEE NILES'S LOOK OF TREPIDATION, AS WE:
FADE OUT.

End of Act One

ACT TWO

Scene H

FADE IN:

INT. FRASIER'S LIVING ROOM – NIGHT – NIGHT/4

Martin, Frasier

SPFX: rain and lightning

Martin is on the phone in midconversation.

Martin *(into phone)*
No, no the storm's really bad. You shouldn't be driving anyway. Just spend the night. Okay good night, Daphne.

He hangs up the phone.

Frasier
You told her to spend the night?

Martin
Yeah. What's the big deal?

Frasier
You know how Niles feels about her.

Martin
Oh, relax. It's just another one of Niles's little crushes. Don't you remember the thing he had for his dental hygienist, Jodi? He had his teeth cleaned so much his gums hemorrhaged.

Frasier
I suppose you're right. Niles is all talk and no action. Besides he'd never try anything with Maris in the house.

Martin

Maris never got home. She's stuck in Arizona.

Frasier

I've got to get Daphne out of there.

Martin

Why?

Frasier

Why?! This is a recipe for disaster. You've got a vulnerable woman and an unstable man in a Gothic mansion on a rainy night. All that's missing is someone shouting "Heathcliff" across the moors.

Frasier *grabs his coat and heads for the door.*

Martin

Wait for me.

Martin *picks up his coat, too, and follows.*

Frasier

You're not coming.

Martin

Yes, I'm coming along.

They exit, ad-libbing argument.

MUSIC CUE: *the dramatic, opening chords of Beethoven, as we:*
CUT TO:

Scene J

INT. NILES'S CONSERVATORY – NIGHT – NIGHT/4
Niles, Daphne
The music we hear turns out to be **Niles** *at the piano, playing passionately. The room is lit by the fireplace and by several candelabra.* **Daphne** *enters in a silk peignoir.*

Daphne

Oh Dr. Crane, you play beautifully.

Niles

Thank you.

Niles *looks up at* **Daphne** *and he goes completely off-key. He attempts to end the song in a small flourish.*

Daphne

I found this upstairs in the guest room. I hope it's all right.

Niles

I thought you were going to put on some of Maris's clothes. You
know, something bulky from her wool collection.

Niles *sits on the keys of the piano.*

Daphne

I was, but she's quite a bit smaller than me. This was all I could find
that fit. Should I go look for something else?

Niles

No. Yes. No, no, the important thing is that it's big enough and warm
enough and silky enough and I have to make a phone call.

As **Niles** *starts to exit, we:*
CUT TO:

Scene K

INT. FRASIER'S LIVING ROOM – NIGHT – NIGHT/4
Frasier (V.O.), **Niles** (V.O.), **Eddie**

SFX: telephone rings

CLOSE ON: THE PHONE MACHINE AS IT PICKS UP.

Frasier (V.O.)

Hello, this is Dr. Frasier Crane. At the sound of the tone, I'm
listening.

SFX: phone machine beep

Eddie *comes over to listen to the following:*

Niles (V.O.)

Frasier? Frasier, this is Niles. If you're there, please pick up . . .
Frasier? . . . I'll just keep stalling in case you're there . . . All right, I
guess you're not there. When you get in, give me a call, okay? Bye.

Eddie *ponders this, as we:*
CUT TO:

Scene L

INT. FRASIER'S CAR – NIGHT – NIGHT/4
Frasier, Martin

SPFX: rain

The rain beats down on the car as **Frasier** *and* **Martin** *speed through the night.*

Martin

This is stupid.

Frasier

It is not.

Martin

Look, nothing is gonna happen between them anyway.

Frasier

But what if it does? He's my brother and he loves his wife. Oh, I know, I know. Their marriage isn't everyone's cup of tea, but on some twisted, bizarre level it works for them. And if he did anything stupid to hurt his marriage, he'd be the one to suffer. And I don't want to see my brother suffer.

Martin

Well, I just don't see where you get off telling a grown man what to do. *(then)* Hey, slow down. You're going to miss the turn on to Roosevelt.

Frasier

Dad, I let you come along specifically on the condition that you wouldn't give directions.

Martin

I'm not giving you directions, I'm telling you which way is faster.

Frasier

But if we take Roosevelt it'll add ten minutes.

Martin

Only in sunshine. In rain it's faster.

Frasier

What, do the laws of spatial relationships suddenly change when it rains?

Martin

You get better traction on Roosevelt. Of course you wouldn't need it if you bought the all-weather tires like I told you to, but no, you have to get those fancy German ones . . .

They begin to ad-lib bickering about Germans, rain and tires, both talking at once and neither hearing the other, as we:
CUT TO:

Scene N

A black screen. In white letters appears "Colonel Mustard and Miss Scarlet in the Conservatory . . ."

FADE IN:
INT. NILES'S CONSERVATORY – NIGHT – NIGHT/4
Niles, Daphne

Daphne *is sitting by the fire drinking her wine and dabbing her eyes with a Kleenex as* **Niles** *enters from outside with an armful of firewood.*

> **Niles**
> We'll have to make this last. It's all that's left of the firewood.

Daphne *lets out a whimper.* **Niles** *sits down beside her.*

> **Niles** *(cont'd)*
> Oh no, don't worry. If this runs out there's an antique sideboard in the drawing room that I suspect is a reproduction. *(realizes)* Oh, it's Eric, isn't it?

> **Daphne** *(nods)*
> I don't know why I'm being so silly. We weren't together long enough for anything to really happen.

> **Niles**
> Sometimes the most powerful feelings come from the promise of what might happen. . . . *(looks at her longingly)* Just the anticipation can make all the little hairs on your neck stand on end.

Daphne *stares into the fire, as* **Niles** *quickly smooths down his neck hairs.*

> **Daphne**
> Dr. Crane . . .

> **Niles**
> Yes, Daphne.

> **Daphne**
> We're losing the fire.

> **Niles**
> No, we're not. It's burning with the heat of a thousand suns!

> **Daphne** *(indicates fireplace)*
> But it's down to its last embers.

> **Niles**
> Oh, I'll put some wood on it.

As **Niles** *crosses to the fireplace to restoke the fire, we:*
CUT TO:

Scene P

INT. FRASIER'S CAR – NIGHT – NIGHT/4
Martin, Frasier

The car has stalled. **Frasier** *tries the key, but the engine won't turn over.*

Martin
You flooded it, you flooded it. You had to keep pumping the gas and you flooded it.

Frasier
You can't flood a fuel injected engine.

Martin
Then it must be the rain.

Frasier
It's not the rain. It has nothing to do with the rain. I don't believe this. We're so close to the house. I can see the gargoyles.

Martin
If we'd taken Roosevelt . . .

Frasier
Then we'd be stuck on Roosevelt!

Martin
Never could admit it when you made a mistake.

Frasier
Call the auto club. I'm gonna make a run for it.

Frasier *girds himself against the storm and jumps out. He slams the door shut.* **Martin** *rolls down the window.*

Martin *(yelling)*
You'll make better time if you take the shortcut around the fountain. *(beat, then)* Well same to you.

As we:
Cut to:

Scene R

INT. NILES'S CONSERVATORY – NIGHT – NIGHT/4
Daphne, Niles, Frasier
Niles *and* **Daphne** *are on the floor, reclined on pillows in front of the fire.*

Daphne
It's always been my problem. I guess I fall in love too fast. The minute I feel that spark, I give my heart away.

Niles
Daphne, you must stop being so hard on yourself. What you see as a fault is also your greatest gift. To be so open and warm and loving . . .

Daphne

And foolish.

Niles

No, you're not foolish. You're perfect.

Daphne

But it was wonderful to be wrapped up in a man's arms.

Niles

Well, it feels equally wonderful to wrap your arms around a woman. If it's the right woman, under the right set of circumstances . . .

They are very close to a kiss. If **Niles** *made his move right now, she'd probably be his.*

SPFX: *flash of lightning and clap of thunder*

SFX: *Maris's antique clock begins playing music*

Daphne

Dr. Crane, your glockenspiel has sprung to life.

Niles

Oh. *(realizes)* Oh, the clock. My God, it hasn't run like that in years. Maris will be so delighted. Maris . . .

Daphne

You really love her don't you?

Niles

You know, I do. Love's a funny thing, isn't it? I mean, sometimes it's exciting and passionate, and sometimes it's something else. Something comfortable and familiar. That newly exfoliated little face staring up at you across the breakfast table, or sharing a little laugh together when you see someone wearing white after Labor Day . . .

Daphne

I hope someday someone will feel that way about me.

Niles

Don't worry, Daphne. You're a very special person. And someday a man worthy of you will come along, just as soon as the gods create him.

Daphne

That's one of the loveliest things anyone has ever said to me. Thank you, Dr. Crane. You're a good friend.

She kisses him on the cheek. At this moment **Frasier** *appears like a specter at the window, or like Dustin Hoffman in* The Graduate.

SPFX: lightning flashes

Frasier *(primal scream)*

STO-OOOOOOP!

Niles *and* **Daphne** *react.* **Frasier** *runs around the side and in a second comes bursting through the door. He is soaked.*

Frasier *(cont'd)*

Have you two gone mad? You'll regret this for the rest of your lives.

Niles

Frasier . . .

Frasier

Look at you two, here, alone, the fire, the candlelight, the nightie.

Daphne

Dr. Crane, you didn't think that Dr. Crane and I were . . . *(appalled)* Dr. Crane! You have some nerve to imply that your brother would do anything so deplorable. Why just moments ago he made a beautiful speech about how much he loves his wife. How he cherishes her excruciating little face and how they laugh at white people. *(then, to Niles)* That didn't sound right.

Niles

Close enough.

Frasier

Well, I certainly didn't mean to suggest . . . Of course, I didn't think you were . . .

Daphne

Then just exactly what was it that you wanted us to stop?

Frasier

Well I wanted you to stop . . . standing here in silence. This is a night for music. Niles, come join me at the piano. Daphne, pour us all some wine.

Frasier *and* **Niles** *cross to the piano and sit.* **Daphne** *pours some wine.*

Frasier *(cont'd)*

Are you sure everything's all right?

Niles

Yes, and thank you for coming over. Everything is going to be fine. You see, my glockenspiel is working again.

As **Frasier** *reviews his* Gray's Anatomy, *we:*

FADE OUT.

End of Act Two

Scene S

END CREDITS
FADE IN:
INT. NILES'S CONSERVATORY – NIGHT – NIGHT/4
Frasier, Niles, Daphne, Martin

SPFX: rain

Frasier, **Niles**, *and* **Daphne** *sit around the piano, drinking wine and singing merrily. Outside a wet and frazzled* **Martin** *appears. He peers through the window angrily. As he starts to limp quickly around the side to the door we:* FADE OUT.

End of Show

Season Two

Slow Tango in South Seattle

The Matchmaker

A Room with a View

An Affair to Forget

When Frasier finds a story from
his past has been novelized, Roz
tries to calm him down . . .

. . . and Bulldog does the reverse.

Slow Tango in South Seattle

Episode #40572-026

Written by
Martin Weiss

Created by
David Angell/Peter Casey/David Lee

Directed by
James Burrows

ACT ONE

Scene A

A black screen. In white letters appears, "Slow Tango in South Seattle."

Frasier (V.O.)

Hello, Steven. I'm listening.

FADE IN:
INT. RADIO STUDIO – DAY – DAY/1
Frasier, Roz, Steven (V.O.)
Frasier *is on the air.*

Steven (V.O.)

Well you see, Dr. Crane, my wife Tracy and I are having a baby. I know we're getting a little ahead of ourselves, but there seems to be a lot of different advice about whether it's okay to let your kid climb into bed with you in the mornings and . . .

Frasier

Stop right there, Steven. It's okay. I know I'll always cherish the times my son crawled in with my wife and me – finally there was someone for us to cuddle. All relationships need that kind of close and undivided attention. Isn't that so, Roz?

We see **Roz** *is reading a book, not listening.*

Roz

Uh-huh.

Steven (V.O.)

But what if you and your wife enjoy, you know, making love in the mornings.

Frasier

Trust me. Once the baby's born that won't be an issue any more. This is Dr. Frasier Crane on KACL. We'll be back after these messages.

Frasier *takes off his headset and walks into* **Roz's** *booth.*

Frasier *(cont'd)*

Roz, how can you be reading now?

Roz

I don't know. It's something I picked up in elementary school and it just stuck.

Frasier

What is it that's so captivating?

Roz *shows him what she's reading.*

Frasier *(cont'd)* *(sees title)*
Slow Tango in South Seattle. Oh, not you too. Why is it every woman I see is carrying that book?

Roz
Because it's impossible to put down. Here, read the first paragraph. I guarantee you'll be hooked.

Frasier *(reading)*
"There are tangos that come flowing from the wine-colored sea, from the rust of a hundred sunken ships. This is one of those dances."

Roz
Well . . .?

Frasier
There are books that make your stomach rumble and lurch and force your lunch ever upward. This is one of those books.

Roz
Men have no soul. *(re: book jacket)* Except for this one. The future Mr. Roz Doyle, Thomas Jay Fallow.

Frasier *(amazed)*
Thomas Jay Fallow?

Roz
Do you know him?

Frasier
Yes. He used to drop into a neighborhood bar I frequented in Boston. He was a little pretentious. He stuck out like a sore thumb.

Roz
God, you used to drink with Thomas Jay Fallow?

Frasier
Actually, I spent most of my time helping him get through his writer's block. In the future I'll remember to use my powers for good and not evil.

He disdainfully casts the book down.

Roz
Well, I don't care what you think about him. He's going to be a guest tomorrow on Amber Edwards's "Book Chat." I want to meet him and you're going to introduce us.

Frasier

Oh, but if I see him, I'm going to have to read his book and tell him how much I liked it. You know how hard it is to lie to someone's face.

Roz

Oh it's easy for someone as sophisticated, charming and articulate as you.

Frasier

Maybe you're right.

Roz

See how easy it is?

As we:

Fade out.

Scene B

A black screen. In white letters appears, "He Was Not Yet a Man, Yet Oh So Much More Than a Boy."

Fade in:

INT. FRASIER'S LIVING ROOM – THE NEXT MORNING – DAY/2

Daphne, Niles, Martin, Frasier, Eddie

Daphne *and* **Martin** *are on the floor trying to do leg extensions.* **Eddie** *is playfully interfering, barking and getting in the way.*

Daphne

Eight, nine . . . Stop that, Eddie.

Martin

He just wants to play. Huh, boy?

Daphne

Well therapy is not a game. *(to Eddie)* Stop, I said. *(Eddie doesn't)* He's completely ignoring me.

Sfx: doorbell

Daphne gets up to answer it.

Martin

He doesn't like taking orders.

Daphne *(pointedly)*

I can't imagine who he gets that from.

She opens the door to **Niles**, *carrying a framed photo.*

Daphne *(cont'd)*

Oh, hello, Dr. Crane.

Niles

Hello, Daphne.

Martin *(from floor)*

Hey, Niles.

Niles

Ah. I see you're doing your exercises.

Daphne

That's right, and if someone doesn't let us get on with them he's going to get a little spank on his fanny.

Niles *reacts.*

Martin *(getting up)*

Oh, leave Eddie alone.

Niles

Oh, Eddie.

Martin *(to Niles)*

What's up?

Niles

Well, when I brought you a beer in your room the other day, I couldn't help but notice you had photos of Frasier and Frederick and an autographed one from someone named Ken Griffey, Jr., but none of Maris and me. So, I brought you this.

He hands **Martin** *the framed photo.*

Martin

Gee, thanks. *(a beat)* Uh, why is Maris wearing jodhpurs? She didn't start horseback riding did she?

Niles

No. She wanted to take it up but unfortunately her little quadriceps are so tight she's incapable of straddling anything larger than a border collie. Still, the wardrobe suits her.

Daphne

Yes, not everyone looks so natural carrying a riding crop.

Before **Niles** *can respond, an agitated* **Frasier** *enters from the hallway, carrying a book.*

Frasier

I simply do not believe this. This is outrageous!

Martin

What are you yapping about?

Frasier

I'm yapping about this. *(re: book)* This book! It's written by someone I knew. He's taken an incident from my own life. Something very personal that I told him one night in confidence and he's turned it into this trash.

Martin

You must be making a mistake.

Frasier

Why? Because no one would be so low as to steal another man's life?

Martin *(opens book's flyleaf)*

No, because I've heard your stories. Nothing that's happened to you is worth $14.95.

Frasier

Oh, he stole my story all right, but does he thank me? No . . . He doesn't even list my name in his acknowledgments.

Martin

What's it about, anyway?

Frasier

That isn't important.

Daphne

It's about his first time.

Frasier

Thank you, Daphne.

Daphne

I just started the book, but I rather like it.

Niles

Your first time doing what?

Frasier

Changing a flat tire – what do you think?

Niles

Ohhh.

Martin

So this whole book is about the night you conceived Frederick?

Frasier

Very amusing, Dad. You'll be happy to know that wasn't my first time.

Martin

Hey, I'm happy to know it wasn't your only time.

Niles

So just who was this charitable lass?

Frasier *hesitates a beat.*

Daphne

His piano teacher.

Martin

What?! Your piano teacher?!

Frasier

Thank you again, Daphne.

Daphne

Well it's not like it's a secret. It's all right here in black and white . . . about your awkward, teenage lunging. And how you used to call your chest hair your "rug of love."

Martin *and* **Niles** *burst out laughing.*

Frasier

Well not all of it's true. He did take some literary license.

Daphne

Then you're not really able to bring a woman to hidden realms of ecstasy with your pantherlike prowess?

Frasier

Well, that part he got right.

Martin

Boy, this really fries me, knowing that woman was taking advantage of my kid. Plus I was shelling out ten bucks a week for piano lessons so you could get your hedge trimmed.

Niles

Wait a minute. We're not talking about Miss Warner, are we?

Martin *(to Niles)*

Don't tell me this was going on during your lessons, too?

Niles

No. You'll be relieved to know that I was actually studying music, while Frasier was getting his Rachmaninoffs.

Frasier

Look, this wasn't some tawdry, older woman lusting after young

flesh. We cared about each other. Clarice introduce me to a world I'd
never known . . . and wouldn't know again for six and a half years.

Daphne

It's true. As Mr. Fallow put it, she saw your sensitive, poetic side.
And you couldn't help noticing the way her ripe, heaving bosom
would brush your cheek whenever she reached for the metronome.

Frasier

The heaving bosom, the metronome – how could someone who drank
so heavily remember so much?

Niles

Yet still conveniently forget who told him the story.

Frasier

Well, he's going to get a little reminder today.

He crosses off. **Martin** *and* **Niles** *stare after him for a beat, then both grab
for the book, as we:*
FADE OUT.

Scene C

FADE IN:
INT. RADIO STUDIO – DAY – DAY/2
**Roz, Frasier, Thomas Jay Fallow, Bulldog, Gil Chesterton,
Amber Edwards**
Thomas Jay Fallow *is on the air with* **Amber Edwards**. *He is reading from
his book.* **Amber** *listens with rapt attention.*

Thomas

"I budded when you kissed me. I withered when you left me. I
bloomed a few months while you loved me."

Through the window we see **Roz** *in the hall, holding a copy of the book and
staring at* **Thomas** *adoringly. Behind her* **Frasier** *gesticulates angrily. We
see but do not hear him ranting.*

Amber

What was the *New York Times* book reviewer thinking? That's
beautiful.

Angle on the hallway, where **Frasier** *has been ranting to* **Roz**. *Now we see*
Thomas *and* **Amber** *in the booth but we do not hear them.*

Roz

Would you calm down?

Frasier

Not until I have exacted my pound of flesh.

Roz

Could you at least wait until I've had my book signed?

Frasier

Why not let me sign it? It's my story. By the way, Roz, you haven't let anyone around here know that, have you? They'd have a field day with me.

Roz

Hey, give me credit for a little discretion, will ya?

Bulldog *comes down the hall and immediately spots* **Frasier**.

Bulldog

Hey, Piano Boy! Way to pound those keys!

Roz

I knew I couldn't trust Father Mike to keep his trap shut.

Frasier

Bulldog, please, I don't want it commonly known.

Bulldog

Hey, it's no big deal, Doc. It just so happens that when I was sixteen I had a similar experience with an older woman who introduced me to the mysteries of love. Of course, she was a pro . . .

Roz

Oh yuck.

Bulldog

Hey, it was a birthday present from my dad, okay?

Frasier

Thank you for that Norman Rockwell moment, but aren't you due in some smelly locker room somewhere?

Bulldog

Want to know the ironic thing, Doc? All I wanted was a bike.

Bulldog *exits.* **Frasier** *glares at* **Roz**.

Roz

Oh, come on. How'd you expect me not to tell? You can't keep something that juicy bottled up. I only told one person.

Gil Chesterton *comes down the hall and sees* **Frasier**.

Gil

Hello, Frasier, Roz.

Roz

Hi, Gil.

Gil

I was just jotting down my latest restaurant review when I came up
with the perfect sandwich to name after you at Rosenthal's Deli.

Frasier

Please don't keep us in suspense.

Gil

"Frasier Crane's Double Decker." It consists of aged pheasant, spring
chicken, and of course plenty of tongue.

Frasier *(to Roz)*

I'll get you for this.

Roz

You already have. I won't be able to fantasize about teenage boys any
more without seeing your face.

Bulldog *comes back through, sees* **Gil**, *and starts to goof on* **Frasier** *by
quoting lines from the book.*

Bulldog *(to Gil)*

"Ravish me, my young maestro."

Gil

"I'm your rhapsody, play me."

Bulldog

"I long to tickle the ivories of your loins."

Gil

My vessel yearns to dock in the magnificence of your harbor.

Bulldog *laughs, then realizes.*

Bulldog

Hey, that's not from the book.

They turn the corner and exit.

Frasier

Doesn't that woman ever have to break for a commercial?

They go into **Roz's** *booth, which is now occupied by* **Amber's** *engineer.
From in here we can hear* **Amber** *and* **Thomas**.

Amber

One thing I must ask you – what was your inspiration for this wonderful love story?

Frasier

Don't make a sound. This is his last chance.

Thomas

Well Amber, it was actually given to me . . . by God.

Frasier

"By God"?! Can you believe this guy's grandiosity? I'm God and he knows it!

Amber

We'll be right back with the divinely inspired Thomas Jay Fallow after this station break.

The on-air light goes off.

Amber *(cont'd) (to Thomas)*

Will you excuse me? I want to call my ex-husband and say, "Okay, let's try again."

She exits, leaving him alone in the booth. **Frasier** *enters.*

Frasier

Thomas Jay Fallow?

Thomas *(surprised)*

Frasier . . . Frasier Crane. What are you doing here?

Frasier

So my name hasn't entirely escaped your sievelike memory.

Thomas

Why would it?

Frasier

Well, it didn't seem to make it into your acknowledgments, you egomaniacal thief!

Thomas *(excited)*

You read my book?

Frasier

I didn't have to read it. I lived it. Not that anyone would know that from reading your three pages of acknowledgments, in which you thank everyone from your kindergarten teacher to the man who designed the typeface. But no mention of me. Of course, why should you? All I did was provide you with the very story which you've ruthlessly merchandised into a multimillion dollar treacle machine.

A beat.

Thomas
Is there more?

Frasier
It figures a hack like you wouldn't recognize a forceful climax.

Thomas *looks at him for a long beat, then begins to blink. Tears come to his eyes and he sniffles.*

Thomas
I don't know what to say . . . You're right.

Frasier
Well, that's a start.

Thomas
No, you're right. *(he starts crying)* I'm so sorry . . . How could I be so thoughtless? I owe you everything.

Thomas *buries his face in the lapels of* **Frasier's** *jacket.*

Frasier
I don't know about everything.

Thomas *is weeping as* **Roz** *enters.*

Roz
God, Frasier, what did you say to the poor man?

Amber *enters.*

Amber
Thomas, what happened?

Roz
Frasier made him cry.

Thomas *lets out another sob. Several more women stream in from the hallway, coming to* **Thomas's** *aid and casting accusing glances at* **Frasier**. *As the women huddle and fuss over* **Thomas**, *and* **Roz** *presents her book for his signature, we:*
FADE OUT.

End of Act One

ACT TWO

Scene D

A black screen. In white letters appears, "The Tears it Takes a Summer Wind to Dry . . ."

Niles (V.O.)
Maris is reading *Slow Tango in South Seattle.*

FADE IN:
INT. FRASIER'S LIVING ROOM – THAT EVENING – NIGHT/2
Niles, Martin, Frasier, Daphne, Eddie
Niles *is talking to* **Martin**.

Niles *(cont'd)*
I think it's put thoughts in her head. This morning I found her cooing over the college student who skims the koi pond.

Martin
I wouldn't concern myself.

Niles
So you think it's just innocent flirting?

Martin
No, I just wouldn't concern myself.

Frasier *enters from outside. He's a bit down.*

Frasier
Hi Dad, Niles.

Niles
Congratulations, Frasier. Maris was listening to "Book Chat" today during her seaweed wrap and heard Thomas Jay Fallow acknowledge his enormous debt to you.

Frasier
Yes, I had a little talk with him at the station.

Niles
Did he seem properly contrite?

Frasier
I made him cry.

Martin
That's my boy. You must be feeling pretty good.

Frasier

Actually, Dad, the whole thing has left me strangely unsatisfied.

Martin

Why? You told him off, didn't you?

Frasier

Yeah?

Martin

So?

Frasier

I still feel sort of empty. I don't know why. I've been twisting it around in my mind all day.

Martin

You kill me, you know that. You get exactly what you want and you're still not happy. Life is not hard. You make it hard. You don't just let things happen and enjoy them. You analyze everything to death. You could learn a big lesson from this dog. You know what makes him happy? A sock. Come on, Eddie.

Martin *and* **Eddie** *exit.*

Niles

Ignore him. Obviously what's troubling you goes deeper than your usual malaise.

Daphne *enters carrying the book.*

Daphne *(to Frasier)*

Shame on you!

Frasier

What for?

Daphne

What for? You just ran out on her, leaving her bed as empty as a swallow's nest after fall's first frost, and you ask me what for?

Niles

Is this true?

Frasier

I'd been accepted at Harvard, what else was I going to do?

Daphne

So you make off in the middle of the night without so much as a kiss on the forehead.

Niles

You never said good-bye?

Frasier

I promised I'd call her at Christmas.

Daphne *"hmmphs!" disapprovingly and exits to the kitchen.*

Frasier *(cont'd) (calls after her)*

Well I didn't say what year.

Niles

Aha.

Frasier

Aha, what?

Niles

Aha, this. I have a theory.

Frasier

Well why else would you say "aha"?

Niles

Just listen. You thought you were angry at Thomas Fallow for failing to thank you for the contribution you made to his life. But perhaps the person you're really angry at is yourself. You never thanked Miss Warner for the contribution she made to your life.

Frasier

No, but I'm sure she understood. I was seventeen years old.

Niles

Well, perhaps she didn't. She was a vulnerable, lonely, middle-aged woman. It could be that her feelings for you were genuine. Feelings that you crushed when you disappeared without so much as a thank you or a good-bye.

Frasier

Yes, well, thank you and good-bye.

Niles

Fine, then. I'll just leave you with this thought. Your encounter with Thomas Jay Fallow was unsatisfactory because it didn't provide you the closure you were seeking. For that, you would have to make amends with Miss Warner.

Niles *exits.* **Eddie** *enters with a sock in his mouth and drops it on* **Frasier's** *foot.*

Frasier *(calling off)*

Very funny, Dad!

AND WE:

FADE OUT.

Scene E

FADE IN:

INT. FRASIER'S LIVING ROOM – LATE THAT NIGHT – NIGHT/2

Frasier, Daphne

Frasier *is sitting in his chair in the dimly lit room reading the novel.*

Frasier (V.O.)

"He had been a teenage Balboa, an explorer of the rising pinnacles and gently curving slopes of my body, and in one explosive burst of discovery he had staked claim to the Pacific Ocean that was my soul. But now he was leaving. Going. Vanishing like a solitary boat on the lonely horizon. Departing like a train, rolling ceaselessly through the night. Exiting swiftly, like –"

Frasier *sighs in exasperation and turns a couple of pages, then reads on.*

Frasier (V.O.) *(cont'd)*

"And so, he was gone. And now, in the cool of the evening I play my piano and his last words resonate through the notes. 'I'll come back to you, my cherished one. In a world of constant flux, my love will never change.'"

Frasier *lets the book rest in his lap.* **Daphne** *crosses through and swats him with her book. On his look we:*

FADE OUT.

Scene H

A black screen. In white letters appears, "I Feel Older Since His Shadows Left My Door."

FADE IN:

EXT. CLARICE WARNER'S FRONT PORCH – DAY – DAY/3

Frasier, Mrs. Warner, Clarice, Man

Frasier *approaches a screen door. Through the screen he sees an older woman playing the piano. He is somewhat taken aback.*

Frasier

Time, the subtle thief of youth.

He knocks on the door. **Mrs. Warner** *leaves the piano and answers the door.*

Mrs. Warner

Hello, may I help you?

Frasier

Ms. Warner?

Mrs. Warner

Yes?

Frasier

I, I'm Frasier Crane.

Mrs. Warner

I'm sorry. My memory isn't what it used to be. But, please come in.

Frasier *follows* **Mrs. Warner** *into the living room.*

Frasier

Surely, you must have some recollection of me. A fair-haired boy outside your door, at the piano, on the piano?

Mrs. Warner

I'd like to.

Frasier

Well before all the memories come flooding back to you, I should tell you we had a romance that didn't have the happiest ending. That's why I'm here. The night we walked in the summer storm and I kissed the raindrops off your nose, I promised we'd always be together. But I didn't keep that promise. You helped a shy adolescent take his first uncertain steps toward becoming a man, and how did I repay this kindness? By running off and leaving you with nothing but your memories.

Mrs. Warner

And not many of those either.

Frasier *(pained)*

Oh.

He takes her hand and begins to pat it.

Frasier *(cont'd)*

Can you ever forgive me?

Mrs. Warner

You're so sweet. Of course I can forgive you.

She hugs **Frasier.** *An attractive woman in her very-sexy early sixties,* **Clarice Warner,** *enters the room.*

Clarice

Mother, what's going on here?

Mrs. Warner

Oh, Clarice.

Frasier *(stunned)*

You're Clarice?!

Mrs. Warner

This is Frasier Crane. Apparently we were quite an item at one time.

Clarice

Frasier? What are you doing here?

Frasier

Making an enormous mistake.

Mrs. Warner *(rising)*

Why don't I make us all some iced tea.

She heads out. On her way, she passes **Clarice**.

Mrs. Warner *(cont'd) (to Clarice)*

Hands off. This one's mine.

Mrs. Warner *exits.*

Clarice

I can't believe you're here. I mean, look at you.

Frasier

Look at you. You look incredible.

Clarice

Well, sure, compared to my mother.

Frasier

No, no, I mean even if I hadn't seen her.

Clarice

You came because of that book, didn't you?

Frasier

Yes, and let me say right off I'm sorry. That story was told to Mr. Fallow in confidence. He had no right to put it in print.

Clarice

There's no need to apologize. I mean, it's not like you mentioned my name. You didn't, did you?

Frasier

No, I would never do that.

There is an awkward beat of silence.

Clarice

So, are you married?

Frasier

Divorced. You?

Clarice

No, I never married.

Frasier *does a slight grimace.*

Frasier

I actually came here to apologize about more than just the book. You see, I never felt quite right about the way I left things. I always felt as if I had abandoned you. It was selfish and cowardly.

Clarice

Frasier relax. I always felt guilty for shortchanging you on your music lessons. Do you still keep it up?

Frasier

What? Oh, the piano – yes, yes. Look, it's very kind of you to let me off the hook . . .

Clarice

Oh, I could never be mad at you, Frasier.

Frasier

It's funny, I was so nervous about coming here but now it feels just like old times.

She smiles. **Frasier** *takes a seat at the piano bench and accidentally hits the metronome. It begins to go back and forth.*

Clarice

Oh, let me get that.

She reaches across **Frasier** *for the metronome, and brushes against him.*

Frasier

At the risk of sounding forward, would you like to go out and get a cup of coffee with me?

Clarice

Thanks, but I'll have to say no.

Frasier

If you think I'm uncomfortable about the age difference, please rest assured that's no longer an issue.

A man in his late twenties appears at the door, knocks, and enters.

Man

Hi honey, ready to go?

He gives her a kiss.

Clarice
Yeah sweetie, I'll be right out.

The man exits. **Frasier** *looks crestfallen.*

Frasier
Are you and he . . .?

Clarice *shrugs.*

Clarice
I wasn't interested in forty-year-old men then, and I guess I'm still not. Great to see you again though. *(calling off)* Bye, Mom.

Clarice *exits, leaving* **Frasier** *in shock.* **Mrs. Warner** *enters with the iced tea.*

Mrs. Warner
Good, we're alone now.

She sets down the tea, dips a finger into the pitcher and dabs her nose.

Mrs. Warner *(cont'd)*
Did you see what I did? I put a raindrop on my nose.

She sits down on the couch and invitingly pats the place next to her. As all the color drains from **Frasier's** *face [a really good actor could do this], we:*
FADE OUT.

End of Act Two

Scene J

END CREDITS
FADE IN:
INT. CLARICE WARNER'S LIVING ROOM – LATER THAT DAY – DAY/3
Frasier, Mrs. Warner
Frasier *and* **Mrs. Warner** *are side-by-side at the piano playing a duet.* **Frasier** *does not look particularly happy to still be here.* **Mrs. Warner** *slides a little closer to him on the piano bench.* **Frasier** *discreetly slides a little farther away.* **Mrs. Warner** *slides toward him.* **Frasier** *slides away again, and we:*
FADE OUT.

End of Show

The Matchmaker

Episode #40572-028

Written by
Joe Keenan

Created by
David Angell/Peter Casey/David Lee

Directed by
David Lee

Frasier's new boss puts smiles on Daphne and Frasier's faces . . .

. . . but not for long.

ACT ONE

Scene A

A black screen. In white letters appears, "Where There's Smoke . . ."

FADE IN:

INT. FRASIER'S LIVING ROOM – NIGHT – NIGHT/1

Frasier, Daphne, Martin, Eddie

It's the middle of the night and the apartment is dark.

SFX: smoke alarm

Frasier (O.S.)

Oh my God! Fire! Fire!

Martin *rushes in from the hall, wearing pajama bottoms and a T-shirt.*

Martin

Eddie! Eddie, where are you, boy?

Frasier (O.S.) *(banging on door)*

Dad! Dad, wake up! Dad, are you in there?

Martin *crosses into the kitchen.*

Martin

Eddie! Here, Eddie!

Frasier *rushes in, dressed in pajamas. He turns the lights on.*

Frasier

Dad! Dad, where are you!?

Martin *reenters from the kitchen.*

Martin

You seen Eddie?

Frasier

No! What's burning? What's on fire?

Martin *(calling)*

Eddie!

SFX: the alarm stops

Daphne, *very agitated, enters in her nightgown.*

Daphne

It's all right! False alarm. The one over my bed went off.

Frasier

Oh, thank God!

Daphne *(to Martin)*

And don't worry about Eddie. He's back in my room. *(then)* The
noise the bloody thing makes! It would be less upsetting to just wake
up on fire.

Martin

What the hell triggered it?

As **Daphne** *speaks* **Eddie** *trots in, a pack of cigarettes in his mouth.*

Daphne

Who knows? I was dozing quite peacefully when it started screaming
away for no reason at all.

Frasier

I see. No reason at all . . .

He moves to **Eddie** *and removes the pack of cigarettes from his mouth.*

Frasier *(cont'd)*

And what have we here? Eddie, you've been smoking in Daphne's
room.

Daphne

Bad dog.

Frasier

Daphne.

Daphne

Oh, I know, I know. You have a no-smoking rule. I'm sorry. But every
now and then I feel a bit tense and I find a ciggy can be very soothing.

Martin

Oh, it's been real soothing. It should only be about an hour till my
heart stops fibrillating.

Martin *heads for the hall.*

Frasier

Wait a minute, Dad.

Martin *turns.*

Frasier *(cont'd)*

You really thought the apartment was on fire?

Martin

I think you have to assume that when the alarm goes off.

Frasier

And in that harrowing, possibly life-threatening instant, the very first thought to enter your mind was . . . "Where's Eddie?"

Martin
No, that was my second thought. My first thought was, "Where's my pajama bottoms?"

Frasier
Actually, my first thought was you finding your pajama bottoms too.

Martin *goes.*

Frasier *(cont'd)*
God, three A.M. Of course, this would happen the night before I have an early meeting. *(a hand on the light switch; to Daphne)* Aren't you going back to bed?

Daphne
No, I'll sit up a bit. I'm feeling a bit blue.

Frasier
Is it anything you'd like to discuss?

Daphne
No, you need your sleep. It's nothing important.

Frasier *nods and heads off down the hall. During the following, he stops and turns back.*

Daphne *(cont'd)*
Just this feeling that my life's a gaping sinkhole and I'm just marking time while the flower of my youth rots on the vine.

Frasier *(eager to go)*
Well, if you're sure . . .

Frasier *starts down the hall.* **Daphne** *emits an achingly poignant, Ophelia-like sigh.* **Frasier,** *defeated, turns.*

Frasier *(cont'd)*
I really do wish you'd tell me about it.

Daphne
Well, if you have to know, it's my love life.

Frasier
Really? Have you been seeing a man?

Daphne
Only when I close my eyes and concentrate.

Frasier
I see – going through a little drought.

Daphne

Small wonder. I'm cooped up here most of the time. And when I do get out it's usually with your father. People see us and assume I'm his daughter or else his wife – either way it's like having my own personal can of stud repellent.

During the following, **Daphne** *begins smoking another cigarette.*

Frasier

Listen, I know how bleak things can look when you're going through a dry spell, but they always end sooner or later. I remember once in Boston feeling exactly the way you do now – and the very next week I met a lovely, if somewhat loquacious barmaid, fell madly in love and got engaged . . . *(realizing, sadly)* Of course, she left me standing at the altar – but the point is I didn't give up. I took my poor, battered heart and offered it to Lilith, *(thinks)* who put it in her little cuisinart and hit the purée button. But I rebounded. And look how far I've come . . . Divorced, lonely, and living with my father – who cares less about me than he does about his foul-breathed flea resort of a dog.

Frasier *takes the cigarette from* **Daphne** *and begins smoking it. And we:*
FADE OUT.

Scene B

FADE IN:
INT. CAFE NERVOSA – DAY – DAY/2
Frasier, Roz, Niles
Frasier *sits alone at a table.* **Niles** *is at the counter.* **Roz** *enters and crosses to* **Frasier**. *She's a little miffed.*

Roz

I figured I'd find you here. You know, you missed the meeting with the new station manager.

Frasier

Oh God, I completely forgot. Was he insulted?

Roz

No, I covered for you. *(peering at him)* God, you look like you've been ridden hard and put away wet.

Frasier

Thank you. I was up until all hours talking with Daphne, competing to see who had the more pathetic love life. On the bright side, I won.

Roz

Your problems I know about – what are Daphne's?

Frasier
She's just having trouble meeting men.

Roz
Say no more.

Roz *pulls an address book from her bag.*

Frasier *(realizing her intent; leery but diplomatic)*
Oh no, Roz, that's all right, really. You don't have to donate one of
your boyfriends to Daphne.

Roz
Please. I'd be happy to.

Frasier
Still – one hates to break up a collection.

Niles, *carrying two coffees, approaches the table.*

Niles
Here we are. One triple espresso and one mocha latte. *(showing
Frasier his mocha; annoyed)* Do those chocolate shavings look any
different to you?

Frasier
No.

Niles
Well, they do to me. I think they've switched to an inferior
domestic brand.

Niles *takes a sip and scrunches up his nose.*

Niles *(cont'd)*
Waxy.

He takes his handkerchief and dabs his lips. **Frasier** *takes the handkerchief
from him.*

Frasier
I'll have this sent to the lab for analysis.

Then giving the handkerchief back to **Niles**.

Frasier *(cont'd)*
Put that thing away.

Roz *(spotting a name)*
Sven Bachman. An aerobics instructor. You can bounce a quarter off
of . . . Well, just about any part of him.

Frasier *(to Roz)*

I don't think so.

Niles *(to Frasier)*

This place is going to hell in a handbasket. What's next? Humorous napkins?

Roz

This one's perfect – Gunther Dietrich. Loads of fun and he's a runway model.

Frasier

A German narcissist – there's an appealing combination.

Roz

Okay, I'll keep looking.

Niles

Looking for what?

Roz

I'm helping Frasier find a man for Daphne.

Niles

What?

Roz *(off the book)*

Here we go. He's a tennis coach and his name's Paolo –

Niles

For God's sake, Frasier. Paolo, Gunther, Sven? Why not just lather Daphne up with baby oil and hurl her over the wall of a prison yard?

Roz

Excuse me, but I've dated all these guys.

Niles

Where do you think I came up with the imagery?

Roz *(to Niles)*

Listen, you little titmouse . . .

Frasier

Niles, you're completely out of line. *(to Roz)* But he does have a point. We have to remember that you and Daphne are different types of women. Where Daphne is a bit shy and inexperienced, you're more . . . Well, a lot more . . . Actually, you'd be hard pressed to find anyone . . .

Roz

Oh, I get it. Not one man I've ever dated is good enough for Miss Daphne. Is that what you're trying to say?

Frasier

No. That's what I'm trying not to say – and you're not making it very easy.

Roz *(rising)*

I'm outta here.

Frasier

Roz, please . . . Wait.

Roz

No, no, I can't stay. The fleet's in.

Roz *exits.*

Niles

Don't feel bad, Frasier. You did the right thing. When I think of the cads she might have unleashed on that delicate, innocent –

Frasier

Oh, get a grip, Niles! I don't know what sort of twisted fantasy you've concocted for yourself about your future with Daphne. I suspect it involves a comet hitting the earth and the two of you having to rebuild the species, but trust me, it's not going to happen. She needs a man, Niles, one who's in a position to do more for her than just smell her hair – and if I can help her find one, I will. Good day.

Frasier *goes.* **Niles** *sits glumly. At the next table a cigarette burns in an ashtray.* **Niles** *takes the cigarette, wipes it off with his handkerchief, then takes a drag. And we:*
FADE OUT.

Scene C

FADE IN:
INT. RADIO STUDIO – A FEW HOURS LATER – DAY/2
Frasier, Roz, Tom
Frasier *is on the air.* **Roz** *is in her booth.*

SFX: *the high-pitched monotone of the emergency broadcast system*

Frasier *passes the time by thumbing through a magazine and yawning a couple of times. Finally, the tone ends.*

Frasier

And so ends our test of the emergency broadcast system. If this had been an actual emergency, your radio would be melting in your hands. We'll be back after this newsbreak.

Frasier *removes his headset.* **Roz** *crosses in and throws a half-eaten donut in a napkin on his desk.*

> **Roz**
> In the future, please keep your disgusting, half-eaten food off my console. In fact, just stay out of my sight.

> **Frasier**
> You're still mad at me. I can tell.

> **Roz**
> There's that keen sensitivity that keeps you in such demand with the ladies.

Roz *slams the door between their booths.* **Frasier** *opens it.*

> **Frasier**
> Roz, I'm sorry, but I feel very protective about Daphne. The man I'm looking for has to be good-looking, smart, successful.

There is a light knock at the other door to **Frasier's** *booth.* **Frasier** *turns to find* **Tom O'Connor** *at the doorway. He is in his late thirties and seems to glow with all the virtues* **Frasier** *has just enumerated.*

> **Tom**
> Excuse me.

> **Frasier**
> Yes?

> **Tom**
> I'm Tom O'Connor, the new station manager.

> **Frasier** *(shaking his hand)*
> It's a pleasure to meet you. I'm sorry about missing that meeting this morning. I'm sure Roz explained. I overslept.

> **Tom**
> Actually, she told me you had a doctor's appointment.

> **Frasier**
> Well, she knows best. She keeps my appointment book.

> **Tom**
> Say, that's a beautiful tie.

> **Frasier**
> Thank you. I got it in London at this little custom shop. What was the name of it? It's right off Sloane Square. *(trying to remember he shuts his eyes)* What's it called? It's got this stone facade . . . God, I can picture it.

Tom *turns* **Frasier's** *tie around and reads the label.*

Tom

Smythe and Son?

Frasier

No, that's not it. *(opens eyes, sees Tom holding his tie)* Of course, that could be it.

Tom

You know, I just came from London. I spent the last five years there working for the BBC.

Frasier

Really? I love London – the theater especially.

Tom

Me too. I'm a big theater buff. I hated to leave, but . . . well, I'd just gone through sort of a messy breakup. I thought I'd sleep better with a continent between us.

Frasier

I know the feeling. *(the idea strikes him)* So . . . I take it you're unattached?

Tom

Yes, but I haven't given up hope.

Frasier

Well, you may have come to the right place. So, getting back to London, were you fond of the British?

Tom

Yes, very much. I guess I've always had a weakness for people who are just a little eccentric.

Frasier *(the wheels turning)*

Really?

Roz *(into her mike)*

Fifteen seconds.

Tom

Well, nice meeting you –

Frasier

Same here.

Frasier *sits and dons his headphones.* **Tom** *turns to go again.*

Frasier *(cont'd)*

Say, Tom, I know this is short notice, but if you're not doing anything

Saturday, why don't you come by my place for dinner? Nothing fancy.

Tom

Thanks. I'd like that.

Tom *crosses into* **Roz's** *booth. The on-air light goes on.*

Frasier

Welcome back, Seattle. So, whom do we have up next, Roz?

Roz

We have James from Tacoma on line one.

Frasier

Hello, James. I'm listening.

Angle on **Roz's** *booth.* **Tom** *stands facing* **Roz** *with his back to* **Frasier**. **Tom** *and* **Roz** *ad-lib hellos.*

Tom *(to Roz)*

Boy, it's the same every job I take. Word spreads like wildfire.

Roz

What's that?

Tom

Oh, you know. You tell one or two people you're gay and before you can blink it's all over the station.

Roz

They don't call it broadcasting for nothing.

Frasier *notices* **Roz** *talking to* **Tom** *and assumes she's hitting on him.* **Frasier** *wags a finger at* **Roz** *indicating "Get away from him."*

Tom *(re: Frasier)*

He seems like a nice guy.

Roz

He's okay.

Tom

I hope he's more than okay. He just asked me out on a date and I accepted.

Roz

Frasier? Asked you out on a date?

Frasier *begins scribbling on a piece of paper.*

Tom

Yeah, he asked me to come to his place for dinner. So I wanted to ask you is there any particular wine he likes?

Roz
Tom, there's something you should know about Frasier –

From his booth, **Frasier** *holds up a sign. It reads, "Hands off! He's taken!"* **Roz** *reads it.*

Tom
What?

Roz *(to Tom)*
He's nuts about Chardonnay.

Tom
Thanks.

Tom *exits, and as* **Roz** *smiles at* **Frasier,** *we:*
FADE OUT.

End of Act One

ACT TWO

Scene D

A black screen. In white letters appears, "Some Enchanted Evening . . ."

FADE IN:

INT. FRASIER'S LIVING ROOM – EVENING – NIGHT/3

Frasier, Daphne, Martin, Niles, Tom

Frasier *is arranging a centerpiece on the dining room table.*

Martin *(screaming at the TV)*
You overpaid, lard ass bum. You couldn't catch a cold in a snowbank.

Frasier *reacts as if to say his perfect atmosphere has been decimated.*

Frasier
Dad, must you scream at the television? They can't hear you.

Martin
Hey, c'mon, this is a nail-biter. It's the fourth quarter and they're using a rookie quarterback.

Frasier
I don't care if it's the tenth quarter and they're using guns. I am trying to host a civilized dinner.

Martin
Fine. I'll watch the end in my room while I'm putting on my ascot.

Martin *exits down the hallway, as* **Daphne** *enters from the kitchen and sets the table.*

Daphne *(murmuring furiously to herself)*

Does he ask permission first, no, he just barges in and says he's set me up with God knows who and I'm supposed to turn cartwheels like I'm bloody Cinderella . . .

Frasier

Will you relax? I told you it's not a setup. I didn't even tell Tom you'd be here.

Daphne

Oh, an ambush, then? Much nicer. My girlfriends in Manchester used to set me up all the time. And it was always some gangly bounder with a boarding house reach. And he wasn't going for the Coleman's hot mustard, if you know what I mean.

Frasier

Well, I think you'll be pleasantly surprised. And remember, he's nothing more than a co-worker here for a nice dinner. If some spark should ignite, fine, but there's no pressure, none whatsoever. *(beat)* Is that what you're wearing?

Daphne

Why, what's wrong with it?

Sfx: doorbell

Frasier

Oh, there he is.

As he crosses to the door:

Frasier *(cont'd)*

Don't you have something with a little more oomph? What about that strapless thing you have?

Daphne

Do you have any idea how uncomfortable a strapless bra is?

Frasier

Thanks to my fraternity days, as a matter of fact, I do. Just put it on. Trust me. He's worth it.

Daphne

So glad there's no pressure.

Daphne *exits to her room.* **Frasier** *opens the door.* **Tom** *is there, dressed in an overcoat and nice suit, carrying a bottle of wine.*

Frasier

Tom, come on in.

Tom

Hi, Frasier.

He hands **Frasier** *the bottle of wine.*

Tom *(cont'd)*

I don't know. Something told me you'd like Chardonnay.

Frasier

My favorite.

Tom *takes in the apartment and its view of Seattle.*

Frasier *(cont'd)*

So, what do you think?

Tom

It's a hell of a view.

Frasier

It's even better from the bedroom.

Tom

Why don't we just start with a drink? *(noting four places set)* Oh, four places. Who's joining us?

Frasier

Just my little household. My father and his charming physical therapist, Daphne.

Tom

You live with your dad? God, I can't even imagine that. I mean, it's great that you get along so well, but . . . *(confidentially)* doesn't having him here put a crimp in your love life?

Frasier

Not at all. That is, except when I bring my dates home and he tries to steal them.

Tom

You're kidding? He really does that?

Daphne *enters in a sexy, strapless dress.*

Frasier

Oh, yes. He's quite the old rascal. *(then)* Well, look who's here. I'd like you to meet Daphne Moon. Daphne, this is Tom O'Connor.

Tom *(to Daphne)*

Pleasure to meet you.

Daphne

Likewise. Dr. Crane, you didn't take his coat – may I?

Tom *turns his back to* **Daphne** *so that she can help him remove his coat.*
Daphne *looks at* **Frasier** *and elaborately conveys her delight, mouthing,*
"He's gorgeous. Thank you, thank you." **Frasier** *beams and smiles a*
"What'd I tell you?" smile. **Daphne** *folds the coat over her arm.*

Daphne *(cont'd)*

Ooh. This is strange. I'm getting a little flash.

Tom

A flash?

Frasier

Daphne feels she possesses some kind of psychic powers. You know
these English eccentrics. Ha, ha.

Daphne *(to Tom)*

You've just been through a very painful breakup, haven't you?

Tom

Yes. *(then to Frasier)* Wait a minute. You told her that, didn't you?

Daphne

There was a bitter dispute about ownership of opera recordings.

Tom

Whoa, now I am impressed.

Daphne

Well, don't get too impressed. It comes and it goes. Now if you'll
excuse me, I'll nip into the kitchen. I have a bird to baste.

Daphne *exits to the kitchen.*

Frasier

That's our Daphne. Isn't she something?

Tom

She's great. And I love hearing that accent again.

As **Martin** *heads down the hallway, he calls from off-stage:*

Martin (O.S.)

Hey, Frasier, I don't need to put on a tie for this joker, do I?

Martin *enters the room.*

Martin *(cont'd) (spotting Tom)*

Oh.

Frasier
Tom, I'd like you to meet my father, Martin Crane.

Tom *(extending hand)*
Tom O'Connor. Nice to meet you.

They shake.

Martin
Sorry about that joker business. I call everybody joker, or jerk, pinhead, bozo.

Frasier
And yet amazingly, he's free for dinner on short notice. *(exiting)* Well, why don't I open some of this wonderful wine.

Frasier *exits to the kitchen, joining* **Daphne** *who is basting a chicken.*

Frasier *(cont'd)*
Well?

Daphne
Oh, he's a looker. I'm glad you made me put on my lucky bra. He's worth every wire digging into my rib cage.

Frasier
You made quite an impression on him too. He said you were great.

Daphne
Go on . . . My God, will you listen to me, getting carried away like a schoolgirl when I just met the man. I'm not raising my hopes tonight . . . though I'm glad I raised my bosom.

Angle on **Martin** *and* **Tom** *in the living room.*

Martin
Let me tell you, you're gonna love Seattle. It's a real people place. Good food, great bars.

Tom
I've heard that. Any you'd recommend?

Martin
I usually go to a place called Duke's. Great crowd there. A lot of young cops.

Tom
That could be fun.

Martin
Say, you a football fan?

Tom
Yeah. I really missed it while I was living in London.

Martin
We should take in a Seahawks game sometime. Frasier hates it, so it'd just be us.

Tom
Hey, Frasier warned me about you.

Martin
Okay, so I yell at the players too much.

Frasier *reenters with two glasses of wine and a can of Ballantines.*

Frasier
Here you are, Tom *(handing glass to Tom)* And Dad, I selected an amusing little vintage for you, too. *(handing him a beer)* You'll forgive me for not bringing you the pull-tab to sniff.

Martin
Merci beaucoup.

SFX: doorbell

Frasier *crosses to the door, carrying his wine. He opens the door and* **Niles** *is standing there holding a book.*

Niles
Hello, Frasier. Oh, thank you.

He takes **Frasier's** *glass of wine and enters. During the following,* **Niles** *keeps craning his neck to get a look at* **Tom.**

Niles *(cont'd) (proffering the book)*
I just stopped by to return your book.

Frasier
This is your book.

Niles
So it is. You should borrow it, it's absorbing. *(leaning in, sotto)* And who would that remarkably ordinary-looking chap on the couch be?

Frasier
Niles, I know why you're here and you're completely out of line.

Tom *rises to greet* **Niles.**

Tom
Hi, I'm Tom O'Connor.

They shake.

Niles

How do you do? Dr. Niles Crane.

We hear **Daphne** *from the kitchen:*

Daphne (O.S.)

The bird's all done. All I need is a pair of big, strong arms . . .

She enters.

Daphne *(cont'd)*

. . . to haul it out of the oven.

Niles

Well, I don't need to be asked twice.

Niles *hurries into the kitchen past* **Daphne**. **Daphne** *smiles weakly, obviously feeling thwarted and exits back into the kitchen.* **Tom**, **Frasier** *and* **Martin** *stand a moment in slightly embarrassed silence.*

Frasier

That's my brother Niles. He's a little . . . *(lost, to Martin)* How would you explain Niles, Dad?

Martin

I usually just change the subject.

As **Martin** *crosses to the table and sits, waiting for his dinner, we:*
FADE OUT.

Scene E

FADE IN:
INT. FRASIER'S LIVING ROOM – LATER THAT EVENING – NIGHT/3
Frasier, Martin, Daphne, Niles, Tom
Everyone is seated at the table finishing coffee. Everyone's laughing and enjoying themselves, except, of course, for **Niles**. **Tom** *is in mid-story.*

Tom

. . . So halfway through the interview, her stomach starts rumbling and her body mike's picking it up. But I have to ignore it because what am I going to say? "Would Her Majesty like a bicarbonate?"

Daphne *laughs.*

Daphne

I could listen to your stories all night. They're so funny.

Niles

And all involving bodily functions.

Daphne *gets up and starts gathering dishes.*

Tom *(rises)*
Here, let me help with these.

Niles
Many hands make light the work!

Niles *rises. He and* **Tom** *clear the dishes, as* **Daphne** *and* **Frasier** *watch in helpless exasperation.* **Niles** *and* **Tom** *exit into the kitchen. Angle on the kitchen as they cross to the sink.*

Tom
Niles, could I speak with you a moment?

Niles
Yes.

Tom
I was just wondering. Did I say or do anything that offended you?

Niles
No.

Tom
Then maybe it's all in my head because I sensed that you had a problem with my dating Frasier.

Niles
Well, if you must know . . . *(stops)* I'm sorry, what was the question?

Tom
Do you have some problem with my dating your brother?

Niles *starts to open his mouth to say something, then stops. He thinks some more, then:*

Niles
No. No problem at all. I'm sorry if I gave you that impression.

Frasier *enters the kitchen with the remaining dishes.*

Frasier
Now, Niles, I didn't ask Tom to join us for dinner tonight so he'd be stuck in the kitchen talking to you. There're others who might want to have a crack at him.

Niles
Forgive me, brother. He's all yours.

Tom *and* **Frasier** *exit back into the living room.* **Martin** *enters the kitchen carrying an armload of dishes.*

Martin

That Tom's a great guy, huh? So, what do you think, maybe him and
Daphne . . .?

Niles *starts to laugh.*

Martin *(cont'd)*

What's so funny?

Niles

Oh, just a little predicament Frasier's gotten himself in.

Martin

What?

Niles

Put down those plates and I'll tell you.

Angle on the living room. **Frasier, Daphne,** *and* **Tom** *are by the bar.*
Frasier's *pouring port.*

Tom

I can't remember the last time I had such a wonderful evening.

Daphne

We should be thanking you. I can't remember when I laughed so hard.

From the kitchen we hear **Martin** *laughing himself silly.*

Daphne *(cont'd)*

You've still got Mr. Crane going.

Frasier

Daphne, how about a little after dinner music.

Daphne

Good idea.

Daphne *crosses to the stereo.*

Frasier

Quite a woman, isn't she?

Tom

Yes, she's really something. *(then, shyly)* Frasier, I was wondering . . .

Frasier

Yes . . .

Tom

Do you think before the evening's over we could get a little one on
one time?

Frasier

I think that can be arranged.

Frasier *crosses to* **Daphne** *who's just put on some music.*

SFX: romantic music

Frasier *(cont'd) (to Daphne quietly)*

He just asked if he could be alone with you.

Daphne

No. This really is my lucky bra. Keep the wine flowing while I go fix my lipstick.

Daphne *exits to her bedroom, as* **Martin** *and* **Niles** *enter from the kitchen, barely able to contain their mirth.*

Martin

Yeah, I guess I'd better be hitting the old sack. I don't want to stand in the way of young romance.

Frasier

And Niles, I'd appreciate it if you would be running along.

Niles

Certainly. I can see I'm a third wheel here.

Frasier

What? That was surprisingly easy after your attitude all evening toward Tom.

Niles

I was wrong about Tom. If I had to choose a man for Daphne, that's just who I'd pick. *(then, to Tom)* Nice meeting you, Tom. Good night.

Tom *(smiling, embarrassed)*

Good night.

Martin *exits to his bedroom.* **Frasier** *escorts* **Niles** *to the front door.*

Niles

Oh, Frasier, a word in your ear . . .

Frasier *and* **Niles** *exit into the hallway.*

Niles *(cont'd)*

I have something to tell you. Dad wanted to, but I won the coin toss.

Frasier

Well, what is it?

Niles

I talked to Tom in the kitchen and he's feeling romantic.

Frasier

That's why you're leaving.

Niles

But are you aware the object of his affection is not Daphne but you?

Frasier

Me? That's impossible. Tom is not gay.

Niles

He seems to be under that impression.

Frasier

There's obviously been some misunderstanding.

Niles

Well, there's a triumph of understatement. Good lord, Frasier, what did you say to the man to lead him on so?

Frasier

I did not lead him on. I just asked him if he was single, and then we chatted about theater and men's fashion and . . . Oh, my God!

Niles

Ah, the perils of refinement.

Frasier

Do you realize what this means?

Niles

Yes. You're dating your boss. You, of all people, should know the pitfalls of an office romance.

Frasier *(at sea, stammering)*

But . . . But, he said . . . I mean . . .

Niles

I see you're prepared to face your dilemma with eloquence. I'll call you tomorrow. Though, not too early, of course.

Niles *exits into the elevator.* **Frasier** *reenters the apartment. The lights are low, soft music is playing.* **Tom**, *sitting on the couch, smiles an "Alone at last!" smile.* **Frasier**, *at wit's end, returns a smile that combines panic and a demented coquettishness.*

Tom

So . . .

Frasier

So! . . . God, I hate this song!

Frasier *scurries over to the stereo and turns the music off.*

Tom
I've broken my rule for you. I usually don't date guys I work with.

Frasier
And I've sort of relaxed my rule for you too.

Tom
Well, now that we're finally alone, I want you to tell me all about yourself.

Frasier
Yes, I think maybe I'd better.

Frasier *sits on the chair.* **Tom** *pats the couch next to him.* **Frasier** *wearily crosses and sits next to him.*

Tom
You're cute when you're nervous.

Frasier
Then right now I must be downright adorable. Tom, I'm incredibly sorry, but we seem to have gotten our signals crossed here. The truth of the matter is, I'm completely straight.

A beat.

Tom
Hey, if you're not interested just say so.

Frasier
No, no. It's true. I really am. I asked you here tonight because you seemed very nice and you were going on so much about liking English people that I thought, "What a perfect man for Daphne."

Daphne *vamps in from the hall just in time to hear:*

Tom
I can't believe this. You really had no idea that I'm gay?

She stops, reaches behind her back and unhooks her bra. She turns and as she heads off, she rips her bra off, flings it with disgust, and stalks back to her room.

Frasier
Don't take this wrong, but it never even occurred to me you might be gay.

Tom
It never occurred to me you might be straight.

Frasier *(uncertain)*

Thank you. I just feel awful that I've managed to lead you on all night.

Tom

It's okay. Honest mistake.

Frasier

But still, pouring you drinks, raising your hopes, letting you think you'd finally found someone sophisticated and sensitive who could help you mend your shattered heart and . . .

Tom

Frasier, I'll learn to love again.

Frasier

Oh. Yes, of course.

They cross to the door.

Tom

Will you apologize to Daphne?

Frasier

For the rest of my days.

Tom

Does this mean your dad's not gay either?

Frasier

No, Dad's not gay.

Tom

But Niles . . . C'mon!

Frasier

Nope. 'Fraid not.

Tom

So this Maris guy he kept mentioning is a woman?

Frasier

Well, the jury's still out on that one.

AND WE:

FADE OUT.

Scene H

FADE IN:

INT. FRASIER'S LIVING ROOM – LATE THAT EVENING – NIGHT/3
Frasier, Daphne

Frasier *sits smoking and sipping cognac in the dimly lit room.* **Daphne** *enters from the hallway and sees him smoking.*

Daphne *(scolding)*

What, not again?

Frasier

Don't worry, I disconnected the alarm.

Daphne

Pity. I have half a mind to set it off and hope the firemen are cute.

Frasier

Daphne, I want to say again . . .

Daphne

I know, I know. You can stop beating yourself up. I'm not mad anymore. To tell you the truth, I was touched that you made the effort.

Frasier

Thank you.

Daphne

You know, you and your father, you've been good friends to me.

Frasier

Well, when you come down to it, that's all that really counts, isn't it? People who look out for you and whom you look out for. The mutual respect and affection.

Daphne

Absolutely.

Frasier

Amen.

A moment of silence.

Daphne

Of course, it's no substitute for having your bones jumped by an expert, is it?

Frasier

Not remotely, no.

Daphne *picks up a cigarette. As* **Frasier** *lights it for her, we:*
FADE OUT.

End of Act Two

A Room with a View

Episode #40570-041

Written by
Linda Morris & Vic Rauseo

Created by
David Angell/Peter Casey/David Lee

Directed by
David Lee

A harsh word from father to son.

Frasier, the inadvertent peeping Tom, desperately tries to apologize to Daphne.

ACT ONE

Scene A

FADE IN:

INT. FRASIER'S LIVING ROOM – LATE MORNING – DAY/1

Frasier, Martin, Niles, Eddie

Frasier *walks down the hall from his room. He is preparing to leave for work, tying his tie. He looks for something on the coffee table. We find out later it is a book. He lifts a newspaper on* **Martin's** *table, it's not there. He calls for help.*

Frasier

Dad?

No answer.

Frasier *(cont'd)*

Daphne?

A beat.

Frasier *(cont'd)*

Anybody home?

There's no answer. **Frasier** *opens the lid of the piano bench, hoping to find the book, no luck. Standing at the piano, he takes a moment to noodle a few notes of a classical piece. He hits a piano key that sounds flat. He hits it a few more times in succession then segues smoothly into a blistering rendition of "Great Balls of Fire." Fully enjoying this rare moment of having his home all to himself,* **Frasier** *plays and sings with joyous abandon.*

Frasier *(cont'd) (singing)*

"You shake my nerves and you rattle my brain. Too much love drives a man insane. You broke my will, but what a thrill. Goodness gracious, great balls of fire!"

He spins around on the piano stool. As he spins he sees the front door open and hears **Martin** *and* **Niles,** *he effortlessly segues back into the classical piece.* **Martin, Niles,** *and* **Eddie** *enter.*

Martin

I think you're making too big a deal out of this.

Niles

But I've never seen Maris this angry. Her eyes were as dead as a shark's.

Martin

When your mother got mad at me, I'd just grab her, bend her backwards and give her a kiss that made her glad she was a woman.

Niles

I can't do that with Maris. She has abnormally rigid vertebrae. She'd snap like a twig.

Frasier

Let me guess, Maris has moved into the east wing again?

Niles

Lock, stock, and slumber mask. *(sighs)* Sunday was her fortieth birthday. She said in no uncertain terms that she wanted no acknowledgment of it whatsoever. And in a moment I live over and over in my dreams, I believed her.

Frasier

What? No party? No gifts? No nothing?

Niles

Say that while weeping into an ermine lap robe and you've got her down perfectly.

Martin

Why don't you just buy her a nice bottle of perfume?

Niles

She gets hives.

Martin

How about candy?

Niles

Hypoglycemic.

Martin

Then just get her a dozen roses.

Niles

Allergic

Martin *(giving up)*

Gum?

Frasier

Oh for God's sake, Niles, just talk to her. Tell her you made a mistake. She's obviously a little touchy about her age, but it's not like this is the first time she's turned forty.

Niles

I know. I'll throw her a great big party this weekend. It'll be a costume ball with a Louis Quatorze theme, right down to the powdered wigs and crushed velvet pantaloons. May I presume you're both coming down with colds?

Frasier *and* **Martin** *cough and nod.*

Niles *(cont'd)*

I thought so.

Niles *exits.* **Frasier** *and* **Martin** *ad-lib "Good-bye and good luck."* **Frasier** *resumes looking for his book.*

Frasier

Dad, I can't find a book the station manager lent me and I promised to return it today.

Martin

What's it called?

Frasier

The Life and Times of Sir Herbert Beerbohm Tree. It's a wonderfully witty history of the English theater.

Martin

Oh, all right, you caught me. I've got it hidden under my pillow. I only let myself read one chapter every night.

Frasier

Fine, so you didn't pick it up.

Martin

Ask Daphne when she comes home. She was looking for something to put her to sleep last night. That book sounds like it could put her into a coma.

Martin *exits to his room.* **Frasier** *thinks for a beat, then heads down the hall to* **Daphne's** *room. And we:*

CUT TO:

Scene B

INT. DAPHNE'S ROOM – CONTINUOUS – DAY/1

Frasier, Daphne

The room reflects the fact that it was originally **Frasier's** *study. Imposed upon this is the personality of* **Daphne Moon.** *Included among her things is a collection of English tea pots on wall shelves.*

The door opens. **Frasier** *lets himself in. His book is in plain sight on the night table next to* **Daphne's** *bed. He crosses purposefully to the book, picks it up and is heading directly back to the door when his eyes drift to an intriguing photograph tucked in the mirror frame across the room.* **Frasier** *can't resist the temptation to look at the photo. He walks to the mirror, picks up the photo and looks closely. It is* **Daphne** *with Prince Charles. They stand on a moor, Charles is wearing his kilt. They look extremely happy.* **Frasier** *ponders this for a beat, then tucks it back into the mirror frame.*

Frasier *looks around the room taking in the details. He sees a small decorative box, opens the lid to peek in but quickly closes it when music starts playing.* **Frasier** *picks up a prescription pill bottle on a dresser. He is reading the label, his back to the door, when* **Daphne** *appears in the doorway. Flustered,* **Frasier** *absentmindedly slips the pills into his pocket.*

Daphne

Dr. Crane. What are you doing in here?

Frasier *(guilty)*

Daphne! I thought you were out. Not that I come in here when you're out. I simply needed my book. Which I have. *(displays it)* See?

She watches him coolly.

Frasier *(cont'd)*

So I'll be off now. Me and my book. See Frasier go.

Frasier *quickly exits as* **Daphne** *watches in cool silence. And we:*
FADE OUT.

Scene C

FADE IN:
INT. FRASIER'S LIVING ROOM – THAT EVENING – NIGHT/1
Frasier, Martin, Niles, Daphne
Martin *and* **Frasier** *sit at the dining room table,* **Daphne** *is in the kitchen preparing dinner.* **Niles** *is on the phone.*

Niles *(into phone)*

Nadia, tell Mrs. Crane I want to speak to her, and don't take no for an answer. *(a beat as he waits for Maris to get on, then he speaks low so as not to be heard)* Nadia, tell her please, please, please come to the phone.

Niles *hangs up the phone and crosses to the dining room table and sits.*

Martin

Maris hung up on you, huh?

Niles

Oh no, now she's got Nadia doing her dirty work. She's Maris's hatchet maid.

Martin

What happened to that Louis the Fourteenth birthday party idea?

Niles

Disaster there too. She reminded me that an entire branch of her family tree was slaughtered by the Huguenots

Martin

Oh, yeah.

Frasier

Well for now forget about Maris and have a nice meal in a more convivial atmosphere.

Daphne *enters from the kitchen carrying a large roast and a carving knife on a platter. She slams it down on the table and exits to the kitchen.* **Niles**, **Martin**, *and* **Frasier** *exchange a look.*

Niles *(sotto)*

What's she mad about?

Martin

Beats me.

Daphne *reenters from the kitchen carrying a bowl of carrots and a bowl of creamed onions. She pleasantly puts them down in front of* **Niles** *and* **Martin**, *her warm attitude in contrast to a moment ago.*

Daphne

Here's your favorite, Mr. Crane, creamed onions. And Dr. Crane, I made my special glazed carrots just for you.

She picks up the carving knife.

Daphne *(cont'd) (to Frasier)*

You. Carve.

Daphne *sticks the knife into the roast and exits to the kitchen.*

Martin

Well, we don't know what, but we sure as hell know who.

Daphne *enters carrying a plate of dinner for herself.*

Daphne

If anyone needs me, I'll be eating in my room. *(pointedly to Frasier)* You know where that is.

She exits to her room.

Martin

What'd you do?

Frasier

This morning I went into her bedroom.

Martin

What?

Niles

Frasier, how could you? No matter how irresistible the force pulling you down that hall, exciting every molecule of maleness in your body, it must be fought.

Frasier

Oh, Niles, I went in to retrieve a book. *(beat)* What's the big deal? She goes into my room all the time and it doesn't bother me.

Martin

It doesn't matter. Women are different.

Frasier

That's sexism talking.

Martin

That's thirty-five years of marriage talking. Women protect their privacy. You know how they are about their handbags. You never go in there. It's always, "Bring me my purse." A husband could say, "Honey, I'm being robbed. There's a man holding a gun to my head and I don't have any money." The wife would say, "Bring me my purse."

Niles

Dad, once again your simple, homespun wisdom has pricked the balloon of Frasier's pomposity.

Martin

Well, when you got a bum hip, you look for something to pass the time. *(to Frasier)* You were wrong. You owe her an apology. Go do it.

Martin *begins serving himself.*

Frasier

All right. I will go to Daphne's room and apologize.

Frasier *gets up and heads toward the hall to* **Daphne's** *room.* **Niles** *gets up and starts to follow him.*

Frasier *(cont'd) (without looking back)*

Alone, Niles.

Niles *circles back to sit and we:*
CUT TO:

Scene D

INT. HALLWAY OUTSIDE DAPHNE'S ROOM – CONTINUOUS – NIGHT/1
Frasier, Daphne
Frasier *comes down the hall to* **Daphne's** *closed door. He composes himself and knocks.*

Daphne (O.S.)

Yes?

Frasier *(sweetly)*

Daphne, it's Dr. Crane.

Daphne (O.S.) *(coldly)*

Yes.

Frasier

Could you open the door, please?

After a beat, the door opens a crack. **Daphne** *stares out at him.*

Frasier *(cont'd)*

This morning I behaved quite insensitively. I did need the book. Nonetheless, I was wrong to go into your room without your permission and I'm sorry.

She stares at him.

Frasier *(cont'd)*

And I'll never do it again.

She continues to stare at him.

Frasier *(cont'd)*

Ever.

She continues to stare.

Frasier *(cont'd)*

I'm being very nice.

She says nothing.

Frasier *(cont'd)*

Well, good night, Daphne.

He turns and heads down the hall. **Daphne** *opens the door.*

Daphne

Oh, wait. I'm being much too hard on you. I'm just a little sensitive about my privacy.

Frasier

No need to explain. It was all my fault and it'll never be an issue
again.

Daphne

Thank you for being so understanding. I suppose my problem goes
back to growing up in a house full of boys. My brothers were all
snoops. They never gave me a moment's peace. Oh, it was a filthy
little rite of passage for the Moon boys – when they reached a certain
age, they'd sneak into the bathroom and peek at me in the shower.

Frasier

All eight of them?

Daphne

Well, all except for my brother Billy, the ballroom dancer. He never
peeked at me. Though he did peek at my brother, Nigel.

Daphne *exits back into her room. As* **Frasier** *reacts and heads down the
hallway, and we:*
CUT TO:

Scene E

FADE IN:
INT. FRASIER'S KITCHEN/LIVING ROOM – A SHORT TIME LATER –
NIGHT/1
Frasier, Martin, Niles, Daphne
Frasier, Niles, *and* **Martin** *are clearing the dinner dishes.* **Martin** *is scraping
them into the sink.* **Daphne** *is still in her room.* **Frasier** *is also making
coffee. During the following,* **Frasier** *gets a bag of coffee beans and pours
them into the grinder.*

Frasier

Coffee, Dad?

Martin

Why not? I'm up six times a night anyway. I might as well be alert.

During the following, **Frasier** *exits back to the living room to clear the
remaining dishes.* **Martin** *flips on the disposal. We hear a hum. It's jammed.*

Martin *(cont'd)*

Oh, geez. *(turns it off)* The disposal's jammed. *(to Niles)* You want to
stick your hand down there and see what's stuck?

Niles

Dad, it's me. Niles.

Martin *(weary)*

Yeah, I know. I'm asking you because you got skinny little fingers.

Niles

Skinny little freshly manicured fingers. *(off Martin's look)* Are you sure it's off?

Martin

Positive.

Niles *(as though directing a crowd through a bullhorn)*

Move away from the switch.

Martin *(sotto)*

Oh, geez.

Martin *takes a step backwards. With a look of great distaste,* **Niles** *inches his hand into the garbage disposal.*

Niles

It's wet and slimy and God knows what. It's like sticking my hand into the mouth of hell.

Frasier *reenters, puts down the dishes and hits the button on the coffee grinder.* **Niles's** *hand shoots out of the garbage disposal.*

Niles *(cont'd)*

Yaaa! *(covering eyes and offering hand)* Somebody count, somebody count!

Frasier

They're all there, Niles. Sorry.

Martin

Give me a call when the coffee's ready.

Martin *exits.* **Frasier** *goes to the sink to unjam the disposal. He pulls a spoon out of the disposal.*

Niles

Well, I better get home. Maris will be missing me.

Frasier

I thought she's not speaking to you.

Niles

She's not. But what fun is it not speaking to someone if they're not there to not speak to?

Niles *exits to the living room and heads for the door.* **Frasier** *follows.*

Niles *(cont'd)*

Oh, by the way, I'm out of cash. I need something to tip your garage attendant.

Frasier

Oh, of course.

Frasier *reaches into his pocket and pulls out not only a dollar bill, but also* **Daphne's** *pill bottle.*

Frasier *(cont'd)*

Oh, perfect.

Niles

What?

Frasier

These pills.

Niles

I was thinking money, but you know him better than I do.

Frasier *hands* **Niles** *the dollar.*

Frasier

No, it's Daphne's prescription. While I was in her room, I must have inadvertently . . . knocked it into my pocket.

Niles

An interesting phenomenon. I can't walk through a drugstore without aspirin and decongestants leaping into my trousers.

Frasier

Okay. I was curious, I looked around a little. *(reading the label)* "One before bedtime." Great. Daphne's sure to discover they're missing when she turns in tonight.

At this point, **Daphne** *enters. She carries a rolled up exercise mat under her arm and heads toward* **Martin's** *bedroom.*

Daphne

Oh, you're heading off, Dr. Crane?

Niles

Yes. Yes, I am.

Daphne

Say hello to your wife.

Niles

I'll certainly try.

Daphne *(yelling down hallway)*
Mr. Crane, time for your exercises.

Daphne *exits down the hallway.*

Frasier
Okay, this is my chance. I've got to put them back.

Frasier *dashes into the hallway to* **Daphne's** *bedroom.* **Niles** *heads after him.*

Frasier *(o.s.) (cont'd)*
Alone, Niles.

Niles *spins on his heel, crosses to the door and exits.*
CUT TO:

Scene H

INT. HALLWAY OUTSIDE DAPHNE'S ROOM/DAPHNE'S ROOM –
CONTINUOUS – NIGHT/1
Frasier, Daphne (o.s.), **Martin** (o.s.)
Frasier *dashes down the hall toward* **Daphne's** *room, pill bottle in hand. He throws open the door and enters. He runs toward the table where he picked up the pills, puts them down, pauses to adjust the bottle just so, and runs back to the door. He opens the door and stops dead when he hears* **Daphne** *and* **Martin** *in the dining room.*

Martin *(o.s.)*
The Sonics game is on. I'll do my exercises tomorrow.

Daphne *(o.s.)*
Fine. If you change your mind, I'll be in my room.

Frasier *gets a panicked look on his face. He shuts the door and frantically looks around for an escape route. He checks the window, it's seventeen stories down. He looks under her bed to hide, it is too small. We hear* **Daphne** *right outside her room.*

Daphne *(o.s.) (cont'd) (yelling to Martin)*
I just thought a man who spends half his life prattling on about sports might actually want to move a muscle of his own once in awhile.

Martin *(o.s.)*
Ha, ha.

Frasier *looks around the room for a place to hide, he finally runs into the closet and closes the door at exactly the same moment* **Daphne** *enters. During the following, we intercut between* **Daphne's** *bedroom,* **Daphne's** *closet and* **Daphne's** *bathroom.* **Daphne** *goes into the bathroom. We hear water running in the sink.*

After a beat, the closet door opens and **Frasier** *peeks out. The coast appears clear. He takes a few steps out of the closet, heading for the door. He hears the water stop running and* **Daphne** *humming, as she heads back into the bedroom. He can't make it to the door and runs back into the closet, closing the door behind him just as* **Daphne** *enters with a glass of water. She goes to the prescription bottle and takes her medication. She then begins to undress.*

CUT TO:

INT. DAPHNE'S CLOSET – CONTINUOUS – NIGHT/1
Frasier
Frasier *is mortified seeing* **Daphne** *through the slats. He turns his face away.*

The closet door opens and **Daphne's** *bra and panties fly past* **Frasier** *into a hamper in her closet.* **Daphne's** *hand reaches in to grab her robe.* **Frasier** *sees that she cannot reach it so, to assist her, he puts the robe within her reach by hanging it off his index finger. She takes it.*

CUT TO:

INT. DAPHNE'S ROOM – CONTINUOUS – NIGHT/1
Daphne, Frasier, Eddie
Daphne, *now dressed in her robe, goes back into the bathroom. After a beat,* **Frasier** *peeks out again, sees the coast is clear, and makes another dash for the door. He gets farther this time and is nearly to the door and safety when* **Daphne**, *still humming, reenters from the bathroom. This time* **Frasier** *is forced to hide on the side of the bed. She stops at a dresser to brush her hair. As she does, he jumps over the bed to the other side.*

Daphne *walks across the room to her closet to get a nightgown.* **Frasier** *sees he's exposed and has no choice, but to duck into the bathroom.*

We see **Eddie** *nuzzle open the bedroom door and enter. Neither* **Daphne** *nor* **Frasier** *see him enter.* **Daphne** *exits to the bathroom.*

CUT TO:

INT. DAPHNE'S BATHROOM – CONTINUOUS – NIGHT/1
Frasier, Daphne, Eddie
Daphne *enters.* **Frasier** *is hiding behind the bathroom door.* **Daphne** *pulls back the shower curtain, steps in, then throws her robe out. The shower curtain is clear plastic with an opaque design. We can see* **Daphne's** *face and she can see into the room, but her body is modestly covered. She sees* **Eddie** *enter the bathroom and start to drink from the toilet.* **Frasier** *does not see* **Eddie** *and assumes* **Daphne** *is talking to him.*

Daphne

What are you doing? That's disgusting, you filthy thing.

Angle on **Frasier** *behind the door. He is mortified.*

Daphne *(cont'd)*

Get out of here right now! Get out!

Frasier *comes out, surprising* **Daphne**.

Frasier

Daphne, I can explain . . .

Daphne *screams.* **Frasier** *screams too and runs out. And we:*

FADE OUT:

End of Act One

ACT TWO

Scene J

FADE IN:

INT. CAFE NERVOSA – THE NEXT MORNING – DAY/2

Frasier, Niles, Roz

Frasier *is seated at a table. He looks glum.* **Niles** *enters in a very up mood.*

Niles

Good morning, Frasier.

Frasier *grunts in reply. A waitress passes:*

Niles *(cont'd)*

Çara mia, prego uno mezzo latte decaffinato. And a bran muffin. No, *due* bran muffins. Maris and I burned up a lot of energy last night . . . *(sotto to Frasier)* a lot of energy . . . And I have to replenish my body.

Niles *coyly whistles a happy tune while he smooths a napkin on his lap.* **Frasier** *watches him closely.*

Frasier

Is that a love bite on your neck?

Niles

Hang the euphemism, Frasier. It's a hickey.

Frasier

Hmm. Well, when one considers Maris's limited lung capacity, that's quite a feat. So, I take it you and Maris achieved détente.

Niles
Twice.

Frasier
What magic words did you use to melt your little glacier?

Niles
When I got home, I sat her down, stared deeply into her eyes and said, "Here are the keys to your new Mercedes."

Frasier
You bought her a Mercedes?

Niles
Yes. *(then)* The things that tiny woman can do when properly motivated . . .

Frasier
Niles . . .

Niles
My little vixen had to go for a B-12 shot this morning.

Frasier
Niles, if you're through marinating in your own testosterone, I have my own problem. Remember last night when I went to put Daphne's pills back in her room? Well, she caught me again.

Niles
You're joking.

Frasier
No. I was so embarrassed, I left the house before she got up this morning. I left a note trying to explain what I was doing, but . . . well, considering the circumstances, I honestly don't see how Daphne can forgive me this time.

Niles
Oh, come now. How bad could it be? It's not as if you . . . you . . . saw her naked or something.

Frasier *looks at* **Niles**. **Niles** *stares for a beat, then realizes.*

Niles *(cont'd)*
You did. *(takes a deep breath)* Well, there goes my afterglow.

Niles *composes himself.* **Roz** *approaches the table and sits. They ad-lib hellos.* **Roz** *eyes* **Niles**.

Roz
So, Niles, you got a little last night, didn't you?

Niles *reacts.*

Roz *(cont'd)*

I can always tell. *(patting Frasier on the hand)* Don't worry. You'll meet somebody.

The waitress crosses over with **Niles's** *coffee and bran muffin.*

Roz *(cont'd) (to waitress)*

Nonfat cap please.

Niles

Roz, this was a private conversation. I was helping my brother with a problem of some delicacy.

Roz

Don't worry. Shower Boy told me all about it.

Frasier

I'm mortified about this and I can't think what I can possibly do to make it up to Daphne.

Niles

Nothing says "I'm sorry" quite like an in-dash CD player and a passenger-side airbag.

Frasier *(to Roz)*

Maris got angry at him so Niles bought her a Mercedes.

Roz

Woof.

Frasier *(to Niles)*

But if you're suggesting I buy my way out of my problem, the answer's no. It's the coward's way out.

Niles

Just remember, this coward has a hickey.

Roz *(to Niles)*

Buy me a Mercedes and I'll make your neck look like a relief map of the Andes.

Frasier

Don't encourage him. I happen to believe that bribery is an unhealthy way for a couple to deal with conflict.

Niles

And during which of your failed marriages did you hone this theory?

Frasier *and* **Niles** *ad-lib bickering:* "You're being defensive." "I am not.

That's merely a rebuttal," etc. Finally:

Roz

Oh, knock it off! *(to Frasier)* I agree with your brother.

Niles

Roz, you agree with me?

Roz

Keep your voice down. I know people here.

Frasier

What do you mean you agree with him? You think any woman can be bought off? Don't you find that insulting?

Roz

A woman's only going to forgive you if she wants to. A gift just helps grease the wheels a little. Didn't you ever hear that story George Burns tells about Gracie Allen? *(off their looks)* Gracie has her eye on this sterling silver centerpiece. George says it's way too expensive. Case closed. A few months later, George is going through some mid-life crisis and cheats on Gracie with some starlet.

Niles

George cheated on Gracie?

Frasier

Yes, Niles. And Ward Cleaver got it on with Lumpy's mother. It's a tough world out there.

Roz

Anyway, George becomes overcome with guilt. It eats at him for months. Finally, the only thing he can do to make himself feel better is to go out and buy her the silver centerpiece. Fast forward to seven years later, George overhears Gracie talking to a girlfriend. She says, "I wish George would cheat again. I really need a new centerpiece."

Roz *laughs.*

Roz *(cont'd)*

I love that story. It's got it all: lust, passion, intrigue, silverware, a fur coat . . .

Frasier

Wait a minute. You didn't mention a fur coat.

Roz

You don't think the starlet walked away empty-handed, do you?

Off **Frasier** *and* **Niles's** *reaction, we:*

Smash cut to:

Scene K

INT. FRASIER'S LIVING ROOM – LATER THAT EVENING – NIGHT/2
Frasier, Martin, Daphne, Niles, Eddie
Frasier *enters the front door.* **Martin** *comes out of the kitchen.*

Martin
Oh, Dr. Crane, I'm glad you're here. I need your advice. I have a son who's a total numbnut.

Frasier
Hello, Dad. Love your icebreaker.

Martin
You better get her to stay, Frasier. She knows my moods, she knows how to handle me and I like her.

Frasier
She's talking about quitting?

Martin
Yeah. Now go in there and apologize.

Frasier *gathers himself and starts for* **Daphne's** *hallway.*

Frasier
I can't go in there.

Martin *heads to his room.*

Martin
Of course you can't. Because I asked you to go in there. Of course, when I said don't go in there, what'd you do? You went in there. Now I say go in there, so you won't. That's why I love Eddie. He does what I tell him to. Come on, Eddie.

Martin *exits down the hallway.* **Frasier** *stops* **Eddie** *from following* **Martin** *by holding him by the tail.*

Frasier
He's defying you too, Dad!

Daphne *enters from the hallway and sees* **Frasier** *holding* **Eddie.** **Frasier** *turns to see* **Daphne** *watching him.* **Frasier** *looks guilty.* **Daphne** *rolls her eyes and starts to move off to the front door.* **Frasier** *finally lets* **Eddie** *go.* **Eddie** *runs to* **Martin's** *room.*

Frasier *(cont'd)*
Daphne, wait. We have to talk. I feel terrible.

Daphne *(suckering him in)*
Oh, now, Dr. Crane, your note explained everything, you've got nothing to feel bad about.

Frasier
Oh, well, I'm glad to hear that.

Daphne
A servant like me doesn't deserve privacy anyway. Matter of fact, why don't we just get everything out in the open. *(She dumps the contents of her purse on the dining room table.)* Here's my personal telephone book, a couple of letters from friends I opened today. And my birth control pills. I haven't had much use for these lately, as I'm sure you know. And here's my driver's license. As you can see I'm a full two years older than I originally disclosed – also, four pounds heavier. But it's in a spot that doesn't show – to most people.

Frasier
Listen, I know how hard it must be living in someone else's home.

Daphne
Yes, it is hard. But I put up with it because I happen to love this job. All I ever asked for was one room. A little corner I could call my own. I never minded that it was a damn-sight too small and I was up to my eyeballs in your precious earth tones and your African knickknacks. But now I have to put up with you in there too. *(picking up an African statue off the table)* And that's one leering love god too many.

Frasier
Daphne, you're absolutely right. You should have a place to call your own. If you agree to stay, I'll happily pay to have your room redecorated. Make it yours. Paint, wallpaper, new upholstery, whatever you need to feel comfortable.

Daphne
How about a dead bolt, an electrified fence and a German police dog?

Sfx: doorbell

Frasier
Daphne, I assure you, as long as we live under the same roof, I will never ever set foot in your room again.

Daphne
All right, then, I'll give it another try.

Daphne *opens the door,* **Niles** *is there.*

Niles

Evening all.

They ad-lib hellos.

Daphne *(very happy)*

Good evening, Dr. Crane.

Niles

You're awfully chipper, Daphne.

Daphne

I'm quite excited really. Your brother has just offered to pay to have my room redecorated.

Niles

Really?

Daphne

As a matter of fact I may just take a trip downtown and start looking at fabrics. I'm thinking of doing the whole thing in pinks and yellows.

She exits. **Frasier** *pours himself a sherry.*

Frasier

She really is determined to keep me out of there.

Niles

So, you're putting things right with Daphne by opening up your checkbook?

Frasier

Oh, Niles, I know what you're thinking. It's merely a gesture.

Niles

Oh, I see. When I do it, it's a bribe. When you do it, it's a gesture.

Frasier

Our situations are completely different. You paid Maris off because you're afraid of her.

Niles

Oh, and you're not the least bit intimidated by Daphne?

Frasier

No.

Niles

Then it wouldn't alarm you if I were to, say, do this?

Niles *darts toward* **Daphne's** *bedroom.*

Frasier
Niles. Niles! Where are you going?

Frasier *runs after him carrying his sherry. And we:*
CUT TO:

Scene L

INT. HALLWAY OUTSIDE DAPHNE'S ROOM/DAPHNE'S ROOM –
CONTINUOUS – NIGHT/2
Frasier, Niles, Martin, Daphne, Eddie
Frasier *finds* **Niles** *standing outside* **Daphne's** *doorway. He puckishly challenges* **Frasier** *by sticking one foot into* **Daphne's** *room.*

Niles
Uh oh, my foot's in Daphne's room.

Frasier
Get out of there.

Niles
Why? You're not afraid of getting . . . *(jumping across the threshold)* . . . in trouble, are you?

Frasier
Niles.

Niles *jumps back out.*

Niles
Now we're safe.

Frasier
Stop it.

Niles *jumps in and out again and again.*

Niles
Trouble. Safe. Trouble. Safe.

Frasier *(over Niles)*
You're acting like a child. Get out of there!

Niles
Trouble. Safe. Trouble . . .

This time **Niles** *accidentally knocks over an earring tree full of jewelry.*

Frasier
Look what you've done now.

He rushes into **Daphne's** *room to pick it up.*

>   **Frasier** *(cont'd)*
>
> She's going to find out.

>   **Niles**
>
> So you'll just write her a bigger fatter check.

>   **Frasier**
>
> No, Niles, she'll quit.

>   **Niles**
>
> What?! *(suddenly panicked)* Why didn't you say so? Help me pick
> these up.

Frasier *has put his glass of sherry on the night table to pick up the jewelry.*
Niles *knocks it over onto the bed.*

>   **Frasier**
>
> Oh my God

Niles *looks for something to mop up the sherry. He grabs a towel from the
bottom of a pile of folded laundry on* **Daphne's** *bed. The laundry falls over
and spills to the floor.* **Frasier** *and* **Niles** *frantically try to mop up the sherry
and refold* **Daphne's** *laundry.*

>   **Frasier** *(cont'd)*
>
> Pick it up. Pick it up.

Martin *enters with* **Eddie**, *they talk over one another.*

>   **Martin**
>
> My God, what are you two doing?

>   **Frasier**
>
> It's Niles's fault.

>   **Niles**
>
> It is not.

>   **Frasier**
>
> Never mind. Just help us clean up this mess.

*The three guys work like crazy to get everything picked up and back into its
place.* **Martin** *is sprawled across her bed trying to mop up the sherry.*
Frasier's *got his head under the bed looking for a stray pencil.* **Niles** *is
refolding her lingerie. He's got a teddy tucked under his chin in order to
fold it.* **Eddie** *sits on the bed with a bra in his mouth.* **Daphne** *enters in time
to see this very incriminating tableau as* **Frasier** *peeks out from under her
bed, we:*

>   **Daphne**
>
> What in bloody hell?

CUT TO:

Scene N

EXT. CAR DEALERSHIP – DAY – DAY/3
Daphne, Frasier, Martin, Niles, Eddie
We see **Daphne** *in the driver's seat of a shiny new convertible.* **Eddie** *is in the passenger seat. She happily plays with the steering wheel. She presses a button and to her delight the roof starts to come up.*

Daphne
Oooo!

Angle on **Frasier** *who stands with* **Niles** *and* **Martin** *and a salesman.*

Frasier
What about this sporty little subcompact? Bet you could park that anywhere.

Daphne *stops the roof from rising and sits up to peer out the dealership windows.*

Daphne
Is that a Mercedes dealership across the street?

Frasier *pushes* **Daphne** *back down onto the seat as we:*
FADE OUT.

End of Act Two

Scene P

END CREDITS
FADE IN:
INT. DAPHNE'S ROOM – NIGHT – NIGHT/3
Daphne, Eddie
Daphne *enters her room and starts to get ready for bed. Before she undresses, she checks the closet, the bathroom, under the bed, and anyplace else humanly possible for a person to hide. Once positive that she's alone, she begins to take off her blouse. At that point we see* **Eddie's** *nose poke out from underneath a pile of laundry. He starts to watch her.* **Daphne** *spots him and shakes her finger at him. She opens her door and* **Eddie** *scurries out.*
AND WE:
FADE OUT.

End of Show

An Affair to Forget

Episode #40570-044

Written by
Anne Flett-Giordano & Chuck Ranberg

Created by
David Angell/Peter Casey/David Lee

Directed by
Philip Charles MacKenzie

Larking around on the set, David Hyde Pierce prepares to enter the sensory deprivation tank.

Niles is comforted by Frasier, Martin, and Eddie after yet another fight with Maris.

ACT ONE
Scene A

FADE IN:
INT. RADIO STUDIO – DAY – DAY/1
Frasier, Roz, Gretchen (V.O.)
Frasier *is on the air.* **Roz** *is in her booth.*

Frasier
You're on KACL with Dr. Frasier Crane. We have time for one last call. Go ahead, Gretchen, I'm listening.

Gretchen (V.O.) *(German accent)*
Well you see, Dr. Crane, my husband is a fencing instructor, and lately he spends all his time with his wealthy new student. He's with her day and night. I'm afraid there's some . . . bumsen going on.

Frasier
Is this merely a suspicion or do you have any evidence?

Gretchen (V.O.)
No, it's just a feeling.

Frasier
Well, unfortunately in these matters, there's no simple way to know for sure.

Roz
Oh yes, there is.

Frasier
Well this is your lucky day, Gretchen. Sitting in with us today, we have one of the world's five leading "bumsen" experts.

Roz
If you want to know if a man's cheating, you offer him two choices for dinner: One that's really rich and fattening and one that's light and sensible. If he picks the one that's calorie packed, he doesn't mind turning into a bloated pig, which means he's happily married and you're in the clear.

Frasier
You know Roz, when I hear advice like that, I think there ought to be a law against two or more women gathering at a water cooler. Now Gretchen . . .

Gretchen (V.O.)
Does it really work, Roz?

Roz

Trust me. If he chooses the diet plate, it means he's staying in shape for his new squeeze, and you should get yourself a lawyer who can sue the sweat off a racehorse.

Gretchen (V.O.)

I'm going to do it. Thank you for your help, Roz. You too, Dr. Crane.

Frasier

Don't mention it.

She hangs up.

Frasier *(cont'd)*

"Dr. Crane and Friends" will be back tomorrow with more advice and *(pointedly to Roz)* fewer recipes. Thanks for listening, Seattle.

They sign off. **Roz** *enters* **Frasier's** *booth.*

Roz

I know you hate it when I butt into your show.

Frasier *(but you still do)*

And yet . . .

Roz

You'll forgive me when you find out the wonderful thing I'm doing for you. You see there's this great woman who lives in my building. She's bright and funny and . . .

Frasier

Stop right there. I do not go on blind dates. They're a hideous waste of time. No, thank you, no.

Roz

She's not for you, she's for your father.

Frasier

What time should he pick her up?

Roz

Oh this is great. She'll be so excited. *(then)* Wait a minute. So blind dates are okay for him, but not for you?

Frasier

Yes. That also goes for games with balls, domestic beer, and giant trucks that roll over smaller ones.

As they head out the door, we:
FADE OUT.

Scene B

FADE IN:

INT. FRASIER'S LIVING ROOM – LATE AFTERNOON – DAY/1

Niles, Martin, Daphne, Frasier, Eddie

Niles, **Martin**, *and* **Eddie** *are sitting at the table. They have a model ship kit.* **Niles** *reads the instructions.*

Niles *(reading)*

"So you want to build a three-masted schooner . . . Step one – take inventory of all parts."

Martin

We don't need to read all the instructions.

Niles

Yes, we do. It says right here in bold face, "Read all instructions."

Martin

Just hand me the right side of the hull.

Niles

You'll get your hands on that piece at step sixteen and not a moment sooner.

Martin

Can we just get started here?

Niles

Okay, Dad. *(reading instructions)* "So you want to build a three-masted schooner . . ."

Martin *rolls his eyes.* **Daphne** *enters from the kitchen. As she crosses by, she looks at the picture on the box.*

Daphne

Oh, look at that. What a beautiful ship. I bet you'll have fun building that.

Martin

Not half as much fun as we're having reading about it.

Daphne

Did I ever mention one of my ancestors was a mutineer on the HMS *Bounty*?

Martin

No kidding.

Daphne

From what we could gather he made it safely to Pitcairn Island where he was quite fruitful and multiplied. For all I know there's a girl who looks exactly like me running around the South Seas, frolicking in the surf, all brown skinned and bare breasted.

Niles *snaps a mast which he's been holding in his hand.* **Martin** *and* **Daphne** *both look at him.*

Niles *(reading instructions)*

"So you want to build a two-masted schooner . . ."

Daphne

Schooner? I thought it was a frigate.

Niles

No, a frigate has a fore and aft main sail.

Daphne

No, that's a brigantine.

Niles

Oh yes, you're right. Then what's a frigate?

Martin

That's when you just don't give a damn anymore.

Martin *exits to the kitchen for a beer.* **Frasier** *enters from outside, coming home from work.*

Frasier

Hello all.

Daphne *and* **Niles** *ad-lib hellos.*

Frasier *(cont'd)*

So, Niles, will you be spending the evening with us?

Niles

Yes. As much as my Maris misses me, she feels that family comes first. She insisted I come over and spend quality time with Dad.

Frasier

She wanted you out of the house, huh?

Niles

Like a Jehovah's Witness.

Martin *reenters from the kitchen, beer in hand, and crosses back to the dining room table.*

Frasier

Dad, I have a proposal for you. There's a woman in Roz's building who's very interested in going out with you. Roz says she has a terrific personality.

Martin

So I guess that makes me the pretty one.

Frasier

Just hear me out. She likes sports, she likes beer . . .

Martin

Yeah, so does Duke.

Frasier

But Duke won't kiss you good night at the end of the evening.

Martin

He will if he's had a few. Tell Roz thanks, but no thanks.

Daphne

Well, I think you're making a mistake. Trying new things is what keeps us all young and vibrant.

Niles

You're right, Daphne. For weeks all Maris did for excitement was float in her sensory deprivation tank, now she's taken up fencing. I've never seen her more vital. She practices with her instructor late into the evening.

Frasier

Maris has a fencing instructor?

Niles

Yes. Gunnar was the Bavarian champion three years running.

Frasier

He's Bavarian?

Niles

You're full of questions I've already given the answers to.

Frasier

Oh, am I?

Niles

So recapping, he's Bavarian and he doesn't speak a word of English so Maris gets to brush up on her German while she parries and thrusts.

Martin

So Maris is learning German . . . *(aside to Frasier)* Just when you thought she couldn't get any cuddlier.

Niles *picks up a model piece. He reacts, then opens his hand. A piece of the boat is stuck to it.*

Niles

Dad, did you touch the spanking aft?

Martin

Yeah, I preglued it for you.

Niles

Well you might have said something. The instructions on the glue specifically say, "Avoid contact with skin." Though of course you wouldn't know that.

Daphne

Not to worry. This type of thing used to happen to my brothers all the time. I can get that off with some nail polish remover. Come with me.

Niles *and* **Daphne** *cross through the living room toward the powder room.*

Niles

So your brothers used to build a lot of models?

Daphne

Actually, I suspect they just sniffed a lot of glue.

Niles

That can cause brain damage, you know.

Daphne

Well, that confirms it.

They exit into the powder room.

Frasier

Dad, we need to talk. It's about Niles.

Martin

Boy, I can't tell you how many times I heard that from your mother.

Frasier

I took a call today from a German woman who suspects her husband – a fencing instructor – is having an affair with his wealthy new client.

Martin

And . . .

Frasier *(determined)*

German fencing instructor . . . Wealthy new client . . .

Martin *(equally determined)*

And . . .

Frasier

Well, don't you find that incriminating?

Martin

No. I find that a coincidence. Seattle's a big city. There must be a bunch of German fencing instructors, each one of them with dozens of students.

Frasier

Yes, but are they wealthy students?

Martin

No, most of them are inner-city kids who are trying to work their way out of the ghetto with nothing but a foil and a dream.

Frasier

Yes, well, somewhere in that slag heap of sarcasm there may be a kernel of truth. Maybe I am letting my imagination get the best of me.

Martin

Just trust me. Forget it.

Martin *goes back to making the model.*

Martin *(cont'd)*

C'mon. Help me put this model together.

Frasier *crosses to the table.*

Frasier

Boy, Niles has always loved these models. Remember that Christmas when Mom gave him "The Visible Man and Woman," and he had to glue all the internal organs in place?

Martin

All I remember is you two fighting over it.

Daphne *reenters from the powder room.*

Frasier

Niles was getting on my nerves so I snuck into his bedroom and stole his ovaries.

Daphne

There's a story I'm glad I missed the beginning of.

Daphne *continues on into the kitchen, as we:*
FADE OUT.

Scene C

A black screen. In white letters appears, "Bavarians at the Gate."

FADE IN:
INT. RADIO STUDIO – NEXT DAY – DAY/2
Frasier, Roz, Gretchen (V.O.)
Roz *is in* **Frasier's** *booth setting up for the show.* **Frasier** *enters.*

Frasier
Sorry I'm late, Roz.

Roz
Hey, Frasier. Did you have a chance to ask your dad about the date?

Frasier
Yes, he said he'd love to go, if not for the problem with the horses.

Roz
What horses?

Frasier
The wild horses that aren't strong enough to drag him out of the apartment.

Roz
Darn it. I already got her hopes up. I don't suppose you'd consider going out with her?

Frasier
Sorry. I've been on my share of pity dates.

Roz
Yes, but this time you wouldn't be the one being pitied. *(off his look)* Listen, we've got some great callers today. Get this. Line three is a guy who just found out his girlfriend is his long-lost sister.

Roz *starts out, then turns back:*

Roz *(cont'd)*
Oh yeah, and that German woman is calling back about her husband's affair.

Frasier
Gretchen?!

Roz
Yeah.

Roz *exits into her booth.*

Frasier
I want her first!

Roz
Are you kidding? What am I supposed to tell the guy dating his sister?

Frasier

Tell him to hang on and relax, we've all been there.

Roz *cues him.*

Frasier *(cont'd)*

Hello Seattle. You're listening to Dr. Frasier Crane on KACL 780.
Let's get right to the phones. Roz?

Roz

We have Gretchen calling back about her husband's affair. She thinks
she has more evidence.

Frasier *quickly punches the button.*

Frasier

Hello, Gretchen, I'm listening.

Gretchen (V.O.) *(crying)*

Oh, Dr. Crane, Gunnar picked the diet plate!

Roz *looks knowingly at* **Frasier.**

Frasier

Gunnar . . .? Still that's no proof. Proof is phone bills, credit card
receipts, lipstick on the collar . . .

Gretchen (V.O.)

I found a love letter he wrote to her.

Frasier

Well, how long were you going to keep that a secret? Work with me
here, Gretchen. What does it say?

Gretchen (V.O.)

"Mein kleine leberknodel . . ."

Frasier

I'm sorry, I don't speak German

Gretchen (V.O.)

It means "my little liver dumpling."

Frasier *(hopeful)*

Maybe he's writing to you.

Gretchen (V.O.)

It can't be me. He says he loves her beautiful little body, as thin as
his sword, and her skin as white as bratwurst, and that she's his
Nichteinmenschlichfrau.

Frasier

What is that?

Gretchen (V.O.)

I don't know if there's a word in English. The closest translation is "not quite human woman."

Frasier

Oh dear God, it is her!

Gretchen (V.O.)

What?

Frasier

I mean, it's not you.

Gretchen (V.O.)

What should I do?

Frasier

I don't know! I need time to think. Let's go to commercial.

And on **Frasier's** *desperation, we go to commercial.*
FADE OUT.

End of Act One

ACT TWO

Scene D

FADE IN:
A black screen. In white letters appears, "An Affair to Forget."
INT. RADIO STUDIO – MOMENTS LATER – DAY/2
Frasier, Roz, Gretchen (V.O.)
Roz *cues* **Frasier** *that they're out of commercial.*

Frasier

We're back. Gretchen I've considered your problem and I think the only course of action is for you to immediately confront your husband and insist he end this affair.

Gretchen (V.O.)

But what if he won't?

Frasier

He has to! Innocent people are being hurt. Remind him of how much he means to you, remind him of all your years together. Are there children?

Gretchen (V.O.)

No.

Frasier

Damn. Still, it's got to be a clean break. He must never see this woman again, even accidentally.

Gretchen (V.O.)

We never had these problems back home.

Frasier

Then maybe that's where you should return, to the stable influence of Bavaria.

Gretchen (V.O.)

How did you know we were from Bavaria?

Frasier

Well . . . I'm a master of dialects and I noticed there was a glottal quality to the occlusion of your dipthongs. Your pronunciation screams Bavarian.

Gretchen (V.O.)

I'm originally from Austria.

Frasier

Do you want to split hairs or do you want your husband back? I'm sorry Gretchen, it's time for another commercial.

Roz

Another commercial?

Frasier *(firmly)*

Yes, Roz, another commercial!

Roz *plugs in a cart and they go off the air. She runs into* **Frasier's** *booth.*

Roz

What is going on?

Frasier

What makes you think something's going on?

Roz

Well, when the person giving advice sounds crazier than the person calling in, I've got to think something's going on.

Frasier

Nothing's going on.

Roz

Wait a minute. You know who it is, don't you?

Frasier *(caught)*

Who?

Roz
The leberknodel.

Frasier
All right. Yes, I do know. But the husband's a close friend of mine. No one you know. How can I tell him? He'll be crushed.

Roz
Don't they teach you anything at Harvard? You never tell the person who's being cheated on. You confront the person who's doing the cheating.

Frasier
Oh no, that's out of the question.

Roz
It's easy. Just tell her you know she's been mattress surfing with another guy and if she doesn't knock it off you'll tell her husband.

Frasier
You don't understand. This isn't an easy woman to talk to. She doesn't deal well with confrontation. I once questioned the political correctness of her serving veal. An hour later we found her locked in the garage with the engine running on her golf cart.

Roz
Whoa, it's Maris.

AND WE:

FADE OUT.

Scene E

A black screen. In white letters appears, "It's a Sensory Deprivation Tank."
INT. NILES'S SPA – LATER THAT DAY – DAY/2
Frasier, Marta, Niles

We're in a corner of a room in which a sensory deprivation tank sits prominently. Other doors suggest a steam room or sauna, etc. Pegs on the wall hold white terrycloth robes.

Frasier *is escorted into the room by* **Marta***, a 78-year-old Guatemalan maid. She points at the sensory deprivation tank.*

Marta
Missy Crane esta en la caja.

Frasier
Mrs. Crane is in the box?

Marta
En la caja.

Marta *exits.* **Frasier** *knocks on the tank.*

Frasier

Maris? This is Frasier. We've got to talk about Niles.

There's no answer.

Frasier (cont'd)

Look I know you've been deceiving him. We have to talk about this, so will you please come out of there?

A beat.

Frasier (cont'd)

You are in there, aren't you?

There is a knock from inside the tank.

Frasier (cont'd)

Look, you can't hide in this ridiculous deprivation tank forever. *(Softening)* I know you're having an affair. I care about you and Niles and I want to help you do what's best for your marriage.

The door to the tank slowly opens . . . And a sopping wet and miserable **Niles** *emerges.* **Frasier** *is aghast.* **Marta** *reenters and puts towels on the tank.*

Frasier (cont'd)

Oh God, Niles, I'm so sorry. *(turns to Marta)* Marta, you said Mrs. Crane was in the box.

Marta (re: Niles)

Si, Missy Crane.

Frasier (indicates Niles)

No, that's Mister Crane!

Marta (realizes her mistake)

Oh, Mister Crane!

She shrugs and exits, practicing saying "mister," "mister," as she goes. **Frasier** *searches for something to say to* **Niles**, *then:*

Frasier

Towel?

He offers **Niles** *a towel, and we:*
FADE OUT.

Scene H

A black screen. In white letters appears, "To the Victor Goes the Spoiled."

FADE IN:
INT. FRASIER'S LIVING ROOM – LATER – NIGHT/2
Frasier, Martin, Niles, Daphne, Eddie
Frasier *and* **Martin** *are nervously waiting for* **Niles** *to appear.*

Martin
So, he didn't say anything about what happened with Maris?

Frasier
Dad, he was on a car phone. He was breaking up – in both senses.

Martin
I'm worried about him. He's always been such a sensitive kid.

Frasier
Yes, but when he gets here, it's important not to let him know how worried we are. We'll only fuel his anxieties.

Martin
You're right. If we coddle him, he'll think this is the end of the world.

SFX: the doorbell rings

Frasier *and* **Martin** *exchange a look, then go to the door and open it.* **Niles** *is there.*

Frasier
Hello, Niles.

Martin
Hello, Son.

There's a beat, then **Niles** *holds out his arms in a needy gesture and the two of them step forward and envelop him in their arms. They move him to the couch while ad-libbing coddling words such as, "It's okay," "It happens, it happens . . ." "It's not over yet," "Don't worry about this, it's gonna be fine."*

Martin *(cont'd)*
Sit down, Son.

Niles *sits on the couch.* **Eddie** *jumps up next to him and licks his face.*

Martin *(cont'd)*
Frasier, pour him a brandy.

Frasier
Actually, I'm out of brandy, but I do have an excellent sherry, two types of port, oh, and a new twelve-year-old single-malt scotch. It's a little on the peaty side.

Martin

Just pour him a drink!

Frasier *pours him a scotch.*

Martin *(cont'd)*

What happened?

Niles

Nothing.

Frasier

But when I left you were storming up to Maris's room to have it out
with her.

Niles

Yes, and with each step I thought of another question to hurl at her,
but when I reached the door, I froze.

Martin

That's okay, Son. There's nothing wrong with taking your time
figuring out the best way to handle this.

Niles

I turned around, walked out of the house, got in the car and started
driving.

Frasier

Well I'm glad you ended up here.

Frasier *puts a drink down in front of him.*

Niles

Actually I ended up at the Oregon border check, but I had some fruit
in the car so I had to turn back. What am I going to do? She's my
whole life.

Frasier

Look, I'm sure whatever Maris is feeling for Gunnar, it's just
infatuation. *(hinting)* You know how you can be in love with one
person and still be infatuated with someone else?

Niles

No.

Frasier

Boy, you are upset.

Niles

Of course I'm upset. I've been vanquished by a dashing, young,
"Ubermann." First Poland and France, now me.

Frasier

Look, she may have succumbed to his Teutonic charms temporarily, but in the long run she's going to choose the man who's also smart and sensitive.

Niles

Oh Frasier, that's just something we used to tell ourselves in chess club. The truth is women don't want men like us. Men of intellect. They want men of action. Men like Gunnar.

Frasier

Well, the first course of action you should take is to talk to Maris.

Niles

But I'm not sure I should talk to her. Maybe if I just sit tight, this whole thing will blow over. Why open that wound?

Frasier

That wound has already been opened, and you're the one who's been hurt. Talk to her. Someone once told me: "To understand all is to forgive all."

Niles

That's the biggest load of drivel I've ever heard in my life. What simpleton's almanac did that come from.

Frasier

It came from a letter you wrote me when I was having my problems with Lilith. You urged me to reach out to her and find out why she did what she did.

Niles *(trying to get it)*

"To understand all is to –"

Frasier

All right, that part was hackneyed but there was some good stuff in the letter. I still have it. Let me get it.

Frasier *exits.*

Niles

Frasier's right, isn't he, Dad?

Martin

Eh . . .

Niles

You sound dubious.

Martin

Well, you know, something like this happened between your mother and me, too.

Niles

And you handled things differently?

Martin

Yeah. First, I took it up with the other man. I told him if he went near your mother again, he'd be the other woman. *(beat)* It took a whole lot more than that to keep our marriage together, but at least it showed her how much I cared.

Niles

So what would you have me do? Go grab the guy by the scruff of the neck and escort him out of my house?

Martin

Could ya do that?

Niles

Well, I have fantasized about it, and it does sound like a way to go, but I'm so confused. A minute ago what Frasier was saying sounded good, too.

Martin

Hey, suit yourself. Frasier's very smart, very sincere and very divorced.

Niles

Well, I do have to talk to Maris eventually. At least your way I'll be going at it from a position of strength. I'm going to do it, Dad. I'm going to stand up to him. Maris has fencing practice tonight but it's Gunnar who's going to be taught a lesson!

Martin

That's my boy. Are you gonna do it right now?

Niles

Yes, Dad.

He throws back his scotch.

Niles *(cont'd)*

I'm pumped, I'm psyched . . . and I'm fairly sure I just swallowed an entire twist of lemon.

Niles *exits as* **Frasier** *enters from the hallway with a letter.*

Frasier

Where's Niles?

Martin

He just left.

Frasier

What? Has he gone to talk things through with Maris?

Martin

No, he's gone to have it out with this guy and set him straight.

Frasier

And you let him go? What if this guy doesn't want to talk? What if he wants to fight?

Martin

It's okay. He's still better off. He'll have found his manhood.

Daphne *enters.*

Martin *(cont'd)*

I tell ya, I'd be proud if Niles traded a couple of teeth for his cajones.

Daphne

I've got to stop walking in on the middle of conversations.

She crosses into the kitchen, and we:
FADE OUT.

Scene J

A black screen. In white letters appears, "Get Out Your Dictionaries."

FADE IN:
INT. NILES'S CONSERVATORY – LATER – NIGHT/2
Niles, Frasier, Gunnar, Marta
Gunnar *is seated on the couch, with his fencing equipment, waiting for* **Maris. Niles** *arrives and steps into the room.*

Niles

There you are. *(Gunnar looks up)* Yes, I'm talking to you, strudel boy. No one seduces my wife and gets away with it!

Frasier *steps in, with* **Marta.**

Niles *(cont'd) (to Gunnar)*

You probably thought because of my refined bearing and swimmer's build I wouldn't put up a fight for the woman I love, but you're dead wrong, because real men have a thing called honor. But you wouldn't know that, would you?

Frasier

Niles . . .

Niles

You wouldn't know how decent people behave.

Frasier

Niles . . .

Niles

You wouldn't know the meaning of the word "rectitude."

Frasier

Niles! He wouldn't know the meaning of anything you're saying. He doesn't speak English, remember?

A beat.

Niles

Damn.

Gunnar *(to Marta)*

Worüber ist er so böse?

Marta *(shrugs)*

Ich weiss nicht.

Niles

Marta, you speak German?

Marta

¿Que?

Frasier

Uh . . . *¿Habla alemán?*

Marta

Sí. Trabajé para una familia alemána en Guatemala quien lleguen despues de la guerra.

Frasier *(to Niles)*

She worked for a German family who turned up in Guatemala right after the war.

Niles

Good, then she can translate for me. Tell her to tell him –

Frasier

Wait Niles.

Niles

Why?

Frasier

Look at him. If he knew you were calling him "strudel boy" he'd be wiping his feet on your face.

Niles

Oh hang that, Frasier. If there are going to be scuffs, they're going to be scuffs of honor. *(to Gunnar)* How dare you steal my wife! *(to Frasier)* Translate!

Frasier

Oh all right. *(to Marta) Señor Crane quiere que preguntas a Gunnar, "¿Como se atrevez a robar mis zapatos?"*

Marta *(to Gunnar)*

Was fällt Dir ein meine Schuhe zu stehlen?

Finally understanding, **Gunnar** *draws his sword on* **Niles***.*

Gunnar

Schweinehund!

Niles *grabs one of* **Gunnar's** *other fencing swords.*

Niles

Fine. You challenge me. *En garde.*

Frasier

Oh, yes, that's just what we need, a fourth language. Niles, you can't fight him.

Niles

Are you forgetting I've been fencing since prep school?

Frasier

So what? The man was born with a sword in his hand. He probably performed his own Caesarean!

Gunnar *has begun to parry and thrust.* **Niles** *scrambles to defend himself.*

Niles

Oh my God, he's gonna kill me.

Frasier *ad-libs, "Duck! Parry! Thrust! Etc." as the fight quickly turns into an amusing, brilliantly choreographed rout, ending with* **Niles** *flat on the floor.* **Gunnar** *stands over him, the point of his sword against the soft flesh of* **Niles's** *neck.*

Gunnar

Entschuldige Dich sofort! Ich habe nicht Deine Schuhe gestohlen!

Niles *(strained voice, to Frasier)*

Is he giving up?

Marta *(to Frasier)*
¡Pideme perdon! ¡No robo sus zapatos!

Frasier *(to Niles)*
He says he wants you to apologize. He did not steal your shoes.

Niles
Shoes?? What does he mean he didn't steal my shoes?

Frasier
Oops, sorry. I guess I mistranslated.

Niles
How could you confuse "wife" with "shoes"?

They go into one of their ad-lib bickerings, with **Frasier** *saying, "It's been a long time since high school. You're in no position to complain," and* **Niles** *saying, "You should have studied harder. Maris is not footwear," etc.*

Gunnar *presses his sword harder against* **Niles's** *neck.* **Niles** *yelps.*

Frasier *(to Marta)*
Not shoes, wife! I mean, *¡no zapatos, esposa!*

Marta *(giggles)*
Ohhh! (to Gunnar) Nicht Schuhe, Frau!

Gunnar
Frau?

Sadly he takes the sword from **Niles's** *neck and casts it aside.*

Gunnar *(cont'd)*
Ja, ich probat. Maris ist unwiderstehlich.

Marta *(to Frasier)*
Si, yo probado. Maris es irresistible.

Frasier *(to Niles)*
He tried. Maris is irresistible. *(then, to Marta, in Spanish)*
¿Irresistible?

Marta *(shrugs, then to Gunnar)*
Unwiderstehlich?

Gunnar
Ja.

Marta
Si.

Frasier
O-kayy.

> **Gunnar**
>
> *Aber sie hat mich abgewiesen.*

> **Marta**
>
> *Pero me desecha.*

> **Frasier**
>
> But she refused him.

> **Niles**
>
> Really?

> **Frasier**
>
> *¿Verdad?*

> **Marta**
>
> *Wirklich?*

Gunnar *nods.* **Marta** *nods.* **Frasier** *nods.*

> **Niles**
>
> What did Maris say?

> **Frasier**
>
> *¿Que decía?*

> **Marta**
>
> *Was hat sie gesagt?*

> **Gunnar**
>
> *Ich liebe Niles.*

> **Marta**
>
> *Me amo a Niles.*

> **Frasier**
>
> I love Niles.

> **Niles**
>
> She loves me! She loves me! My marriage is whole again.

Niles *hugs* **Frasier,** *then* **Marta.**

> **Niles** *(cont'd)*
>
> Maris!

Niles *exits up the stairs.*

> **Frasier**
>
> Now if I can just do the same for Gunnar and Gretchen.

> **Gunnar**
>
> Gretchen?

Frasier *(to Marta)*

Tell Gunnar his wife loves him very much. I mean – *Diga a Gunnar que su esposa le ama mucho.*

Marta *(to Gunnar, pointing at Frasier)*

Deine Frau liebt ihn sehr.

Gunnar *reacts, draws his sword on* **Frasier**.

Gunnar

Schweinehund!

Frasier *(to Marta)*

Not me, she loves him! Marta, damn your pronoun problems!

Frasier *grabs* **Niles's** *sword and tries to fend off* **Gunnar's** *advances, as we:*
FADE OUT.

End of Act Two

Season Three

Moon Dance

*A passionate embrace
on the dance floor . . .*

. . . but is it all an act?

Moon Dance

Episode #40570-063

Written by
Joe Keenan & Christopher Lloyd
and
Rob Greenberg & Jack Burditt
and
Anne Flett-Giordano & Chuck Ranberg
and
Linda Morris & Vic Rauseo

Created by
David Angell/Peter Casey/David Lee

Directed by
Kelsey Grammer

ACT ONE

Scene A

FADE IN:

INT. RADIO STUDIO – DAY – DAY/1

Frasier, Roz, Marianne (V.O.)

Frasier *is on the air.* **Roz** *is in her booth.*

Frasier

We have thirty seconds left. I think we have time for one quick call. *(pushing a button)* Hello, Marianne, I'm listening.

Marianne (V.O.) *(very excited)*

Oh my God, I'm really on?

Frasier

Yes, your problem please . . .

We hear a dog barking over the line.

Marianne (V.O.)

Lucky, Lucky, get down! George, get the dog.

Frasier

Fifteen seconds . . .

Marianne (V.O.)

Oh my God, oh my God, this is so exciting.

We now hear a baby crying over the line.

Marianne (V.O.) *(cont'd) (calling off)*

Honey, get the baby. George, get your son!

Frasier

Ten seconds . . .

Marianne (V.O.)

Okay, okay, here it is, Dr. Crane. If my husband and I don't have sex in the next two days, I'm going to a department store and pick up a stranger.

In the background we hear someone say, "Hello!"

Marianne (V.O.) *(cont'd) (calling off)*

Oh, Timmy, look who's here, Nana and Pop Pop! *(then)* I'll call you back.

She hangs up.

Frasier

To all you Mariannes out there, sex with a stranger is never the

answer. Better to pack the kids off with Nana and Pop Pop, lock
Lucky in the basement, lead your husband to a sturdy kitchen table
and let the postman ring twice. *(then)* That's all, listeners. I'll be on
vacation next week, but on Monday be sure to tune in to my
replacement, noted podiatrist, Dr. Garreth Wooten. He'll be
discussing his newest book, *(picking up a copy) Bunions and Blisters
and Corns.* Oh My!

Frasier *hits a button. They're off the air.* **Roz** *enters* **Frasier's** *booth.*

Roz
I hate it when that foot freak subs for you. He's always trying to feel
my arches. Couldn't you just have Frederick visit you here?

Frasier
Sorry Roz, the taxi's waiting to take me to the airport.

Roz
I hope it goes well. I hated family trips. My father was always
dragging me through a gazillion museums.

Frasier
The only museums my father ever brought me to had the word "wax"
written over the door.

They share a laugh.

Roz
Have a great time.

She gives **Frasier** *a hug.*

Roz *(cont'd)*
And don't forget to bring me a really great present.

Frasier
How'd you like me to bring you a nice T-shirt from Colonial
Williamsburg?

Roz
How'd you like me to give your home phone number to a bunch of
people with webbed toes?

Frasier
It happens to be a very nice vacation spot. Frederick and I are going
to dip candles, tan leather, churn butter . . .

Roz *(imitating the commercial)*
"Frederick Crane, you just finished the first grade! What are you
going to do now?" "I'm going to Butter World!"

Frasier *reacts, then picks up his garment bag and exits. And we:*
FADE OUT.

Scene B

FADE IN:
INT. FRASIER'S LIVING ROOM – DAY – DAY/1
Martin, Daphne, Niles, Eddie
Martin *is in his chair with the newspaper.* **Daphne** *enters with a basket of laundry.*

Martin

Hey, Daph – Bring that laundry over here, will you?

Daphne

What for?

She crosses with the laundry.

Martin

I was just reading about this intelligence test you can give your dog. You throw a towel over his head, and see how long it takes him to shake it off. *(calls)* Eddie!

Eddie *trots in with a soft toy banana in his mouth and drops it on the floor.*

Daphne

And the faster he takes the towel off, the smarter he is?

Martin

No, the faster he folds it. *(then, to Eddie)* Sit down, boy. Good.

He takes a towel and tosses it over **Eddie's** *head.*

Martin *(cont'd)*

They ranked all the dogs and the smartest is the Border collie. He did it in seven seconds. Come on, boy! Take it off! *(looks at watch)* Six, seven . . . Okay, next smartest was the poodle. I know he's as smart as a poodle. *(looks at watch)* Okay, so he's no poodle. *(looks at watch)* A dachshund . . . a German shepherd . . . a labrador.

Daphne

If you ask me, he's refusing to do that trick because he knows if he does it right, you'll have him doing it every time we have company.

Martin

Hey! I bet you're right. He's putting one over on me and that takes real intelligence.

SFX: doorbell

Daphne *(under her breath)*

Not really.

Martin *takes the towel off* **Eddie's** *head as* **Daphne** *crosses to answer the door.* **Niles** *is there with the newspaper.*

Daphne *(cont'd)*

Hello, Dr. Crane.

Niles

I appreciate the false cheer, Daphne, but surely you've read this. *(re: the paper)* Today's society page.

Martin *(covers his ears)*

Don't tell me, don't tell me, don't tell me! I'm saving it for after dinner!

Niles *(opens it)*

Apparently Maris is going on a three week cruise. Her friends threw her a bon voyage party. Look at this photo – Maris on the arm of a new beau, Pierson Broadwater. How could she be ready to date so soon? Especially Pierson. The man is a first-class feeb. He once wore his yachting cap backward so he'd look "with it."

Daphne *(looks at paper)*

She's just standing there, barely touching him, with only the tiniest bit of a smile on her face.

Niles

You can practically hear the zing, zing, zing of her heartstrings.

Daphne *(scoffing)*

Oh, Dr. Crane.

Daphne *exits down the hallway with the basket of laundry.*

Martin

I think you're overreacting.

Niles

No, I'm not. Broadwater is just the latest in a parade of escorts. According to Marta, my ex-maid and current mole, the gigolos have been swarming around Maris like ants on a Snickers bar.

Martin

Son, you've got no reason to believe Maris is involved with anyone. She's probably just getting out of the house, having a little fun. You might consider it yourself. Ever since you two separated you've been holed up like a fugitive.

Niles

Dad, if you're suggesting I start dating again, save your breath.
Women don't exactly find me irresistible.

Martin

You've had lots of girlfriends.

Niles

Oh, let's count them. There's Maris. Dora, my childhood pen pal
from Costa Rica. And I seem to recall a little girl in the fourth grade
who lured me to a stairwell to show me her underpants.

Martin

Oh come on, you're exaggerating.

Niles

All right, perhaps I am. But let's face it. I've never been God's gift to
women.

Martin

Hey, Niles, I think your problem is you still think of yourself as that
same geeky kid you were in high school. But you've come a long
way since then. And you're not doing yourself any favors staying
home every night. Just think about it.

Martin *exits to the kitchen.* **Niles** *unfolds the paper and looks at Maris's
picture.*

Niles *(whining)*

Pierson Broadwater . . .?!

Daphne *reenters.*

Daphne

Wine, Dr. Crane?

Niles

Well, wouldn't you?

AND WE:
FADE OUT.

Scene C

FADE IN:
INT. ELEVATOR IN FRASIER'S BUILDING – EVENING – NIGHT/2
Martin, Daphne, Eddie
Daphne *and* **Martin** *are returning from walking* **Eddie**.

Daphne

Oh, let it go. The man had a right to be proud of his dog.

Martin

I just don't like show-offs, okay? *(as the show-off)* "Ginger, catch the Frisbee!" "Ginger, roll over!" "Ginger, do my taxes!"

Daphne

Just because Eddie's not clever at tricks –

Martin

The hell he isn't. He just likes the kind that give him a chance to use his brain. Eddie is a thinker.

RESET TO:
INT. HALLWAY OUTSIDE FRASIER'S APARTMENT – CONTINUOUS – NIGHT/2
Martin, Daphne, Eddie
The elevator doors open and **Daphne** *exits.*

Martin *(cont'd)*

Just watch. Open the door for him.

Daphne *opens the apartment door.* **Martin** *steps out of the elevator and addresses* **Eddie** *who's still in the elevator.*

Martin *(cont'd)*

I taught him the names of all of his chew toys. *(to Eddie)* Eddie, get your banana. *(to Daphne)* Now he's thinking. You can see the little gears turnin'. "Which one's the banana?" . . . Now he's thinking, "Where the heck did I leave the banana?"

The elevator doors close.

Daphne

Now he's thinking, "Wait, we passed a fruit stand on Oak Street."

Martin *pushes the elevator button and the doors open.* **Eddie** *runs out.*

RESET TO:
INT. FRASIER'S LIVING ROOM – CONTINUOUS – NIGHT/2
Martin, Daphne, Niles, Eddie
Martin, Daphne, *and* **Eddie** *enter.* **Niles** *is there.*

Daphne *(cont'd)*

Dr. Crane!

Niles

Hello. I hope it's all right I let myself in.

Martin

Fine. What's up?

Niles

I just came by to ask you a question. Are you free Saturday night?

Martin

Sure.

Niles *(boasting)*

Well, I'm not. *(then, for effect)* I have a date.

Daphne

Bravo, Dr. Crane.

Martin

Hey, no kidding? Who is she?

Niles

Marjorie Nash – *(proudly)* the "fruit at the bottom" yogurt heiress. I bumped into her at the Frye museum. Before I knew it, your advice was thundering in my ears and I found myself asking her out. We'll be attending our club's winter dance, the Snow Ball.

Martin

Good for you.

Daphne

What's she like?

Niles

She's terribly haughty and rumors persist about her husband's death, but heck, a date's a date.

Daphne

The Snow Ball . . . sounds very glamorous.

Martin

I didn't know you could dance.

Niles

Well, just because we're going to a dance doesn't mean . . . Oh dear, you don't suppose she'll actually want me to?

Martin

Well, let's see, what do you have at a ball? A dance floor, an orchestra . . . I think you should be prepared for anything.

Niles

That never occurred to me. I've taken Maris to dozens of these and she never once asked to dance. Maris dislikes public displays of rhythm. *(panicking)* This is terrible. My first date is a miserable failure before it even begins. I'll just have to cancel.

Daphne

Oh, Dr. Crane, all you need are a few dancing lessons. I'd be happy to give you some.

Niles

You would?

Daphne

Oh yes, growing up I used to practice all the time with my brother Billy, the ballroom dancer.

Niles

I could never prevail upon you that way. It's much too much trouble. *(grabbing a chair)* We'll need to move this, won't we?

Martin

I'll just get out of your way.

Daphne and **Niles** *move the coffee table to clear a little dance floor. During the following,* **Niles** *will awkwardly follow* **Daphne's** *instructions.*

Daphne

We'll start with a box step. It's very simple. Here – take my hand like so and put your other one round my waist. Now . . . start with your left foot.

Niles

Which one?

Daphne

Oh, hush. Step toward me, then bring your right forward and over and slide the left over to meet it. Then the right goes back, the left back and over, the right slides next to it and that's it. Once again now. *(repeating the moves)* One two three, one two three, one two three, one two three . . .

Niles

This is boring, yet difficult.

Martin

There's no trick to dancing. It's a matter of coordination. Hell, if you can ride a bike or skip rope or kick a ball you can certainly . . .

Martin and **Niles** *exchange a look, then* **Martin** *exits to his room, and we:*
DISSOLVE TO:

Scene D

We hear the final strains of "Isn't It Romantic?"
FADE IN:

INT. FRASIER'S LIVING ROOM – A FEW HOURS LATER – NIGHT/2
Niles, Daphne, Martin, Eddie
Niles *and* **Daphne** *are finishing a dance. We cannot see* **Niles's** *face. He's still no Astaire but his dancing has improved.*

Daphne
You're really doing very well, Dr. Crane. Earlier you seemed a bit tense. You've really relaxed now, haven't you?

Reverse angle – or they spin around – to reveal **Niles's** *face over* **Daphne's** *shoulder. He appears completely intoxicated.* **Martin** *enters from the kitchen.*

Niles
Yes – two – three. Thanks – two – three.

They finish with a little flourish.

Martin
Hey, you two are looking pretty sharp.

Daphne
I think we're ready to move on to the samba. *(to Eddie; playfully)* Eddie, fetch me a samba tape . . . Xavier Cugat . . . *(to Martin)* Now he's thinking "The later Hollywood stuff, or the early New York recordings?"

Martin
Now guess what I'm thinking.

Daphne *gives him a look and exits.*

Martin *(cont'd)*
I'm hittin' the sack.

He heads toward his room as **Niles** *continues to move about the room doing a little dance.*

Niles
One – two – three, 'nite – two – three . . .

SFX: his cellular phone rings

Niles *(cont'd)*
One – two – three . . .

He takes the phone from his jacket.

Niles *(cont'd) (into phone)*
Hello – two – three. Oh, Marjorie . . .

Martin *stops.*

Niles *(cont'd) (into phone)*

How are you? . . . Really? . . . Oh, that is a shame. Well, there will be other dances . . . No, no . . . I understand completely.

Niles *hangs up and exchanges a look with* **Martin.**

Martin

Sorry, Son. Well, I guess you won't be needing those dance lessons.

Niles

Guess not.

Martin *continues out as* **Daphne** *reenters.*

Daphne

Now in the samba, you have to hold me a little closer. Ready?

Niles *considers telling* **Daphne** *about the call, then:*

Niles

I'm a dancer. A dancer dances.

As **Daphne** *turns on the music and they begin to samba, we:*
FADE OUT.

End of Act One

ACT TWO

Scene E

FADE IN:

INT. CAFE NERVOSA – AFTERNOON – DAY/3

Niles, Martin, Daphne, Waitress

Niles *is seated. The* **Waitress** *comes by to take his order.*

Niles *(to waitress)*

Nonfat, half-caf latte, with a sprinkle of cinnamon and chocolate. I'm feeling reckless today.

Waitress

Maybe instead of nonfat milk you should go for the two percent?

Niles

I said reckless, not self-destructive.

The **Waitress** *crosses off.* **Martin** *and* **Daphne** *enter.*

Daphne

Well, look who's here. My dancing partner. Hello, Fred.

Niles

Hello, Ginger.

Daphne

It's a little joke we have.

Martin

Oh. Well you'll have to say it again so I can get the words exactly right when I tell it to my friends at parties.

Niles

Look, Daphne, I got some new CDs. Tonight we master the mambo and the conga. I can feel myself growing a pencil-thin moustache just saying them.

Martin

You're having more lessons tonight?

Daphne

Oh, yes, I've never seen anyone quite so eager to learn. I'll just go get us some coffees.

She crosses to the counter.

Martin

Why didn't you tell her your date canceled and you don't need any more lessons?

Niles

I would've, but the dear thing is having so much fun.

Martin

I think you're the one having so much fun. You think I haven't noticed the way you look at Daphne?

Niles

What are you implying!

Martin

You know damn well what I'm implying. Take my word for it. You're sticking a fork in a toaster here.

Niles

Well my muffin's stuck. Besides, what's the harm in a few dance lessons?

Martin

It's nighttime, you're alone, there's music playing, you got your arms around her – you're gonna end up saying something you can't take back.

Niles

I will not.

Martin

You will. You're a man. Look, something happened when I was
separated from your mother. There was this pretty coroner in the city
morgue. I guess I always had a crush on her. Any time we found a
dead body I'd say, "Okay, boys, I'll take it from here." So, one night I
asked her down to the corner bar.

Niles

Coroners have their own bars?

Martin

No, corner, Niles. The bar on the corner. Anyway, we had a few
drinks, the lights were low, Sinatra was on the juke box – suddenly it
all started pouring out. I told her how I felt. I knew the second it was
out of my mouth it was a mistake. She let me down easy, but we still
had to go on seeing each other all the time and it was very
uncomfortable. After that the morgue was a pretty chilly place.

Daphne *returns with cups of coffee.*

Daphne

The smell of freshly ground coffee always takes me back to Grammy
Moon's kitchen – the hours we spent trying to sober that old woman
up. What time are we going to start your lesson tonight, Dr. Crane?

Martin *looks at* **Niles**.

Niles

Actually, we don't have to worry about that anymore. I just got a call
from Marjorie – something came up so I won't be going to the ball.

Daphne

Oh, I am sorry.

Niles

Quite all right. Thank you for all your help.

Daphne

It seems such a shame to waste all that hard work. I hope you don't
think I'm being too forward, but what would you think of our going
to the dance together?

Martin

He's already taken up enough of your time. He couldn't ask you to do
that.

Daphne

But it would be as much fun for me as it would for him. I'd love a
chance to put on a pretty gown and have an elegant evening out. What
do you say, Dr. Crane?

Martin

Tell her what you say, Dr. Crane.

Niles

Pick you up at seven?

As **Martin** *rolls his eyes, we:*
FADE OUT.

Scene H

FADE IN:
INT. FRASIER'S LIVING ROOM – EVENING – NIGHT/3
Frasier, Martin, Daphne, Niles, Eddie
Martin *is in his chair, reading the newspaper,* **Eddie** *comes up to him with a
little toy pig in his mouth. He puts his chin on* **Martin's** *leg.* **Martin** *takes the pig.*

Martin

No, Eddie. That's not your banana, that's Mr. Pig. *(showing Eddie
pictures in a book)* Listen to the difference: banana, pig, banana, pig.
(then rubbing Eddie's head) I still love ya, ya little pinhead. Go sit down.

Eddie *sits in a chair.* **Frasier** *enters.*

Martin *(cont'd)*

Boy, am I glad you're back. Listen –

Frasier

Dad, stop. I am still officially on vacation until ten A.M. tomorrow.

Martin

It's about –

Frasier *(a la Jimmy Burrows)*

Bup, bup, bup, bup, bup . . . I don't want to hear about how hard
Daphne pushed you to exercise, or the boring foreign film Niles made
you sit through, or the progress of Eddie's on-again, off-again
romance with the ottoman.

Martin

But you don't understand.

Frasier

Dad, please, for all intents and purposes, I am not here.

SFX: doorbell

Daphne *enters from the hallway. She is dressed in a beautiful gown and looks absolutely stunning. She crosses to the door.*

Daphne
I'll get it. I'm so excited. This is my first ball. I hope he likes the way I look.

She opens the door to **Niles**.

Daphne *(cont'd)*
Hello.

Niles *enters. He is wearing a tux and is holding a perfect single rose. He's taken by how beautiful she looks.*

Niles
I thought I'd found the most perfect English rose . . . until now.

He hands the flower to **Daphne**.

Daphne
Oh, you. Shall we go?

Niles
Our carriage awaits.

They head out.

Martin *(warning)*
Niles, you get her home at a decent hour. I'm gonna be waiting up.

Daphne
Oh, Mr. Crane. *(she laughs)*

They exit.

Martin *(calling after them)*
And your carriage better have a full tank. I don't want to hear you ran out of gas.

We hear **Daphne's** *off-screen laugh.* **Martin** *shuts the door.*

Frasier
What the hell was that?

Martin *crosses to the kitchen.*

Martin
Eddie, did you hear someone? It couldn't be Frasier, he's still on vacation.

Frasier
Was that a date? Dad?

Martin *exits into the kitchen. Clearly, he's not going to answer him.* **Frasier** *crosses to the front door, opens it, then slams it.*

Frasier (cont'd)

Hi, everyone, I'm home.

Frasier *follows* **Martin** *into the kitchen, and we:*
FADE OUT.

<h2>Scene J</h2>

FADE IN:
INT. COUNTRY CLUB BALLROOM – NIGHT – NIGHT/3
Niles, Daphne, Lacey and Andrew Lloyd, Conductor
It is a beautiful room, richly appointed. Through the windows we see the starry night sky, perhaps a moon. A crystal chandelier hangs above the dance floor. Tables set with china, crystal, candles, and beautiful floral centerpieces surround the dance floor. There is an orchestra and a bar. Waiters serve the guests. Sophisticated couples in formal attire dance and mingle. The atmosphere reeks of old money. Since it's the "Snow Ball" it's elegantly decorated with a winter theme.

Niles *enters with* **Daphne** *on his arm. She is impressed by the surroundings.*

Daphne (re: room)

Oh, Dr. Crane. It's so beautiful. It's like a dream.

Niles (looking at Daphne)

Isn't it though? *(beat)* Just for tonight could you call me Niles?

Daphne

When I was in school I knew a boy named Niles and I called him Niley.

Niles

Just for tonight could you call me Niles?

She smiles. They cross through the room. As they go:

Niles (cont'd)

You're a vision. Everyone's looking at you.

Daphne

You look awfully handsome yourself . . . Niles.

Niles *laughs giddily.*

Niles

Would you like some champagne?

Daphne

That would be lovely.

Niles
Back in a moment.

Niles *walks a few steps away to the bar.*

Niles *(cont'd) (to bartender)*
Two champagnes, tout de suite.

Lacey *and* **Andrew Lloyd** *approach.*

Lacey *(dripping with pity)*
Niles dear . . . *(she air-kisses him on both cheeks)* How are you?

Niles
Fine. *(he air-kisses her on both cheeks)* Thank you.

Andrew
Haven't seen you for ages. We feel terrible about you and Maris.

Lacey
Oh, yes. We were just devastated. Everyone's talking about it.

Niles
Oh. How is everyone?

Lacey
Devastated.

Daphne *approaches from behind* **Niles**, *to overhear.* **Niles** *is not aware she's there.*

Lacey *(cont'd)*
We were just saying that to Maris when we ran into her and Barclay Paxton at the Breeder's Cup.

Andrew
No, she was with Carlo Binaldi at the Breeder's Cup. She took Barclay to Billy and Binky's birthday bash.

As **Andrew** *and* **Lacey** *walk off:*

Lacey
But anyway, Niles, if there's anything we can do to cheer you up just let us know.

Niles *(sotto)*
How about a murder-suicide pact?

Niles *turns to see* **Daphne**. *He hands her a glass of champagne.*

Daphne
Well, they weren't very nice.

Niles

Everyone in our set seems to have this idea that while Maris is living the high life, I'm sitting home crushed and lonely.

Daphne

Oh, never mind those gossipy twits. Tonight, you're all mine. Now, take me in your arms, Niles, and let the music carry us away.

Daphne *puts out her arms.* **Niles** *moves to her. They start the first step of a dance when the music stops.*

Conductor

Thank you. We'll be back in ten minutes.

Niles *(feigning exhaustion)*

Whew!

AND WE:
DISSOLVE TO:

Scene K

INT. COUNTRY CLUB BALLROOM – AN HOUR LATER – NIGHT/3
Niles, Daphne, Lacey and Andrew Lloyd, Claire Barnes
Niles *and* **Daphne** *dance a waltz. He is more comfortable now, smiling and nodding to his social acquaintances as they dance by. They finish dancing with a little flourish.* **Daphne** *laughs.*

Daphne *(heading toward table)*

Oh, I can't remember when I've had a better time. I'm on cloud nine.

Niles

I'd have to look down to see cloud nine.

They move toward a table.

Niles *(cont'd)*

You look ravishing. Daphne, that is the most exquisite gown.

Daphne

Thank you. It was way out of my price range, but did you ever see something and say, "I just have to have it"?

Niles *(head swimming)*

Where's my chair?

The lights dim. The dance floor is engulfed in colored light. A mirrored ball descends from the ceiling, sending spots of light around the room. The orchestra begins to play a tango.

Daphne

Ah, a tango.

She stands, takes his hand and leads him toward the dance floor.

Niles
But, you never taught me this.

Daphne
You'll love it. It's perfect for you. This is a passionate, hot-blooded dance that rose up from the slums of Buenos Aires.

Niles
The parallels between me and an unemployed gaucho aside, maybe we should sit this one out.

He heads off, but she grabs his hand and pulls him back very close to her.

Daphne
Nonsense! There's only rule in the tango. Our bodies must be in continuous contact with not a sliver of daylight between them.

Niles
I'll do my best.

They begin to dance.

Daphne
Loosen up. Don't be afraid. Daphne won't let anything happen to you.

Niles
I don't think . . .

Daphne
Don't think. Just feel. You're an Argentine slum dweller. You have no house, no car, you don't know where your next meal is coming from, but none of that matters because tonight you have the tango.

Niles
Oh Mama, I've got it all!

Niles *really starts to get into it.*

Daphne
That's it. You're dazzling, you're brilliant. But I feel you're holding back.

Niles
I am.

Daphne
This is no time for inhibitions.

Niles
I know.

Daphne

Let it out, Niles. Let everything out.

Niles

Oh Daphne, I adore you.

At just that moment in the dance, they switch directions and **Daphne** *turns her face away. We see* **Niles** *is stricken with horror. He just did what* **Martin** *warned him of. Then, to his amazement:*

Daphne

I adore you too.

Niles

What?

Daphne *(a little louder)*

I adore you too.

Niles

Oh, how I've longed to hear those words.

Daphne

How I've longed to say them.

Niles

You're beautiful. You're a goddess.

Daphne

I don't ever want this moment to end.

Niles

Then let's not let it.

Niles, *inspired, tangos like a man possessed. There is, in fact, not a sliver of daylight between them. Other couples, including* **Lacey** *and* **Andrew**, *give up the dance floor to watch them. The music reaches a crescendo.* **Niles** *dips* **Daphne**, *his face close to hers. The music ends. The crowd applauds.*

Niles *(cont'd)*

This is the most glorious night of my life.

Daphne

Mine too.

Niles *looks into* **Daphne's** *eyes, and kisses her. She kisses back. The lights come up.* **Niles** *pulls* **Daphne** *up as they move off the dance floor, toward their table.* **Niles** *is walking on air.*

Niles

I'm a new man. Do you have any idea what I'm feeling?

Daphne

Of course I do. *(she indicates the Lloyds)* Your friends look positively dumbstruck. From now on there'll be no more of that "Oh, poor Niles" attitude.

Niles

Far from it.

Daphne

I knew you were a good dancer, but I had no idea you were such a good actor. "I adore you, Daphne. You're a goddess, Daphne." We fooled everyone, didn't we?

Niles

Oh. Yes, we did, didn't we?

Daphne

Rich people. You'd think they'd be a lot smarter. What a bunch of gits.

Niles

Go easy on them. Given the right circumstances anyone can be fooled.

Daphne

Well, what do you say, another dance?

Niles

No, thanks. It's getting late and I've done enough dancing for one night.

Daphne

All right. I'll just go powder my nose and we'll be off.

She exits. **Niles** *watches her go. An attractive woman in her late thirties taps him on the shoulder. He turns to see* **Claire Barnes**.

Claire

Niles, Claire Barnes. I was an associate in your attorney's office.

Niles

Of course. Claire. It's good to see you again.

Claire *(handing him her card)*

I heard about you and Maris and I just wanted to give you my card and let you know that you can call me any time.

Niles

Thank you, but I'm happy with my attorney.

Claire

I meant to go dancing.

Niles

Oh. Thank you.

Claire *smiles at him and exits.* **Niles** *stares at the card as* **Daphne** *approaches.*

Daphne

Well, Dr. Crane, are you ready?

Niles *(looking across the room at Claire)*

No . . . I don't think I am. *(He leaves her card on a nearby table.)*

Daphne

I beg your pardon?

Niles

Oh, Daphne, yes, of course. Shall we?

Daphne *gives him a confused look, takes his arm and they start out.*

Daphne

We had a time tonight, didn't we?

Niles

Yes, we certainly did.

Daphne

And to think you almost didn't come to the ball. It's such a shame when people let fear stop them from trying new things.

Niles

Excuse me.

Niles *breaks away from* **Daphne**, *runs back to the table and grabs the card. He runs back to* **Daphne**.

Niles *(cont'd)*

I'm ready now.

She takes his arm and they exit. And we:

FADE OUT.

End of Act Two

Season Four

The Two Mrs. Cranes

Mixed Doubles

Ham Radio

Daphne and Roz battle for the attention of Daphne's ex-boyfriend, Clive.

Face-off between the two "Mrs. Cranes."

The Two Mrs. Cranes

Episode #40570-073

Written by
Joe Keenan

Created by
David Angell/Peter Casey/David Lee

Directed by
David Lee

ACT ONE

Scene A

FADE IN:

INT. FRASIER'S LIVING ROOM – DAY – DAY/1

Frasier, Daphne, Martin, Niles

Frasier *and* **Niles** *sit at the dining room table.* **Frasier** *reads a newspaper while* **Niles** *probes his muffin with a pair of tweezers.*

> **Frasier** *(looks up from paper)*
>
> Niles, what are you doing?

> **Niles**
>
> This fruit muffin contains a number of things I don't care for. Currants . . . A husk of something . . . *(flicking something onto his plate)* Away wrinkly thing.

> **Frasier**
>
> You know, if you and Maris reconcile, I'm going to miss these tranquil mornings. Me reading my paper. You tweezing your muffin.

Frasier *goes back to his paper as* **Martin** *and* **Daphne** *enter through the front door.* **Martin** *has the mail,* **Daphne** *carries groceries.* **Martin** *seems in high spirits. They ad-lib good mornings.*

> **Martin**
>
> Hey, I got a letter from my old army pal, Bud Farrell. The whole platoon's getting together next weekend at his place in Rattlesnake Ridge. Remember I took you boys camping there when you were small?

> **Frasier**
>
> Who could forget the birth of a lifelong reptile phobia? *(to Daphne)* Speaking of old chums, a certain Clive called while you were out.

> **Daphne** *(concerned)*
>
> Clive? Did he sound British.

> **Frasier**
>
> No, he was one of those fiery Mexican Clives. He said he'd call back.

> **Daphne**
>
> I bet he will.

> **Martin**
>
> I can't wait to see the old gang.

Niles

Dad, you're not planning to drive to Rattlesnake Ridge. It's five hours away. You know how your hip stiffens up.

Martin

No problem. It says I can bring a guest. So, who's the lucky one?

Frasier

If my count is correct, Dad, two of us get to be lucky.

Martin

C'mon, they're great people . . . Stinky, Wolfman, Boom-Boom, Jim – mind you, Jim's not his real name. We call him that 'cause he drinks Jim Beam. Just like we call Hank "Bud" 'cause he drinks Budweiser . . . C'mon, you'd love these guys.

Niles

What sherry drinker wouldn't? Alas I have a conference that weekend.

Daphne

And I have my friend Megan's birthday party.

Martin

What about you, Fras?

SFX: the phone rings

Frasier

Please let this be Lilith asking me to give her a kidney that weekend.

Daphne *answers the phone.*

Daphne

Hello? *(uncomfortably)* Oh, Clive . . . Yes, it has been a long time, hasn't it? . . . I'm sorry, I have dinner plans tonight. . . . Well, maybe just a drink then. Say six-thirty? . . . Me too. Bye. *(hanging up)* Oh hell.

Niles

Who is this Clive, anyway?

Frasier

No, wait, wait, I'm a bit psychic . . . ex-boyfriend?

Daphne

Worse. Ex-fiancé.

Niles

You were engaged?

Daphne

Yes, for years. We were mad for each other. He was very sweet, and had the most gorgeous eyes you ever saw.

Niles

But . . .?

Daphne

Oh yes, that too. I just couldn't see a future with him. The man was a total layabout. No ambition, no drive, couldn't hold a job. All he wanted to do was tinker about with his car. His hands were always black from the motor oil.

Niles

What a brutish habit. If God had intended me to work on my Mercedes, he wouldn't have given me Horst.

Daphne

I had to break it off, but I wanted to let him down easily, so I said if we were still free in five years we could try again. And here he is right on schedule. What do I say to him?

Frasier

Be honest. Tell him how you feel.

Daphne

What, and break the poor thing's heart all over again?

Frasier

In the long run it will spare you a lot of unnecessary anguish. A case in point – *(to Martin)* Dad, I have no plans for next weekend but I don't wish to spend it in the middle of nowhere with Budweiser and Boilermaker and their liver-damaged friend, Seltzer.

Martin

Fine. They'll have another one someday.

Frasier *(to Daphne)*

You see? No evasions. *(to Niles)* No convenient conferences. Just simple honesty.

Martin

'Course, I don't suppose Jim'll be there next time. *(off letter)* Says here he just had his third bypass. And poor old Bud –

Frasier

Well, off to work . . .

Frasier *crosses to the coatrack for his jacket.*

Martin

I guess I'll see Bud at Jim's funeral. Or vice versa. Unless I go first.

Frasier

Oh, for God's sake, all right! I'll drive you to your stupid reunion.

Martin

Thanks, Son.

Frasier *exits.*

Martin *(cont'd)*

Guess I should wait a few days before I mention the part about Stinky needin' a ride.

AND WE:

FADE OUT.

Scene B

A black screen. In white letters appears, "Next in the Repertory, 'Cosi Fan Tushy.' "

INT. RADIO STUDIO – DAY – DAY/1

Frasier, Roz, Gil

Frasier *is on the air.* **Roz** *is in her booth.*

Frasier

And in closing I'd like to send a message to Keith the narcoleptic I spoke to earlier. We can continue our conversation when you feel more alert, but meanwhile I urge you to reconsider applying for that air traffic controller position. This is Dr. Frasier Crane, KACL 780 AM.

Frasier *signs off.* **Gil** *enters the booth.*

Gil

Brilliant show, Frasier. Chock full of pithy insights.

Frasier

What do you want?

Gil

A favor. Bonnie Weems, the Auto Lady, just asked me to a dinner party – one of her famous Bring-Your-Own-Antidote affairs. I told her I'd have to check my book. I'm planning to say you and I have ballet tickets that night, so do back me up.

Frasier

Sorry, I can't.

Gil

You've got to. Have you any idea how vile her food is? The local raccoons have posted warning signs on her trash bin.

Roz *enters* **Frasier's** *booth.*

Frasier

No, I mean she already asked me. I told her I can't make it because I'm driving my dad to his army reunion in Rattlesnake Ridge.

Gil

Very clever. I'd use it myself, but I killed my father off to escape her Labor Day clambake.

Gil *exits.*

Frasier

Oh, Roz, I have opera tickets for tomorrow. I don't suppose you happened to remember –?

Roz *(smiting her forehead)*

Your opera glasses! I am so sorry, they completely slipped my mind.

Frasier

I wouldn't mind if you'd actually borrowed them to go to the opera, but no, you just wanted to ogle that bodybuilder across the street from you.

Roz

Hey, I've just looked once or twice. It's not like I copied his name off his doorbell so I could look up his number and call him when he's in the shower so he'd have to walk across his room naked to answer the phone by the picture window. That would be wrong.

Frasier

Roz, I want them back. I refuse to squint through Pagliacci just because you're trying to see "the magic flute."

As FRASIER EXITS WE:
FADE OUT.

Scene C

INT. FRASIER'S LIVING ROOM – EVENING – DAY 1
Frasier, Niles, Daphne, Clive
Frasier *is in the living room.*

Daphne (O.S.)

Dr. Crane, I need your opinion on this outfit. I wanted something that sent no romantic signals whatsoever.

She enters the living room. She wears a long, heavy cardigan over a decidedly dowdy dress.

Frasier
I can't think how you could improve upon that short of wearing a cactus as a corsage. *(then)* You know, five years is a long time to carry a torch. The man may just be stopping by to say hello.

Daphne
I certainly hope so. The thought of rejecting the poor thing again is more than I can bear.

SFX: doorbell rings

Daphne *(cont'd)*
Oh dear, it's him. *(to Frasier)* Anything between my teeth?

Frasier
No.

Daphne
Do we have any spinach in the fridge?

Frasier
Oh, just go!

Daphne *crosses and opens the door to* **Niles**.

Daphne
Oh, Dr. Crane. I was afraid you were Clive.

Niles *("forgetfully")*
Clive? . . . Oh, yes Clive. Was that tonight? Well, don't I feel silly bringing over this thousand-piece jigsaw puzzle.

Frasier
Niles, I'm sure Daphne doesn't need us horning in on her reunion. We're going to dinner.

Niles
Can't we order in? I've already assembled the first kitten and two yarn balls.

Frasier *(firmly)*
I'm getting my jacket.

Frasier *crosses up toward his bedroom.*

SFX: the doorbell rings

Daphne *and* **Niles** *both turn toward the door.*

Frasier *(cont'd)*
Oh, for God's sake Niles, give them some privacy.

Niles *exits reluctantly to the kitchen.* **Frasier** *exits to his room.* **Daphne**
opens the door and there stands **Clive**. *He's handsome, shy, and a bit
tongue-tied.*

Clive

Hello.

Daphne

Hello.

She gestures for him to come in. He does.

Clive

Look at you. You look wonderful.

Daphne

Oh, go on.

Clive

No, I mean it. Very pretty and . . . warm. *(a moment)* So . . .

Daphne

So . . .

They hug awkwardly.

Clive

Oh, God.

Daphne

What?

Clive

I've gotten a spot of axle grease on your sweater.

Daphne

It's all right. It's just a ratty old thing. Please come in. Same old Clive
I see.

Clive *(wiping his hands with a hanky)*

I suppose so.

Daphne

So, what brings you to Seattle?

Clive

My undying love for you. *(then)* Damn. I meant to lead up to that.
Sorry.

Daphne

No, it's all right. Just a bit –

Clive

Abrupt. No "How are you?" No "Nice place you have here" – By the
way, it's lovely. *(pointing at the view)* Is that the Space Needle?

Daphne

Yes.

Clive

Super. Anyway, I remembered what you told me five years ago. I
thought my feelings would change. It is a long time, but –

Daphne

Clive . . .

Clive

No, let me finish. My feelings haven't changed. I think about you
every day and every night. There comes a time in every man's life
when he has to get up the courage to look a woman in the eye and say
–

Niles *enters from the kitchen with a snack bowl.*

Niles

Cheese Nips? *(then "innocently")* Oh sorry, is this a bad moment?

Daphne

No, not at all. *(to Niles)* This is my very dear old friend Clive Roddy.
(to Clive) Clive, this is Dr. Niles Crane . . . my husband.

Clive

Your husband?

Daphne

Yes. *(slipping an affectionate arm around Niles's waist)* Six months
next week.

Clive

Oh. Well – don't I feel a bit . . . Congratulations. *(to Niles)* You're a
very lucky man.

Niles

Believe me – *(putting an arm around Daphne)* it's like a dream come
true.

AND WE:
FADE OUT.

End of Act One

ACT TWO

Scene D

Black screen. In white letters appears: "A Swell of Couples."

FADE IN:

INT. FRASIER'S APARTMENT – CONTINUOUS – NIGHT/1

Frasier, Martin, Daphne, Niles, Roz, Clive, Eddie

The action is continuous.

Clive

I'm certainly happy for both of you. I see you don't wear wedding rings.

Daphne

We don't need rings, because we always have our arms around each other. Don't we, dear?

She gives **Niles** *a peck on the cheek.* **Niles** *gives her one back, decides he likes it, and gives her another.*

Niles

I know it's sickeningly sweet, but it works for us.

Clive

Well, I suppose I should be going.

Niles

No! *(off their looks)* I mean, no, I'm so enjoying having you here.

Daphne

I did promise you a drink.

Clive

Well, I suppose I could stay for a beer.

Daphne

Oh, good. *(to Niles)* Darling, could you give me a hand in the kitchen?

Niles

Certainly, my angel.

ANGLE ON KITCHEN

Daphne *and* **Niles** *enter.* **Daphne** *pours beer.*

Daphne

I'm so sorry, Dr. Crane. It seemed the kindest way to let him down. I didn't mean to put you in such an awkward position.

Niles

When it comes to you no position's too awkward.

ANGLE ON LIVING ROOM

Clive *has wandered up to the window to check out the view.* **Frasier** *enters.*

Frasier

Oh, hello. You must be Clive.

Clive

Yes. And you're –?

Frasier

Dr. Frasier Crane.

Clive

Oh, Niles's brother?

Frasier

Yes. You've met him?

Clive

Just now. Though I used to know his wife quite well.

Frasier

Really? You know Niles's wife?

Clive

Yes, she's one-of-a-kind, that one.

Frasier

Isn't she?

Clive

She certainly can light up a room.

Frasier *(laughs)*

Usually by leaving it.

Clive *reacts.* **Niles** *and* **Daphne** *reenter. They are alarmed to see* **Frasier.**

Niles

Frasier!

Daphne

Oh, Clive, I see you've met . . . my husband's brother.

Frasier

What?

Daphne *(to Clive)*

He's not hard of hearing. He just doesn't listen. It must run in the family. My husband's the same way.

Niles *(demonstrating)*

What?

Clive

I'm not intruding on some family occasion, am I?

Daphne

No, not at all. Frasier lives here . . . I mean, temporarily. You see –

Niles

– He's had a little spat with his wife . . . Maris.

Clive

Oh. *(to Frasier)* Sorry to hear that.

Frasier

Yes, me too. *(to Daphne)* Daphne, I'm parched. Could you show me again where you keep the wine?

Daphne

Of course. *(to Niles; squeezing him affectionately)* Can you spare me a minute?

Niles

Only if you pay the love toll.

He leans toward her touching his cheek which she dutifully kisses.

Niles *(cont'd)*

Oops! Too much – here's your change.

He kisses her back. **Frasier** *and* **Daphne** *exit to the kitchen.* **Niles** *waits till they're gone then turns immediately to* **Clive***.*

Niles *(cont'd)*

Can you stay for dinner?

Clive

Are you sure? Daphne said you had plans.

Niles

They fell through. Daphne would be crushed if you said no.

Clive

Well, if you're sure . . .

ANGLE ON KITCHEN

Frasier

I told you just be honest but did you listen? No, you have to subject us to this ridiculous charade.

Daphne

Just play along. Please. I swear – one drink and he's out the door.

Niles *enters the kitchen.*

Niles

He's staying for dinner.

Frasier

What?

Daphne

How did that happen?

Niles

He just sort of invited himself. Pretty damned cheeky I thought.

Daphne

Oh, dear God.

Niles

Obviously, he still has hopes of winning you back. We'd better keep these displays of affection as realistic as possible.

Niles *exits.*

Daphne

What will I serve? *(opening freezer)* Do we still have that lasagna?

Frasier

You expect me to endure a whole evening of this nonsense?

Daphne

Just do this for me and anything you want, name it, it's yours.

Frasier

Anything?

Daphne *(realizing)*

Except Rattlesnake Ridge.

Frasier *shrugs then calls out to the living room.*

Frasier

Oh, Clive . . .

Clive (O.S.)

Yes?

Daphne

All right!

Frasier *(calling to Clive)*

Is lasagna okay?

Clive (O.S.)

Super.

Daphne

I'm warning you, one thing goes wrong the whole deal's off.

Frasier

Nothing can go wrong. We just have to keep our stories straight and avoid unnecessary complications.

And we hear **Martin's** *voice from the living room.*

Martin (O.S.)

Hey, I see we got company.

Frasier *and* **Daphne** *exchange panicked looks.*

ANGLE ON LIVING ROOM

Daphne *and* **Frasier** *race in.* **Martin** *is removing his coat.*

Niles

Dad!

Frasier

Dad!

Daphne

Dad!

Martin *reacts.*

Daphne *(cont'd)*

Clive, I'd like you to meet my new husband's father.

Frasier

Or, as we sometimes say in this country, father-in-law.

Martin

What?

Daphne

You see? This listening problem all comes from their dad.

Clive *(extending hand)*

I'm Clive Roddy.

Martin *shakes* **Clive's** *hand.*

Martin *(unsure)*

Hi. Marty Crane.

Niles

Oh, Daphne, how remiss we've been. We haven't even given Clive the tour.

Daphne

Oh, yes, quite right. Well, this is the living room . . .

Niles

I think Clive would be far more interested in the master bathroom, the shower being so large and Manchester being so rainy.

Daphne

Oh, it is lovely. Right through here.

Daphne *leads* **Clive** *off.* **Niles** *calls after her.*

Niles

Wait, you didn't pay the toll. *(then, off Frasier's look)* Oh, never mind.

They're gone. **Frasier** *turns to* **Martin**.

Frasier

Go away.

Martin

What for? What the hell's goin' on?

Frasier

Clive is Daphne's old boyfriend. She's trying to let him down easy by pretending she's married to Niles.

Niles

So, this is my place. Frasier's staying with us because he's separated from Maris.

Martin *(to Frasier)*

You couldn't stand her either, huh?

Niles

Very amusing.

Martin

Do I still live here?

Frasier

Yes, but it might be best if you just excused yourself. This is a very complex situation requiring quick thinking, improvisational skills, and a knack for remembering details.

Martin

Gee, I never used any of those skills as an undercover cop.

Niles

Now, Dad, don't be offended.

Martin

We'd better be careful. This oatmeal brain of mine's liable to bungle everything.

Frasier *rolls his eyes as* **Daphne** *and* **Clive** *reenter.*

Clive *(to Frasier)*

So, Daphne tells me you're both psychiatrists.

Frasier

Yes.

Clive

Fascinating. *(to Martin)* Are you a psychiatrist as well, Marty?

Martin

Me? Nah, I'm retired.

Clive

What did you do?

Martin

I was an astronaut.

Clive *(fascinated)*

Really? You actually flew space missions?

Martin

A few. Me and Neil Armstrong, Buzz Aldrin. I was the one nicknamed him Buzz. People think it's 'cause he flew fast. Not true. He was scared of bees.

Sfx: the doorbell rings.

Everyone looks to the door with concern. Then **Frasier** *leerily crosses to it.*

Frasier

Who is it?

Roz (o.s.)

Open up. It's me.

Martin

What do you know? It's Maris!

Frasier, Niles, *and* **Daphne** *regard* **Martin** *with as much enraged incredulity as they dare display in front of* **Clive**. **Martin** *smiles contentedly.* **Frasier** *opens the door.* **Roz** *enters and thrusts a pair of opera glasses at* **Frasier**.

Roz
Here, I brought your stupid opera glasses. So are we friends, again?

Frasier *embraces her.*

Frasier
Darling!

Clive *(to Daphne)*
Well, I guess that little tiff's over.

ANGLE ON **Frasier** AND **Roz**

Frasier *whispers into* **Roz's** *ear.*

Frasier *(whispering)*
You're Maris.

Roz *(whispering)*
What?

Frasier *(whispering)*
We're married.

Roz *(whispering)*
What?

Frasier *(whispering)*
Play along! *(then, recovering)* Maris Crane, Clive Roddy.

Clive
It's a pleasure.

Roz
It certainly is.

Frasier
Cupcake . . . *(taking Roz's arm; to all)* Could you excuse me? We need a moment alone.

Frasier *and* **Roz** *cross upstage and out onto the balcony.*

Niles *(to Clive)*
Well, now you've met the whole Crane clan.

Clive
Yes, though, Daphne, I did notice in the phone book, you still go by Moon.

Niles
That must've been an old book. She hyphenates now. It's "Moon-Crane."

Martin *(reminiscing)*
I remember the first time I drove a moon crane. Damn near rolled it

in the Sea of Tranquility.

Niles

So Clive, what do you do?

Daphne *(indicating his hands)*

Still mucking about with cars I see.

Clive

Hmm? . . . Oh, my hands. No, I just helped a lady change a tire on my way here. I don't have as much time for cars as I used to. What with my business and all.

Daphne

Your business?

Clive

Yes. After you left I thought about the advice you used to give me and I decided it made sense.

Daphne

What advice?

Clive

You know, "Get a job, you lazy git." I had to grow up sometime. So I took a business course and opened a sporting goods shop. Next thing I knew I had three of them.

Daphne

Goodness. *(to Niles)* Isn't this ironic? All those years I nagged him to make something of himself and now look at him. A captain of industry and still handsome as ever.

Niles

Yes, well send in the clowns.

Frasier *and* **Roz** *reenter the living room.*

Niles *(cont'd)*

Don't bother, they're here.

Frasier

Well, unfortunately my Maris has to say her good-byes. She has a previous engagement.

Clive

Sorry to hear that.

Roz

Me too. I thought I was available, but apparently I'm not.

Martin

Ah, forget your plans, Maris. Stay for dinner.

Roz

Okay, Dad.

Clive

Lovely. We can celebrate you two being reconciled.

Roz

Well, it's still tentative.

Daphne *eyes* **Roz** *jealously. Just then* **Eddie** *enters and trots right up to* **Clive**.

Clive

Well, look who's here. What's his name?

Everyone looks to everyone else in uncertainty over **Eddie's** *or anyone's agreed upon identity before they all nod and say:*

All *(except Clive)*

Eddie!

FADE OUT.

Scene E

FADE IN:

INT. FRASIER'S LIVING ROOM – LATER THAT EVENING NIGHT/1
Frasier, Martin, Daphne, Niles, Roz, Clive
Niles *and* **Frasier** *clear the table.* **Niles** *keeps a watchful eye on* **Daphne** *who, along with* **Roz**, *only has eyes for* **Clive**.

Martin

So there I am floating twenty feet up in the chamber when some idiot turns off the weightless button. Down I go, right on to this special pickax we used for moon rocks.

Clive *(shaking his head sadly)*

And you still walk with a cane?

Martin

Que será será. (rising) Well, it's time I was hitting the ol' hay.

Frasier

Don't forget your warm glass of Tang.

Clive *(shaking his hand)*

It was an honor to meet you.

Martin

I had fun too. 'Night all.

Martin *exits to his room.*

Clive

Delicious meal, Daphne. I don't remember the last time I ate so
much.

Roz

That explains how you keep that fantastic physique.

Daphne

Yes. You are looking wonderfully firm. *(playfully patting his
stomach)* You used to have that little tummy.

Roz

Do you work out?

Clive

When I can. My shops keep me awfully busy.

Niles

Daphne and I have our own little exercise regimen. We work up quite
a sweat, don't we, darling?

Daphne *(ignoring him, to Clive)*

I can't get over it. It's like you're a whole different person. *(to Niles,
meaningfully)* A whole different person.

Frasier *stands.*

Frasier

Well, who's for coffee?

Roz *(her eyes on Clive)*

More importantly, who's for dessert?

Frasier

Gumdrop . . .

Roz

Just asking.

Daphne

I'll give you a hand.

ANGLE ON KITCHEN

Daphne *and* **Frasier** *enter. They whisper furiously as they put plates in the
sink and coffee and cookies onto serving trays.*

Daphne

Would you please tell Roz to stop flirting? Has she forgotten she's a
married woman?

Frasier

You're one to talk. If you batted your eyelashes any harder you'd blow out the candles.

Daphne

You get rid of her now or it's Rattlesnake Ridge for you.

Frasier

You wouldn't.

Daphne

Wouldn't I? By the way, Stinky needs a ride.

Daphne *exits the kitchen.*

ANGLE ON LIVING ROOM

Daphne *reenters with a plate of cookies for dessert.* **Frasier** *follows.* **Roz** *is reading* **Clive's** *palm.*

Roz

And according to your love line . . .

Frasier

Maris darling, I don't know about you, but I'm completely exhausted.

Roz

See you at home. *(extending her glass to Daphne)* More wine, please.

Daphne

Are you sure that's wise, dear? Remember that blackout you had last month? *(then, with a merry laugh)* What am I saying? Of course you don't.

Niles

That's what I love about her, her sense of humor. *(to Daphne)* Cookie, dear?

Daphne

No thanks. *(with a glance to Roz)* Some of us do look after our weight.

Roz

Now, now, you have to keep your strength up. You are eating for two.

All react. **Daphne** *stares murderously at* **Roz**.

Clive *(to Daphne)*

You're having a baby? Well, when were you planning to spring that news?

Daphne
Well, we don't like to bring it up. It's a sore point around here what with my sister-in-law being barren and all.

Niles
Now now. It's not her fault. My brother is impotent.

Clive *(at a loss)*
Well . . . congratulations. *(then)* Is there a loo I can use?

Niles *(pointing)*
Right by the front door. We call that one Frasier's bathroom. That's why we've monogrammed the towels with his initials.

Clive *crosses and enters the powder room. All watch him go with tight smiles until the door closes.*

Frasier
Have you all taken leave of your senses?

Daphne
She started it. Hanging all over him. *(to Roz)* Oh, by the way, that was my foot you kept massaging.

Roz
What is your problem? Frasier told me we were doing this 'cause you wanted to brush him off.

Daphne
I changed my mind. Didn't you see my signals?

Roz
Gee, I missed them. It must've been during one of my blackouts.

Niles
No need to fight. I'll just flip a coin. *(does so)* Good news, Roz.

Daphne
Sod off.

Clive, *unseen by all four, exits the powder room and watches the following in quiet horror.*

Daphne *(cont'd) (to Roz)*
You'd think with all your dozens and dozens of men you could leave at least one for me?

Roz
Dozens? *(to Frasier)* Did you tell her that?

Frasier
Well, forgive me for keeping track.

Niles

Why are you fighting over the man anyway? He's got all the charm of a cricket bat.

Roz *(to Daphne)*

Hey, you want him so bad, fine, take him.

Daphne

Fat chance I've got now that you've told him I'm pregnant. How am I supposed to get rid of this bloody baby?

Frasier *(noticing Clive)*

Clive. Coffee?

Clive

No thank you. I really should be going.

Daphne

No, please. I know what you must think, but we're not what we seem.

Clive

You certainly aren't. Look, I know I'm a guest here so I've kept silent so far, but I'm sorry, I can't any longer. You are the most appalling family I have ever met. *(to Frasier)* You – breaking up with your wife over a pair of opera glasses. *(to Niles)* And you – looking down your nose at me all the while you show off your posh flat. Well, for your information, I don't think there's anything remotely special about either of your bathrooms. *(to Daphne and Roz)* And you two women, flirting shamelessly with me right in front of your husbands. *(to Roz, then Daphne)* You having just reconciled with Frasier, you carrying Niles's baby. I pity your child, Daphne . . . and I pity any good Manchester girl who comes here to this vile coffee-swilling Sodom and lets it change her the way it's changed you.

Daphne

But I haven't changed. Really. We're not the awful people you think we are.

Frasier

Yes. The truth is we've been lying to you all night.

Clive

Well, I don't care to be lied to anymore. Good-bye. I'll never understand how two men like you could have been spawned by that sweet, courageous old astronaut!

HE EXITS, AND WE:

FADE OUT.

Scene H

FADE IN:

INT. FRASIER'S LIVING ROOM – LATER THAT EVENING NIGHT/1
Frasier, Niles, Daphne
Frasier, Niles, *and* **Daphne** *are there.* **Daphne,** *now wearing a ratty bathrobe, sits glumly eating cookies from a large plate on her lap.*

Niles
I've got another one. He would have wanted you to move.

Daphne
I would've moved.

Frasier
Daphne, I'm sure if you just bide your time a while he'll give you a second chance.

Daphne
This was my second chance.

Niles
You'll get another. I believe that if two people are meant to be together sooner or later they will be. Years may pass, years filled with frustration and missed connections. But the day will come when they just fall into each others' arms and jet off to a beautiful Caribbean Island, though France is nice too.

Daphne
I'm not sure I believe you, but thank you, Dr. Crane.

Niles
You're welcome . . . *("a joke")* . . . Mrs. Crane.

Daphne *(laughs then yawns)*
I guess it's bedtime. 'Night.

Frasier
Good night.

Daphne *crosses to her room.* **Niles** *rises, starts to take his first step toward* **Daphne's** *room, then:*

Frasier *(cont'd)*
Niles. You're annulled.

Niles *sits glumly, takes a cookie and eats it, and we:*
FADE OUT.

End of Act Two

Mixed Doubles

Episode #40570-079

Written by
Christopher Lloyd

Created by
David Angell/Peter Casey/David Lee

Directed by
Jeff Melman

The Crane brothers spy on the neighbor's . . . furniture.

Niles encounters his doppelgänger.

ACT ONE

Scene A

FADE IN:

INT. FRASIER'S LIVING ROOM – DAY – DAY/1

Niles, Frasier, Martin, Daphne, Roz, Eddie

Niles *and* **Frasier** *are upstage, at the telescope.* **Frasier** *is looking through it,* **Niles** *is waiting somewhat impatiently.*

Niles

Don't be greedy. Your turn was up forty seconds ago. Tic, tic, tic, tic.

Frasier

Oh, all right. *(they trade places)* It's the penthouse unit, second window in from the right.

Niles

Scanning . . . scanning . . . *(finding it)* Oh Mama! Utter perfection.

Martin

You two know what you're doing isn't right, don't you?

Frasier

We happen to be looking at an extremely rare Brancusi armchair, not a naked woman.

Martin

That's what I'm talking about.

Frasier

By the way, Dad, I hope you're not settling in there. I have plans for the television tonight. Roz is bringing over a quirky little Hungarian comedy she taped off the satellite dish.

Martin

You know, I don't know why we can't get one of those dishes. Duke says they got a channel that runs nothing but sports bloopers.

Frasier

Question asked and answered.

The front door opens and **Daphne** *enters.*

Daphne

Evening.

Martin

Hey, Daph. You're home kinda early, aren't you?

Daphne

A bit. Something . . . sort of happened.

Martin

What was it?

Daphne

Well, Joe and I were having dinner, everything was nice as could be, and I said, "Don't you like your potato?" And he said, "No, I'm not hungry for potato just now." And I said, "Well, if you don't like your potato you're welcome to try my potato –"

Frasier

Perhaps we could hasten to the post-potato portion of the dialogue.

Daphne

Well, that's when he said it. He said we'd been on-again, off-again for too long without making anything permanent. So maybe it was best if we just broke up.

Martin

Gosh, I'm sorry. But you're sure taking it well. If you'd told me Joe would end up dumping you tonight I'd have bet –

Daphne

Oh God. He dumped me!

And with that, she begins to sob uncontrollably.

Frasier

Deftly done, Dad.

Martin

Well don't just stand there, you two – somebody comfort her.

Niles

Right.

They both move toward her, **Niles** *leading the way. He's obviously quite eager at the chance to hug* **Daphne**. *But* **Frasier** *beats him to it – to* **Niles's** *consternation. Throughout the following* **Daphne** *will remain crying.*

Frasier

That's it, Daphne. Let it all out.

Daphne *(through sobs)*

This is so embarrassing.

Frasier

Never mind how it looks. Expressing our emotions is always

beneficial even when it may come at the expense of our pride *(notices his lapel)* – or a brand new Italian silk jacket.

She's still bawling.

Frasier *(cont'd)*
I don't seem to be doing much good here. Maybe one of you should try.

Niles
Very well.

Again, **Niles** *steps forward but* **Martin** *beats him to it.*

Martin
Now Daphne, you're better off without that guy. He was a bum!

Daphne
He was the best thing in my life! *(cries)*

Martin
Oh. Well then maybe he just wasn't ready for a commitment.

Daphne
He's in love with someone else. *(cries harder)*

Martin
Oh. Well, then maybe you just weren't meant for each other. I mean, you're a champagne and caviar sort of girl – he's steak and potatoes.

Daphne *(sobbing at the memory)*
Potatoes! . . .

Martin
I'm making a mess of this too.

Niles *(stepping forward)*
Here, Dad . . .

SFX: doorbell

Daphne
I'll get it.

She slips away from **Niles** *and opens the door to* **Roz** *who has arrived with cassette in hand.*

Roz
Hi, Daphne.

Daphne *(cries)*
Roz.

Roz

Oh my God, you got dumped.

She hugs **Daphne.**

> **Roz** *(cont'd) (over Daphne's shoulder, to Frasier)*
> You made her open the door?

Frasier

It's what she does.

Martin

You're just in time, Roz. We're not doing such a good job of comforting her.

Roz

Don't worry about it. Come on.

They head to **Daphne's** *room.*

> **Daphne** *(starting to gather herself)*
> I'm sorry about all this. I guess I'm still at the point where I can't even hear his name without crying.

> **Niles** *(sensing an opportunity)*
> Well, let's not give Joe that satisfaction.

Daphne *bursts into tears again,* **Niles** *steps forward to comfort her, but* **Frasier** *holds him back as* **Roz** *steers* **Daphne** *off to her room.*

Martin

Well, I don't know about you two, but I see emotion like that and it gets me all upset. Of course, if we had that sports blooper channel I'd be cheered up in no time.

Frasier

Well, if you're desperate, you could always dig up the home movie of Niles and me learning to play Frisbee.

Martin

Nah, that's just plain sad.

He exits to the hall followed by **Eddie. Niles** *has been staring off after* **Daphne. Frasier** *moves to the liquor cabinet.*

Frasier

Brandy, Niles?

> **Niles** *(distracted)*
> Yes, thank you. *(after a beat)* Frasier, I think I just made an important decision. I'm going to tell Daphne how I feel about her.

Frasier

What?

Niles

I'm going to tell her tonight.

Frasier

You're serious about this?

Niles

I'm dead serious. Maris and I are nowhere near reconciling – she's being as intransigent as ever. I know this is the right decision because I'm perfectly calm about it. *(holds up hand, demonstrating; it shakes)* I'll take that brandy now.

Frasier

Niles, before you do anything this rash, you should consider it from all angles.

Niles

I've spent three years considering Daphne from all angles.

Frasier

Are you sure this is the right moment for this?

Niles

If you're trying to rattle me, it's not going to work. I've been rehearsing this for months. *(getting increasingly nervous)* "Daphne, there's something you and I need to talk about. It's a matter of . . . For a long time now, I . . . well, you and I . . . we . . ." Exactly how is that brandy getting here, by Saint Bernard?

Frasier

I just think you should consider her state of mind. She's still reeling from her breakup with Joe.

Niles

Frasier, I'm not sitting on these feelings any longer.

Frasier

It won't kill you to wait a little longer. At least one more day.

Niles

A day? Oh, all right.

Daphne *and* **Roz** *reenter.*

Roz

If the jewelry's not that good and the sex isn't that good, what have you really lost here?

Daphne
I suppose you have a point.

Frasier
Well, I don't normally endorse the Gabor approach to therapy, but it seems to be working.

Roz
I'm going to take Daphne out and get her mind off her troubles.

Daphne
I want to thank you both for being so supportive. I'm feeling a bit better. Another few days and I'll have completely forgotten old what's-his-name.

Niles *(sensing an opportunity)*
Joe.

It has its desired effect – it starts **Daphne** *crying and* **Niles** *moves in to offer a hug, but* **Roz** *steps in the way and shoos* **Niles** *away, and we:*
FADE OUT.

Scene B

INT. LIVING ROOM – DAY – DAY/2
Frasier, Niles, Martin, Daphne, Eddie
Martin *is with* **Eddie** *in his chair. He's reading the sports section.* **Frasier** *is going through the CD's in the cabinet, looking for one.*

Martin
What were they thinking last night? If you're two for fifteen from behind the arc, why do you still give it to your two-guard instead of jamming it down to your big man in the paint?

Frasier
Eddie, I believe that question was directed at you.

Martin
You know, if you ever took an interest in sports, you'd probably like it. It's graceful, it's dramatic.

Frasier *(finding his CD)*
Thank you, Dad, but for now I'm quite satisfied with the likes of Pavarotti's Pagliacci. You have your big man in the paint and I have mine.

Martin *exits to the kitchen.*

SFX: doorbell rings

Frasier *crosses to the door and opens it.* **Niles** *is there, holding flowers to his chest.*

Frasier

Niles.

Niles

Frasier.

Frasier

Either your boutonniere is way over the top or you're here to pursue last night's plan.

Niles

Look, I know I don't have your support on this, but . . . how to put this?

Frasier

You don't care?

Niles

If you could work the phrase "rat's ass" into that you'd have it. The fact is, I'm tired of being lonely. And it makes no sense going on being lonely when the woman I long for is unattached.

Frasier

Well, as I said to you the time you tried to jump out of the treehouse with an umbrella, "I suppose you know what you're doing."

Martin *reenters from the kitchen, and retakes his seat.*

Martin

Hey, Niles.

Niles

Hey, Dad.

SFX: phone rings

Frasier *goes to it and answers it.*

Frasier

Hello . . . Yes. Would you hold on please? *(covers phone, then)* Dad – is Daphne in her room?

Martin

Gee, I don't know. *(then, screaming)* Daphne!! Hey, Daph! Daphne!!

Frasier

For God's sake, I can yell.

He puts the caller on hold, and exits to the hall.

Martin

I've been waiting thirty years to do that.

Niles

So, you're probably wondering what I'm doing with these flowers.

Martin

Not really.

Niles

Well, I'll tell you. They're for Daphne. I've decided I'm going to tell her how I feel.

Martin

That's great, Niles.

Niles

"That's great"?

Martin

Yeah. You're single now, she's single. Why not?

Niles

Oh, my God. That is so funny.

Martin *(starting to laugh)*

What is? Let me in on it.

Niles

I just never expected that reaction. I thought you'd say something more Dad-like. You know, like –

Martin

You're out of your mind?

Niles

Yes. *(laughs)*

Martin

She'll never go for it in a million years?

Niles *(laughing)*

Stop it!

Martin

Some day you'll look back on this as the stupidest, most idiotic –

Niles *(not laughing)*

Dad, I said stop it.

Daphne *enters from the hall, followed by* **Frasier**. **Niles** *coyly hides the flowers behind his back.*

Daphne

Morning, Dr. Crane.

Niles

Hello, Daphne.

Daphne

Don't you look nice.

She picks up the phone, hits the button.

Daphne *(cont'd) (into phone)*

Hello . . . Yes, Rodney. I'm so glad you called . . . Yes, I enjoyed
meeting you too. Uh-huh. Oh, well, yes, that would be lovely. I'll see
you around four, then. Bye.

She hangs up.

Frasier

Rodney?

Daphne

You won't believe this. Last night, Roz insisted on taking me to this
bar she calls the "Sure Thing."

Frasier

How flattering. They've named a bar after her.

Daphne

She told me whenever she takes a friend there they always end up
meeting someone. Well, I wasn't there ten minutes and she spun my
barstool around and I was face to face with this nice-looking man.

Martin

Rodney.

Daphne

Right. I suppose it's a bit soon for me to be seeing anyone else, but
it's just coffee. Besides, if I wait he might not be available when I'm
ready.

Niles

Timing is everything.

Daphne

I can't wait to tell Roz.

She exits to the hall.

Niles

"Give it a day, Niles."

Frasier

Sorry. I don't know what to say.

Niles

Too bad you didn't have that problem last night.

Martin

Don't let this get you down.

Niles

I won't. I still have a fallback position. *(takes out phone)* I'm not particularly proud of what I'm doing right now. Given how strained our relationship is, I'm sure she'll make me grovel. But she's the only woman who can put an end to my loneliness.

Frasier

You're not going to call Maris.

Niles

Good God, no. *(into phone)* Hello Roz, about this sure thing bar of yours . . .

On **Martin** *and* **Frasier's** *reactions, we:*
DISSOLVE TO:

Scene C

INT. GRANVILLE'S – NIGHT – NIGHT/2
Niles, Roz, Bulldog, Adelle
An upscale place with both a bar and tables with chairs. It's sparsely populated. **Roz** *is at the bar.* **Niles** *enters, a little frazzled-looking.*

Niles

Well, I'm here. I forgot to gargle, I'm wearing mismatched socks, and I'm so nervous I could wet myself.

Roz

Well, we've got your opening line down.

Niles

You're going to have to be patient, Roz. This isn't exactly my milieu.

Roz

Let's make that lesson number one. If you're going to use words like "milieu" you might as well show up here with a sore on your lip and a couple of kids.

Niles

Point well taken.

He takes out a handkerchief and begins wiping off his seat.

Roz

Guess what lesson number two is.

He stops wiping, sits.

Roz *(cont'd)*

Will you relax? You're going to be fine. Just remember, every single woman here came for the same reason – to meet someone. They may be putting up a front that says "Go Away," but they're really praying someone will come talk to them.

Bulldog *comes up behind* **Roz.**

Bulldog *(in Australian accent)*

Hey there Sheila, you're looking good tonight.

Roz

Get bent. *(sees it's Bulldog)* Oh, it's you. Get bent.

Bulldog

I'm using my Australian tourist character tonight. *(to Niles)* I've got a few of 'em I like to rotate, like crops. So what the hell are you doing here?

Niles

At the moment, contemplating the grim fact that you and I are peers.

Bulldog

You're just lucky you came on a night when you can observe the maestro. Watch and learn.

He approaches a woman at the bar.

Bulldog *(cont'd) (as Australian)*

Hey there Sheila. You're looking pretty good up top. How are you down under?

The woman throws her drink in his face.

Bulldog *(cont'd)*

I'll check back with you later. G'day.

He crosses to the bathroom to dry himself off.

Niles

I'm leaving.

Roz

Hey – I didn't come all the way down here to see you wimp out.

Niles

No, you came all the way down here because I promised you the keys to my cabin for the weekend. *(gives her keys)* There you are. There's a bear skin rug in protective cellophane in the closet behind the wet bar.

He starts to leave, she grabs him by the arm.

Roz
Look, I have a perfect matchmaking record in this bar and you are not breaking my streak. Now sit.

He does.

Roz *(cont'd)*
There's just a few rules you need to know. First, when you introduce yourself be as casual as possible. Second, you cannot say enough nice things about her hair. I know it's shallow, but it works. Third, hang on her every word. Be fascinated. Now go.

Niles
What do you mean "go"?

Roz
It's time.

Niles
Are you insane? I'm not ready, I'm not nearly ready.

Roz
Look, I've thrown a lot of babies into the water and they all came up swimming. Go.

Niles
But there's no possible way I can –

She spins his barstool around bringing him face to face with an attractive blond woman who sits alone. This is **Adelle**.

Niles *(cont'd)*
Hello.

Adelle
Hello.

Niles
I hope I'm not bothering you.

Adelle
No, not at all. I'm Adelle.

Niles
Niles. So, Adelle – is that with one "l" or two?

Adelle
Two.

Niles *(fascinated)*

Really.

<small>AS THEY CONTINUE, WE:</small>
<small>FADE OUT.</small>

End of Act One

ACT TWO

Scene D

<small>FADE IN:</small>
INT. FRASIER'S LIVING ROOM – NIGHT – NIGHT/3
Frasier, Martin, Niles, Adelle, Daphne, Rodney, Eddie
Frasier *is at the table;* **Eddie** *is a few feet away. They are staring at each other – intently. It's a stare down.* **Martin** *enters from the kitchen.*

Martin

You're wasting your time.

Frasier

No, I'm not.

Martin

You're not going to win.

Frasier

It's time he learned what it feels like to be stared at. *(to Eddie)* So bring it on. You can't touch me. You've got nothing. I'm – *(then, breaks, clutching his eyes)* Gaah! It was as though his eyes turned into sorcerer's pinwheels and started spinning.

Martin

Just shake hands and say good fight.

SFX: doorbell rings

Martin *crosses to it, opens it.* **Niles** *is there, with* **Adelle**.

Niles

Hey, Dad.

Martin

Hi, Niles. Come on in.

Niles

I'd like you to meet Adelle Childs. Adelle, my father, Martin, and my brother, Frasier.

All ad-lib hellos.

Niles *(cont'd) (to Frasier)*

Are you all right? Your eyes look funny.

Frasier

I'm fine. So Adelle – it's nice to finally meet you.

Adelle

It's nice to meet you too.

Frasier *(handing Niles tickets)*

Here are your opera tickets.

Niles

Thank you.

Frasier

Do you have time for coffee before you go?

Adelle

That would be nice.

Frasier

Splendid. I can debut my Limoges coffee set. There are six unique cups, each representing a different wife of Henry the Eighth. Only last week my antique dealer finally located an Anne of Cleves to complete the set.

Martin *(to Adelle)*

He loves to rub it in – I'm still looking for a Wilma to complete my juice glass set.

Niles *(to Frasier)*

I'll give you a hand.

Frasier *and* **Niles** *start to the kitchen.* **Eddie** *jumps onto* **Adelle's** *lap.*

Martin

Don't mind him. He'll lie down anyplace that's nice and warm. Not that I meant to imply that . . . well that – *(his only way out)* Eddie, get off of there!

In the kitchen, **Frasier** *and* **Niles** *begin making coffee.*

Niles

So: What do you think?

Frasier

She seems nice.

Niles

She's fabulous! I know it's only been three dates, but I feel as though I've been rescued. I no longer have to worry about becoming one of those pitiful losers embittered by a failed marriage, leading a lonely, pathetic life of . . . *(off Frasier's withering look)* fulfillment and good times.

Frasier
Shouldn't you make a beeping noise when you back up like that?

They exit to the living room. **Martin** *and* **Adelle** *have been sitting in uncomfortable silence.*

Frasier *(cont'd)*
Coffee will be ready in a moment.

Adelle
So what were you two whispering about?

SFX: doorbell

Niles *crosses to answer it.*

Niles
Oh, nothing. Just about how whenever you think you've got your life figured out something unexpected happens.

He opens the door to **Daphne** *and* **Rodney Banks**.

Daphne
Sorry, forgot my keys. Hello, all. Everyone, this is Rodney Banks.

Niles
How do you do?

He and **Rodney** *shake hands.*

Rodney
The pleasure is mine.

He removes a handkerchief and wipes his hand. **Niles** *does the same.*

Rodney *(cont'd)*
No offense, but it is the flu season.

Niles
Yes, you can't be too careful.

Daphne
This is Frasier Crane, and his father Martin, and . . .

Niles *(moving Adelle toward Daphne)*
Adelle Childs.

Daphne
Hello. We've just had the most wonderful day at the marina.

Martin
Oh, you've got a boat?

Rodney
Actually, no. I have an inner ear curvature that makes me prone to motion sickness. But there's a bistro there that serves a bouillabaise that's an exact duplicate of the one at Tour D'Argent in Paris.

Frasier
A duplicate you say.

Martin
Can you join us for coffee?

Daphne
Yes, that would be nice.

Frasier
I'll get it. Daphne, you like yours black. Rodney?

Rodney
Generally I take it with one percent milk and just a nuance of cinnamon.

Frasier
I had a feeling you might.

Martin
I'll give you a hand.

Frasier *crosses into the kitchen.* **Martin** *follows. They begin pouring coffee.*

Martin *(cont'd)*
What the hell was that?

Frasier
I know. We should put a red mark on the real Niles so we can tell them apart.

Martin
Niles must be going nuts.

Niles *enters.*

Niles
Can I lend a hand?

Martin *and* **Frasier** *just stare at him.*

Martin
No thanks. Niles, what do you think of Rodney?

Niles

Well, so far I'm not very impressed. Kind of a pretentious fop, isn't he?

Martin

He doesn't remind you of anyone?

Niles

Remind me of anyone?

Rodney *enters.*

Rodney

So Niles – Adelle tells me you're headed to the opera tonight.

Niles

Yes, Khovanshchina.

Rodney

A masterwork.

Niles

I don't think there's a more haunting moment in all of opera than when Shaklovity poisons the prince.

Rodney

Agreed. Although I believe he stabs him.

Niles

No, he poisons him.

Rodney

Well, no sense arguing. Oh, about my coffee, I neglected to mention that I like my milk steamed. But just a dollop of foam, such as might give the effect of a cumulus cloud reflected in a still pond.

Niles

Consider it done.

Rodney *exits. There's a beat, then:*

Niles *(cont'd)*

I want to kill myself.

Martin

Oh come on, Niles. It's funny.

Niles

No, it's not remotely funny. Frasier talked me out of approaching Daphne on the same night she fell for that man.

Frasier

You can't really be mad at me.

Niles

Mad at you? What for? For denying me any chance at a happiness I have only ached for for the last three years of my life? No, Frasier, I'm grateful. Come closer, I'll show you how grateful.

He grabs a knife from the counter.

Frasier

Are you mad?

Martin *(stepping between them)*

Niles!

Frasier

He's got that same look in his eyes that Eddie had!

Daphne *enters,* **Niles** *quickly hides the knife.*

Daphne

Isn't Rodney just great?

Martin

Oh, yeah.

Frasier

Yes, great.

Daphne

I think it was the moment Joe broke up with me I heard a voice say, "Daphne, it's time you went for a completely new type of man."

All we hear is the cold slap of a knife blade against the counter behind **Niles's** *back.* **Daphne** *exits.*

Frasier

I should really be getting Rodney his coffee.

He starts out, but **Rodney** *reenters, carrying a reference book.*

Rodney

Niles, I've taken the liberty of looking up that opera point we were disputing. It says right here it was a stabbing. You don't forget a stabbing.

Niles

No, you don't.

Frasier *(exiting)*

Well, we all have our coffee now. No sense staying in here when we have wide open spaces in the living room.

Frasier *enters the living room, followed by* **Rodney** *and* **Martin.**

Rodney *(smells his coffee)*

Mmm – nothing on earth smells quite so heavenly as a freshly brewed cup of coffee. Well, perhaps one thing does.

He makes a move toward **Daphne.**

Daphne

Stop that. He loves to smell my hair.

From the kitchen we hear a crash, obviously **Frasier's** *coffee set is no longer complete.*

Frasier *(deflated)*

Anne Boleyn?

Niles (O.S.)

Catherine of Aragon.

FADE OUT.

Scene E

INT. CAFE NERVOSA – DAY – DAY/4

Niles, Frasier, Adelle, Rodney

Niles *is at a table alone.* **Frasier** *enters, a bit sheepishly, and approaches him.* **Niles** *sees him, then looks the other way.* **Frasier** *strides over and takes a seat.*

Frasier

Oh for heaven's sake, Niles, not returning my calls and trying to ignore me is the behavior of a pouting adolescent. Are you quite finished? *(then realizing)* You put gum on my chair, didn't you?

Niles

Yes, and now I'm finished.

Frasier *works to remove the gum.*

Frasier

I'm sorry if I steered you wrong, but let's remember, you do have someone wonderful in your life now, don't you?

Niles

I suppose I do.

Frasier

Adelle does make you very happy, doesn't she?

Niles

Yes. Yes, she does.

Frasier

Well then, if you're ever going to follow another piece of advice I give you, follow this one: Adelle is your path to happiness.

At that moment, **Adelle** *and* **Rodney** *enter the cafe arm-in-arm.* **Frasier** *sees them,* **Niles** *doesn't.*

Frasier *(cont'd)*

But let's say I'm wrong.

Frasier *gingerly removes the knife from* **Niles's** *place setting.*

Niles

But you're not wrong. Adelle is a wonderful, affectionate woman.

Frasier *sees* **Adelle** *give* **Rodney** *a kiss.*

Frasier

She is affectionate.

Niles

And she's clearly drawn to a man of my type. Just thinking about her is lifting my spirits. Thank you, Frasier.

Frasier

Niles . . . look.

He indicates the table where **Adelle** *and* **Rodney** *have taken seats and are now holding hands.* **Niles** *looks.*

Niles

I don't believe it! The betrayal! No one treats Daphne like that!

He stands, **Frasier** *grabs him by the arm.*

Frasier

Niles! Whatever you do, don't engage him in a physical fight. The whole thing would just look too weird.

Frasier *lets go of him.* **Niles** *strides over to* **Adelle** *and* **Rodney's** *table.*

Niles

Hello, Adelle.

Adelle *(startled)*

Oh no.

Rodney

I know this may look a tad incriminating, but the truth is –

Niles

Oh, spare me, you ludicrous popinjay. I know exactly what's going on. I was watching you from my table.

Adelle

I was going to call you. You see, Rodney and I, well we . . . well, you saw from your table. I'm sorry.

Niles

I'm sorry too, Adelle. But I'm mostly sorry for Daphne. *(to Rodney)* How do you intend to handle that small matter?

Rodney

I was planning to tell her tonight. We're meeting for drinks at Granville's.

Niles

Why don't you do her a favor and let me tell her? It will be better coming from a friend.

Rodney

Yes, I suppose it would. Please tell her I'm sorry. Sometimes when a man finds the woman he's meant to be with *(takes Adelle's hand)* he's powerless to resist. I hope she understands that.

Niles

I hope she understands it too.

Niles *heads out the door.* **Frasier** *walks over to the table.*

Frasier *(to Rodney)*

I just have one question for you. Do you have an older brother?

Rodney

As a matter of fact I do. He's the pride of the family. Handsome, successful, brilliant. I've always been rather jealous of him.

Frasier

Spooky.

AS FRASIER HEADS OUT, WE:
FADE OUT.

Scene H

INT. GRANVILLE'S – NIGHT – NIGHT/4
Daphne, Niles
Daphne *is there with a glass of wine.* **Niles** *enters.*

Niles

Evening, Daphne.

Daphne

Hello, Dr. Crane.

Niles

You don't seem surprised to see me.

Daphne

I was running late so I called Rodney on his cell phone. He told me everything.

Niles

Oh. I'm sorry.

Daphne

Sorry for you, too. *(re: the wine)* Join me in a little sorrow-drowning?

Niles

Yes, I believe I will. *(to bartender, re: her wine)* One more of these, please. *(then)* You know, I can't say I really blame Adelle. Rodney is that type of man that women seem to go for.

Daphne *(sadly)*

Yes, he is.

Niles

I didn't mean to upset you.

Daphne

You didn't. I guess I'm just more in the mood to hear about his negative qualities right now.

Niles

Well, he is a bit of a know-it-all, and kind of fussy.

Daphne

. . . has to have everything just so, he's a nut about cleanliness, then there's his clothes, his precious shoes . . .

Niles

I don't like this road we're on. *(off her look)* I mean, wouldn't we be better off discussing what's in our future?

Daphne

I suppose. I'll tell you one thing, after the run I've had lately I pity the next man I date – I'll probably rip him to shreds.

Niles

What about the man after that?

Daphne

It's not that I hate all men, but they are an unfeeling lot. Look at Rodney. The minute he heard I'd just broken up with someone he moved right in for the kill. Is that how all men are?

Niles

Not all men, no.

Daphne

Of course they aren't. You're not. You're kind, sensitive. If you ask me, you were too good for that Adelle.

Niles

Thank you, Daphne. But the truth is my heart was never really in that relationship.

Daphne

I thought it might not be.

Niles

There's someone else who's been on my mind too much.

Daphne

I had a feeling, Dr. Crane.

Niles

You did?

Daphne

Yes. As long as you still have feelings for your wife, you know you can't be involved with anyone else. It makes sense to me. I know I'd never get involved with a man who was separated.

Niles

Even if he'd worshiped you since the day he laid eyes on you?

Daphne

And don't think that's not just how they'd put it, too. *(laughs)* No. I think I need to do a bit of separating myself. From Joe, I mean. I'll wait a good long time before I do any more dating.

Niles

I'm glad to hear you say that.

Daphne

It's funny when you think about it: the two of us both coming to this same singles bar this week. This is the very stool I was on when I met Rodney.

Niles

I was right here when I met Adelle.

Niles *points to the empty stool next to* **Daphne**. **Daphne** *laughs to herself.*

Niles *(cont'd)*

What?

Daphne

Oh, I was just thinking: if it had been a different time in both of our lives, we might have actually met. How do you suppose that would have gone?

Niles

What, our conversation?

Daphne

Yes. Just for fun – we could both use a smile.

Niles

Well, I suppose I would have said "Excuse me, is this seat taken," you'd have said "No." Then you'd have said "My name's Daphne," and I'd have said "I'm Niles." Then I'd have said, "What are you doing for the rest of your life?"

Daphne *(laughs)*

You always know just the right thing to say. *(then, as a friend would say it)* I love you, Dr. Crane.

Niles

I love you too, Daphne.

AND WE:

FADE OUT.

End of Act Two

Ham Radio

Episode #40570-089

Written by
David Lloyd

Created by
David Angell/Peter Casey/David Lee

Directed by
David Lee

The show must go on . . . Frasier, Niles, and Roz make a crisis out of a radio drama.

Bulldog freezes up on air.

ACT ONE
Scene A

FADE IN:

INT. CAFE NERVOSA – DAY – DAY/1

Frasier, Niles, Martin

Niles *and* **Martin** *are seated at a table drinking coffee. There is a slightly strained feeling.*

> **Martin**
>
> This is great, spending time like this.

> **Niles**
>
> We don't do it enough.

> **Martin**
>
> Yep, just the two of us.

There's an awkward beat, then **Frasier** *enters, carrying a folder.* **Martin** *and* **Niles** *both excitedly wave him over.*

> **Martin** *(cont'd)*
>
> Hey, Fras! Frasier!

> **Niles**
>
> Come join us!

> **Frasier** *(to the counter person)*
>
> Double cappuccino to go.

Frasier *crosses to join them.*

> **Frasier** *(cont'd)*
>
> Thank you. But I can only stay a moment. I've taken on a very exciting project. This is KACL's fiftieth anniversary. I did some research and found that they used to specialize in live dramas. You must remember those, Dad.

> **Martin**
>
> Oh sure.

> **Frasier** *(to Niles)*
>
> People of Dad's generation would sit around the radio each night, absolutely mesmerized.

> **Martin**
>
> We were a simple people. It was that little orange glow that got us.

> **Frasier**
>
> I happen to think radio drama was marvelous. People actually had to use their imagination. Then TV came along and ruined it.

Martin

Yeah, and it scared us too. We kept wondering how all those little people got trapped in that box.

Frasier

All right, Dad. Anyhow, I've persuaded the station manager to give me thirty minutes of air time to recreate the very first mystery KACL ever aired. *Nightmare Inn.*

Martin

Let me guess: Bunch of people get caught in a storm and everybody wonders who's going to be murdered first.

Frasier

Exactly. And I'm going to direct it.

Niles

Then we can stop wondering.

Martin

What, you don't think your brother knows how to direct?

Niles

No, the trouble is he doesn't know how to stop directing. During our prep school production of *Richard III*, he drove the entire cast crazy with his constant critiquing. I seem to recall a delay on opening night while our Richard chased Frasier around the dressing room, beating him with his hump.

Frasier

It was just a little backstage horseplay to relieve tension.

Niles

You have an Orson Welles complex. By the end of the week, you'll not only be directing, you'll have rewritten the script and be playing the lead.

Frasier

Nonsense. I have no intention of performing. And the only "rewriting" I've done is some cutting – to get it down to thirty minutes.

Martin *has taken the script out of the folder and now reads the title.*

Martin

Frasier Crane's Nightmare Inn.

Frasier

It's just a working title.

ON THEIR REACTIONS, WE:
FADE OUT.

Scene B

FADE IN:
INT. RADIO STUDIO – THE NEXT DAY – DAY/2
Roz, Frasier, Gil, Bulldog, Ian

Frasier

Well, that's it for today, but don't forget to tune in Saturday night for KACL's presentation of *Nightmare Inn.* So set your dials for goosebumps. Till then, this is Frasier Crane reminding you that – *(playfully)* – you never know what's lurking in the shadows.

He gives an evil chortle like the Shadow and clicks off. He takes off his headphones and **Roz** *comes in the booth.*

Roz

Well that should certainly comfort that woman who called about her paranoia. Listen – have we found a leading man, yet?

Frasier

No.

Roz

Well, you could do it.

Frasier

Don't be silly, Roz. It is a juicy role, and a strong voice is required, but I've got my hands full as it is.

His door swings open and **Gil Chesterton** *enters.*

Gil

Oh Frasier, I've had a quick peek at your script and I think I'd be perfect as "Bull" Kragen, the brutish gamekeeper.

Frasier

Um, actually, Gil, I think that might be . . . a little too on the nose. But you know what part you could do? *(consulting script)* "Nigel Fairservice, drummed out of the Royal Air Force under mysterious circumstances."

Roz

With him playing it they may not seem so mysterious.

Gil

I'll take it. After all, Nigel does have that divine speech in the second act about his boyhood in Surrey, "romping with his school chums in the fens and spinneys, when the twilight bathed the hedgerows like a lambent flame."

They both give him a jaw-dropped stare.

Gil *(cont'd)*
Actually I had rather a long peek at the script.

Gil *exits.*

Roz *(checking script)*
Gosh, we've still got a lot of these supporting roles to cast, don't we?

Frasier
I'm working on that. Jennifer in accounting is married to a professional actor who specializes in dialect parts. I'm hoping he'll do six or seven of the smaller roles.

Bulldog *enters.*

Bulldog
Hey Doc: Need one more for your play?

Frasier
Absolutely, Bulldog. But you've got to promise you'll promote us during your show.

Bulldog
Actually I wasn't talking about me. I'm talking about a friend of mine, Maxine. Gifted girl. Athletic, too. I fell in love with her the minute I saw her doing laps.

Frasier
She's a swimmer?

Bulldog
No, a dancer. Come on Doc, you'd really be helping me out.

Frasier
Well we still need a maid and she's only got one line: "Look out – he's got a gun!"

Bulldog
Maxine could knock that line right out of the park.

Frasier
Okay. She can have it – but only if you play a part too. We need someone for the sinister silk merchant.

Bulldog *(thinks, then)*
All right, deal. Maxine's going to be so excited. I gotta remember to

pick up one of those cute little maid outfits on my way home from work.

Frasier
She doesn't have to appear in costume.

Bulldog
Maybe here she doesn't.

Bulldog *exits.*

Roz
Well, we're getting there.

Frasier
Except for the lead. I haven't seen anyone even remotely qualified to play a wily old Scotland Yard inspector. You may be right, Roz. With time running short, I may have to bite the bullet and take on the burden myself.

There is a knock on the door. **Frasier** *opens it to reveal* **Ian** *from accounting, An Englishman with grey hair and mustache, tweedy, smoking pipe – he could pass as a Scotland Yard inspector.*

Ian
Excuse me, Dr. Crane. Is it too late to read for the role of the inspector?

Frasier
I'm afraid that part has already been cast.

And, as **Frasier** *quickly closes the door on* **Ian***, we:*
FADE OUT.

Scene C

FADE IN:
INT. FRASIER'S LIVING ROOM – THAT EVENING – NIGHT/2
Frasier, Roz, Mel, Daphne, Gil, Bulldog
Frasier *is going over the script with* **Roz** *and* **Mel** *(husband of Jennifer in accounting) as* **Daphne** *admits* **Gil** *and* **Bulldog***. As they cross down to* **Frasier***,* **Daphne** *starts setting out soft drinks and cheese and crackers.*

Frasier
Ah, Bulldog, Gil. Right on time. We have to be on our toes tonight, we have a professional actor with us. This is Mel White, our man of a thousand voices.

They ad-lib greetings, take scripts, sit down.

Frasier *(cont'd)*

Mel will be doing Hans, the German butler, both McCallister sisters and Peppo the dwarf – *(reading)* "a little man with a big secret."

Bulldog

The same guy's playing all those parts?

Frasier

Yes, plus "Bull" Kragen and O'Toole the handyman. *(to Mel)* Think you can handle it?

Mel

Just so they don't all talk at once.

Frasier *(bubbling)*

What a joy to work with a professional. Bulldog – where's Maxine?

Bulldog

She's home with food poisoning.

Frasier

Oh, I'm sorry.

Bulldog

Ah, nothing serious. I think she just wrestled in some bad jello.

Frasier

Never mind. She only has one line: "Look out – he's got a gun!" Daphne can do that for tonight.

Gil, who has been thumbing through his script, looks up.

Gil

Oh Frasier . . . *(pointing)* one of Nigel's lines seems to be missing.

Frasier

I had to take out twenty minutes.

Gil

Yes, yes, but that line so neatly defined Nigel's character.

Frasier *(incredulous)*

Saying "gesundheit" when the butler sneezed?

Gil

It shows he's a caring person.

Frasier

It's cut, Gil. Learn to let go.

Gil *(sighs)*

Oh very well. Just so I still have that delicious speech about my boyhood in Surrey . . .

Frasier

Yes, that's still in.

Gil

Romping with my school chums in the fens and –

Frasier *(impatient)*

Yes, yes, that one. Now – I fear we may still be long so I'm going to ask Daphne to time us tonight. And Noel hasn't rounded up all the sound effects yet so I'm also going to have her read those. That's a lot of responsibility for you, but I'm sure you can handle it. Start the watch. Sound effect.

Daphne *starts stopwatch.*

Daphne *(declaiming)*

"Sound of door opening."

Roz, *who has been eating, does her line with her mouth full.*

Roz

"Inspector – thank God you've come."

Frasier

Stop the watch. Roz, I have a line that says "when she opened her lips I caught a hint of some exotic accent." You'll notice it does not say "when she opened her lips cheese fell out."

Roz *(huffy)*

I was hungry, okay? Sorry.

Frasier

Start the watch. *(then)* "This is a grisly business, Miss Thorndyke."

Daphne *(declaiming)*

Sound of door closing.

Roz

"I can't believe any of my guests could be a multiple-murderer."

Frasier

"That's easy for you to say, but my job is to suspect everyone. Please introduce your guests."

Roz

"This is the silk merchant, Mr. Wang."

Bulldog *starts to giggle.*

Frasier

Stop the watch! What's your problem?

Bulldog

Wang? You gotta give me another name. I'll crack up every time I hear that.

Frasier *(struggling for patience)*

All right. All right. What about "Wing?" That's a good Chinese name. Everybody
Change Wang to Wing in your scripts.

Daphne *(declaiming)*

Sound of people changing Wangs to Wings.

Mel

Look, could we move this along?

Frasier

Certainly. *(to others)* That's a professional speaking. *(to Roz)* From your line. *(to Daphne)* Start.

Roz

"This is the silk merchant, Mr. Wing."

Frasier

"Did you witness anything suspicious this evening, Wing?"

Bulldog

"Me no lookee. Me go beddy-by, chop-chop."

Roz

Whoa. Chinese Embassy on line one. You can't say that.

Frasier

Don't worry. I'll adjust his dialogue later. *(to Daphne)* Start.

Gil

"I'm Nigel Fairservice, inspector. I was strolling in the garden when this dreadful tragedy occurred."

Frasier

"Did anyone see you?"

Gil

"Several people. Hans, the German butler –"

Mel *(German accent)*

"Ja, I saw der gentleman."

Frasier *(to Daphne)*

Stop. *(to Mel)* That's wonderful, Mel, but to my ear he's coming across just a bit more Austrian than German.

Mel *(annoyed)*

I've done that accent on both Broadway and London stages.

Frasier *(airily)*

Yes, well, perhaps they have different standards than I do. All right, let's do it again. But this time, people, I want you to make it real. From the dwarf's entrance . . .

INTERIOR DISSOLVE TO:

INT. FRASIER'S LIVING ROOM – TWO HOURS LATER – NIGHT/2

Food is eaten, empty glasses are scattered around, ties have been loosened or removed, people are seated or standing in different places than when we left.

Frasier *(cont'd) (reading script)*

". . . And so, the case was closed and with a grateful shudder I swore I'd never return to Nightmare Inn." *(to Daphne)* Stop. Time?

Daphne *(checking)*

Thirty-two minutes, forty seconds.

Frasier

Damn. I'll have to trim some more before we try again.

Roz

Again? We've done it four times.

Frasier

We'll keep doing it until I'm satisfied. Which reminds me, Mel: I'm not entirely happy with the second McCallister sister.

Mel *(dangerously)*

Oh . . .?

Frasier

Yes, she still doesn't sound sufficiently postmenopausal.

Mel *(rising)*

I see. You also told me my gamekeeper sounded too cultured, my Irishman sounded more Protestant than Catholic, and my dwarf sounded too tall. So let me try this and you tell me how it sounds: *(German)* "I qvit!"

Mel *crosses toward door behind* **Frasier**.

Frasier

Wait, you can't leave.

Mel *exits slamming the door.*

Daphne *(declaiming)*

. . . And with a grateful shudder he swore he'd never return to Nightmare Inn, either.

Bulldog

What do we do now, boss?

Frasier

Not to worry. I have a plan.

Frasier *goes to the telephone and begins dialing.*

Roz

Oh yeah, right. We're doing this thing tomorrow night. Where are you going to find an idiot willing to do six dialect parts unrehearsed?

Frasier *(into phone)*

Niles – I love this new message on your machine. What an expressive voice you have . . .

AND WE:

FADE OUT.

End of Act One

ACT TWO

Scene D

FADE IN:

INT. BROADCAST STUDIO – THE NEXT NIGHT – NIGHT/3

Frasier, Noel, Gil, Niles, Bulldog, Maxine, Roz

It's a larger studio than **Frasier's,** *with a phone on one wall, old-fashioned stand mikes on the floor and a table on which* **Noel** *is setting up his sound effects while* **Frasier** *goes over the script with* **Gil.**

Gil

There's your brother. How is he enjoying the prospect of playing all those parts?

Frasier

Actually, he doesn't know about that yet. If he did he never would've agreed.

Niles *enters, a bit agitated, and crosses to them.*

Niles

Frasier, I thought you said you were going to messenger the script to me this morning.

Frasier

I'm so sorry, Niles. I ended up tinkering with it until the very last minute. But not to worry, with your natural gift you'll be fine. Now come see this. *(quickly distracting)* Noel was just giving us a demonstration of the sound effects.

Noel

Okay. This is my door sound *(opens little door)*, my thunder screen *(shakes it)*, balloons for gunshots *(pops one)* –

Gil

Why not a blank pistol?

Noel

Guns scare me.

Frasier

The mike was picking up his whimpering.

Noel *(indicates tape player)*
This has various kinds of organ music.

SFX: **Noel** *plays tape, which gives a chilling organ sting*

Noel *(cont'd)*
I've also got bells, wind machine, gravel bag, and a coffee thermos.

Niles

What does that do?

Noel

Keeps my coffee warm. Duh.

Noel *inflates several more balloons from the helium tank as* **Bulldog** *enters with* **Maxine**, *his statuesque protégée.*

Bulldog

This is Maxine, everybody. Baby, you go up in the booth and work on your part.

Maxine

Okay.

Maxine *obligingly goes into the booth with a script.*

Frasier *(sotto)*
"Work" on it? Bulldog, she only has one line.

Bulldog

Yeah, but she's got – what do you call it, begins with a "dis?"

Niles

Distemper?

Bulldog

Dyslexia. That's it, she's dyslexic.

Frasier

I wish you'd told me.

Bulldog

She'll be great, it's me I'm worried about. I've got some serious butterflies here.

Frasier

You're on the radio all the time.

Bulldog

That's me being me. This is acting. It's scary.

Frasier

That's all part of the thrill of live performance: butterflies in the stomach, sweaty palms, dry throat, pounding heart. I imagine you have all of those.

Bulldog

I do now.

Roz *enters with a lip full of novocaine and speaking accordingly.*

Roz

Forry I'm wait, Fravier – I just fpent two hourf in va dentist's chair. An emergenfy. Ooh!

Gil

What is the matter?

Roz

Novocaine. He faid it would weah off by now. I keep biting by vip.

Frasier

Dear God. *(checks watch)* And we start in five minutes.

Niles

I don't even know who I'm playing.

Frasier

I'll just cue you once we're on the air.

Niles

But shouldn't I at least prepare a little?

Frasier

Oh Niles, your spontaneity is your greatest asset as an actor. What was it the *Yale Daily News* said about your Tartuffe?

Niles

Oh, I don't know. Something about my having the magnetism of
Marlon Brando, the charm of Danny Kaye, and the range of Laurence
Olivier.

Frasier

Yes. *(sotto, to Roz)* He'll need all of them.

AND WE:

CUT TO:

Scene E

INT. FRASIER'S LIVING ROOM – CONTINUOUS – NIGHT/3
Martin, Daphne, Frasier (V.O.)
Daphne *is seated by the radio.*

Daphne

Hurry up, it's starting.

She turns up the volume as **Martin** *enters from the kitchen with a big bowl of
popcorn. We hear* **Frasier's** *voice doing the intro.*

Frasier (V.O.)

Good evening. This is Frasier Crane welcoming you to KACL's
recreation of the original Mystery Theater. We invite you to follow us
– if you dare – through the looming portals of . . .

SFX: there is a wonderful burst of spooky organ music

Frasier (V.O.) *(cont'd)*

. . . Nightmare Inn.

Daphne

I already know the plot but I'll try not to blurt out the name of the
murderer.

Martin

Good. As a cop I hated it when people did that.

CUT TO:

Scene H

INT. BROADCAST STUDIO – CONTINUOUS – NIGHT/3
Frasier, Roz, Niles, Noel, Gil, Bulldog, Maxine
All are standing at mikes, scripts in hand. **Frasier** *is reading.*

Frasier

. . . In all my years at The Yard I doubt I'd ever seen a fouler night –

Cues **Noel**, *who gives him thunder.*

Frasier *(cont'd)*
– than that on which I was called out to investigate a double murder at the old inn on the moors.

He cues **Noel** *again, who gives him a door knock.*

Frasier *(cont'd)*
The door was answered by Miss Carlotta Thorndyke.

Frasier *cues* **Noel** *to give a door opening effect.*

Frasier *(cont'd)*
Her face was unfamiliar, and when she opened her lips I caught a hint of some exotic accent.

Roz *reads her line holding her lip in her fingers to keep from biting it, giving her an even weirder sound.*

Roz
Inthpector, fank God youf come.

He cues **Noel** *who makes door shutting sound.*

Frasier
This is a grisly business, Miss Thorndyke.

Roz
I campf bewiewe any of by guesps coulb be a mububle-mububer.

She bites her lip, winces, drools, claps a Kleenex to her mouth.

Frasier
That's easy for you to say – *(rolls his eyes)* – but my job is to suspect everybody. Please introduce –

He realizes **Roz** *is ministering to her lip and vamps.*

Frasier *(cont'd)*
– No never mind. I know your guests by reputation. This must be Mr. Wing, the silk merchant. Did you witness anything suspicious, Wing?

He cues **Bulldog,** *who freezes, staring at his script.* **Frasier** *cues him again. His mouth moves but no sound emerges.*

Frasier *(cont'd)*
Ah yes . . . the inscrutable Mr. Wing . . .

He cues **Bulldog** *more furiously.* **Bulldog** *continues to stare at his script as though hypnotized, moving his mouth silently.*

Frasier *(cont'd) (vamping wildly)*
. . . Of course, the inscrutable and mute Mr. Wing, who – who –

He looks wildly around, sees the sound effects table, has an idea.

Frasier *(cont'd)*

– Who wears a bell on his hat. Did you witness anything suspicious, Wing?

Frasier *shakes the bell while shaking his head "no" very agitatedly.*

Frasier *(cont'd)*

No, eh? I'll remember you said that. *(cues Gil)*

Gil

I'm Nigel Fairservice, inspector. I was strolling in the garden when this dreadful tragedy occurred.

Frasier

Did anyone see you?

Gil

Several people. Hans, the German butler –

Frasier *cues* **Niles**. **Niles** *reacts with some surprise.*

Niles

Ja, I saw der gentleman.

Gil

O'Toole, the gardener –

Frasier *again cues* **Niles**, *who reacts, surprised, pantomiming "Me?"*
Frasier *nods and cues him again.* **Niles** *assays a brogue.*

Niles

T'was himself and no mistake.

Gil

– As well as Prudence McCallister.

Frasier

Is that true?

Frasier *cues* **Niles**, *who huffs in silent anger but makes a game attempt at a matronly voice.*

Niles

Yes, I was taking a breath of air.

Frasler *(narrating)*

I tried to shake Nigel's alibi but each witness was adamant. O'Toole – *(cues)*

Niles

Faith and it's true.

Frasier

– Hans – *(cues)*

Niles

Jawohl.

Frasier

– Miss McCallister – *(cues)*

Niles

Mercy, yes.

Frasier

There remained one suspect whose whereabouts had not yet been established . . . Peppo the dwarf, a retired circus performer.

Frasier *cues* **Niles**, *who throws up his hands, giving up. The hell with it.*

Frasier *(cont'd)*

Exactly where were you when the murders occurred, Peppo?

Frasier *cues.* **Niles** *shrugs.* **Frasier** *cues again.* **Niles** *pantomimes "How?"* **Frasier** *looks around, spots the helium tank, points to it. Gritting his teeth,* **Niles** *goes and takes a hit off the tank.*

Frasier *(cont'd)*

Peppo? I'm waiting . . . exactly where were you?

Niles *(helium voice)*

I was at the movies.

Reeling and coughing, **Niles** *goes and slumps in a chair and takes a long drink of water from a glass on the table.*

Frasier

At the movies, you say? Well, one quick phone call can verify that. What's this? Dear God! The phone lines have been cut.

He cues **Noel** *for organ music.*

SFX: organ music

Frasier *(cont'd)*

Now we're really stranded. Totally and completely isolated from any contact with the outside world.

SFX: the actual phone in the studio rings

Noel, *acting on instinct, picks it up.*

Noel

Studio five. *(realizing)* Sorry.

Frasier

Apparently, the phone's been repaired. Hello?

He pulls the cord from the bottom of the phone.

Frasier *(cont'd)*

It's gone dead again. Who knows what other surprises this night may bring?

AND WE:

CUT TO:

Scene J

INT. FRASIER'S LIVING ROOM – CONTINUOUS – NIGHT/3
Frasier (V.O.), **Martin, Daphne**

Frasier (V.O.)

Nightmare Inn will continue after these words from our sponsor.

Martin *turns down the volume.*

Martin

I didn't remember the plots of these things being so goofy.

Daphne

Mr. Wing wasn't mute last night. Dr. Crane must have written that.

Martin

Too bad he isn't playing it.

CUT TO:

Scene K

INT. BROADCAST STUDIO – CONTINUOUS – NIGHT/3
Frasier, Roz, Noel, Gil, Niles, Bulldog, Maxine
Frasier *is scribbling in the scripts as* **Niles** *berates him.*

Niles

Six different roles and six different accents? I have half a mind to walk out of here.

Frasier

I had no choice, but you're doing brilliantly. Although your Hans could be a bit gruffer.

Niles

Don't direct me.

Frasier

Right, right. Sorry. My bigger problem is we're running way over time. *(to Gil)* Gil, at the bottom of page fourteen, after you're shot, just say "I'm dying." Cut the rest.

Gil *(stricken)*
That's my boyhood in Surrey speech.

Frasier
Yes, I know.

Gil
You can't cut that. You can't.

Frasier
Stop whining. We have a play to do.

Gil
I don't care anymore.

Frasier
Quiet. Ten seconds, everybody. Maxine, watch for your cue. And let's pick the pace up, people.

Frasier *claps his hands and everyone takes their places. The on-air light goes on.*

Frasier *(cont'd) (narrating)*
Nightmare Inn – Act Two – I was baffled. They all had alibis. Suddenly Miss Thorndyke pointed, her eyes wide with alarm . . . *(cues Roz)*

Roz
There's someone outside that window!

Frasier *cues* **Noel** *who hits tape. Instead of organ music, however, loud, jingly calliope music comes out.*

SFX: calliope music

Noel *(sotto)*
I forgot to rewind.

He shuts off the tape.

SFX: calliope music stops

Frasier *(struggling)*
Why yes . . . Miss Thorndyke . . . it . . . it appears to be an ice-cream truck . . . but – but never mind that . . . *(flips ahead a page)* Suddenly the storm put the lights out and we were left in darkness. Then, a scream.

Frasier *cues* **Maxine***, who steps forward and reads her one line, giving it her best shot.*

Maxine *(screams, then)*
Look out – he's got a nug.

Frasier *(beside himself)*
A gun. A gun is what he's got.

Frasier *cues* **Noel** *who pops two balloons. Bang! Bang!*

Frasier *(cont'd)*
Just then the lights came back up. A smoking gun lay on the table, the maid lay dead, unable to name her killer. And Nigel Fairservice lay mortally wounded.

Gil
I'm dying –

Frasier
Poor man was gone.

Gil *(stubbornly)*
– Never again to revisit the scene of my boyhood in Surrey –

Frasier *makes frantic "cut" gestures with finger and throat.* **Gil** *pointedly ignores him.*

Gil *(cont'd)*
– Romping with my school chums in the fens and spinneys – *(Frasier grabs a balloon)* . . .

Frasier
Then the lights went out again. *(pops balloon)* Nigel had been shot again.

Gil
Only grazed me. – When the twilight bathed the hedgerows –

Frasier *(popping another balloon)*
The final bullet blew his head clean off his shoulders. *(then)* People, let's try to keep calm. Although it's hard when the killer is among us.

Gil *works the "door" sound effect, knocking and "entering."*

Gil *(now totally ad-lib)*
Hi-ho. I'm Nigel's brother Cedric. I haven't seen him since we were boys in Surrey, romping –

Frasier *pops another balloon.*

Frasier
And so died the last surviving member of the Fairservice family.

CUT TO:

Scene L

INT. FRASIER'S LIVING ROOM – CONTINUOUS – NIGHT/3
Martin, Daphne, Gil (V.O.)

Martin
Boy, I didn't see that one coming.

We hear the ongoing drama on the radio as they listen. First there is another knock and another door opening.

SFX: knock and door opening

Gil (V.O.)
Hello, I'm the ice-cream man. Years ago I went to school with Nigel Fairservice. We used to romp in the fens and spinneys –

SFX: the sound of another bang

Daphne
This is turning into a bloodbath.

Martin
See – that's why I prefer TV. You want to see that stuff.

CUT TO:

Scene N

INT. BROADCAST STUDIO – CONTINUOUS – NIGHT/3
Frasier, Roz, Niles, Noel, Gil, Bulldog, Maxine

Frasier
By this time I was more baffled than ever so I played a hunch. Hans, may I see your fingernails?

Niles
Why?

Frasier
They seem a bit ragged for a butler's.

Niles
All right, all right, I'm not what I appear. None of us is. I'm not a butler, I'm not even *(losing accent)* German.

SFX: **Noel** *plays an organ sting*

During the following, **Frasier** *can't help himself and begins gesticulating like an orchestra conductor directing* **Niles's** *performance.*

Niles *(cont'd)*
Sit down, inspector. You're about to hear a fascinating tale. Each of us

holds a piece of the puzzle to relate to you. When we've finished you'll know the full, dark secret of Nightmare Inn.

Frasier *gesticulates that* **Niles** *should emote from the heart.* **Niles** *gives* **Frasier** *a look that says, "You'd better stop that."*

Roz
Are you sure we should, Hans?

Niles
Be quiet, Mother.

Sfx: **Noel** *plays another organ sting*

Niles *(cont'd)*
Mother and I moved here when I was a small boy after the tragic death of my father.

Frasier *indicates for more emotion.*

Niles *(cont'd)*
I kept the pain of that loss buried deep within me like a serpent coiled within a damp cave.

Frasier *indicates again for more emotion.* **Niles** *gives him a look that says, "That's it," and tosses the script aside.*

Niles *(cont'd)*
Okay, that's it. Never mind all that. I think I'll just take that gun off the table. *(pops balloon)* Sorry about that, O'Toole. I guess we'll never hear your fascinating piece of the puzzle. *(two more balloon pops)* Or yours, Kragen and Peppo. Could you McCallister sisters stand back-to-back? I'm short on bullets. *(another pop)* Thank you. *(to Roz)* What was your name again, dear?

Roz
Miss Thorndyke.

Niles
Thank you. *(balloon)* Also Wing, *(balloon plus bells)* and of course one final bullet for myself, so the mystery will die with me. *(final balloon pop)* Hah.

Niles *folds his arms and beams at* **Frasier**.

Frasier *(floundering)*
Well, then . . . that . . . pretty much wrapped things up. The case was closed and with a grateful shudder I swore I'd never return to Nightmare Inn.

Sfx: organ sting

Frasier *(cont'd)*

Well, we still have . . . *(looks at his watch)* nine minutes remaining. Perhaps we could have a little post-play discussion.

AND WE:

CUT TO:

Scene P

INT. FRASIER'S LIVING ROOM – CONTINUOUS – NIGHT/3
Martin, Daphne, Frasier (V.O.), **Gil** (V.O.)

Martin

What?

Martin *and* **Daphne** *exchange a look.*

Frasier (V.O.)

I suppose, to me, it stands as a morality play about the futility of using violence to solve our problems.

Gil (V.O.)

I agree. It reminds me of a lesson my mother taught me when I was still a boy in Surrey, romping with my –

Gil's *voice cuts off. He is being strangled. We then hear the sound of* **Gil** *being restrained.* **Frasier** *is obviously solving his problem with violence. The mayhem builds: there are sounds of a tussle, then general anarchy. On* **Martin** *and* **Daphne's** *reaction, we:*

FADE OUT.

End of Act Two

Scene R

END CREDITS
INT. BROADCAST STUDIO – LATER THAT NIGHT – NIGHT/3
Roz, Noel
Noel *is cleaning up, putting the sound effect items into a box. He notices some pages from a script, picks them up, crosses to the mike, and dramatically begins to perform. In the hallway,* **Roz** *wanders by, sees him, sneaks in, crosses to the prop table, and pops a balloon with her pencil.* **Noel** *throws his pages in the air, hits the deck, and we:*

FADE OUT.

End of Show

Season Five

Season's greetings from the Frasier *cast.*

The wise man.

Perspectives on Christmas

Episode #40570-106

Written by
Christopher Lloyd

Created by
David Angell/Peter Casey/David Lee

Directed by
David Lee

ACT ONE
Scene A

FADE IN:

A black screen. In white letters appears, "Master Class."

Martin (V.O.)

Yow! Easy!

INT. MASSAGE ROOM – NIGHT – NIGHT/2

Martin, Masseur

A small, low-lit room with a massage table in the center. A **Masseur** *works on* **Martin**, *who is on his back.*

Masseur

Sorry – your neck is tight.

Martin

Yeah, well, I've had a tense couple of days.

Masseur

Well, the holidays will do that to you.

Martin

Yeah, well, this was the worst Christmas ever . . .

CUT TO:

Scene B

INT. FRASIER'S LIVING ROOM – DAY – DAY/1 (**Martin's** VERSION)

Martin, Frasier, Daphne, Niles, Eddie

Martin (V.O.)

It started yesterday . . .

As in the past, the room is abundantly decorated in Christmas regalia. **Frasier** *and* **Martin** *are decorating the tree.* **Niles** *is nearby with a cup of eggnog. There's mistletoe over the door.*

Martin

You know the only part about Christmas I don't like? How quickly it's all over.

Frasier

Yes, come December 26th it's all a memory, with nothing but your light decorating touch to remind us.

Daphne *enters the front door, with* **Eddie** *on a leash. She pauses to remove his leash, directly below the mistletoe.*

Daphne

Afternoon, all.

They all ad-lib hellos.

Niles

That's awfully dangerous, Daphne, standing there under that mistletoe.

Frasier

That's enough eggnog, Niles.

Daphne

The oddest thing just happened. I was walking Eddie past that church over on Chestnut, and he turned to go in, like he assumed that's where we were going.

Frasier

That's strange. He did exactly the same thing when I was walking him yesterday.

Daphne

You're kidding. Mr. Crane – any idea why he'd do that?

Martin

Not a one.

Daphne

Well, don't you think it's strange?

Martin

Look, that dog does a lot of weird things. Yesterday when we were taking a bath together he spent fifteen straight minutes pushing the soap around with his nose, like an otter. Weird.

Martin *moves to the kitchen.*

Frasier

Yes, if he gets any weirder we may have to send "Eddie" to a home.

Frasier *crosses into the kitchen.* **Martin** *is there, pouring himself a glass of eggnog.*

Frasier *(cont'd)*

Well, I'm off. I've still got all my shopping to do.

Martin

All of it?

Frasier

Yes, I'm determined not to settle this year. I want to give gifts that will be remembered and cherished long after the holidays.

Martin
Well, there's nothing more cherished than the gift of laughter.

Frasier
Dad, if you want that *Highway Patrol Bloopers* tape you'll have to buy it yourself. *(off Martin's eggnog)* You're not going to drink that naked, are you? The first mistake in eggnog preparation is failing to garnish it properly with a dash of nutmeg.

Frasier *grabs a spice container and sprinkles some in* **Martin's** *cup.* **Martin** *takes a sip and inhales the spice, sending him into a coughing and wheezing fit.*

Frasier *(cont'd) (checking spice container)*
Of course the second mistake is placing the nutmeg next to the paprika on the spice shelf.

Daphne (O.C.)
Mr. Crane, are you all right?

Frasier
We're fine, Daphne. *(then)* Sorry, Dad.

Frasier *starts out.*

Martin
Oh, Fras – can I talk to you a minute?

Frasier
Sure. What is it?

Martin
Well, the thing Daphne was talking about . . . there is a reason Eddie knows that church. I've been taking him there.

Frasier
Well, I guess the family that bathes together prays together.

Martin
No, there's this priest, Father Curtis, who knows Eddie from the park. One day he asked if Eddie could be in their Christmas pageant. Well, I said okay, then he roped me into playing a shepherd. Then Dutch Gansvört came down with bronchitis and I got promoted to wise man.

Frasier
Dad – apart from stirring my sympathy for someone named Dutch Gansvört, I'm not sure why you're telling me this.

Martin
It turns out the wise man has to sing a song. I told him I could do it, but the song is a killer. I'm going to humiliate myself.

Frasier

Well, you probably just need a little rehearsal. Why don't we work on it tonight?

Martin

You really think that will help?

Frasier

Absolutely. You're a good singer, you're just rusty. We'll start at eight.

Martin

I'm more than rusty. The first time I sang it, the kid playing the Angel Gabriel laughed so hard he wet his cloud.

Frasier

Maybe we'll start at seven. *(calls off)* Niles, hold the elevator.

DISSOLVE TO:

Scene C

INT. FRASIER'S LIVING ROOM – THAT NIGHT – NIGHT/1
Martin, Frasier, Niles, Eddie
Frasier *and* **Niles** *are at the piano and* **Eddie** *is on the couch.* **Martin** *enters with sheet music.*

Martin

All right, this is the song – "O Holy Night." You know it?

Frasier

Of course, Dad. It's a classic. It all builds to that one wonderful note at the end *(singing)* "O NIGHT DIVINE!"

Martin

Yes, yes, that's exactly the note I can't hit. I practice in my room and Eddie ends up burying his head under a pillow.

Niles

Well, not to worry, Dad. We'll get you there. Now, the whole key to singing is learning to control your throat.

Frasier

That's one school of thought.

Niles *(produces a bow tie)*

A good exercise you can do is put this bow tie on and practice making it go up and down by moving your Adam's apple.

Frasier

It will also come in handy should you sing "O Holy Night" with a barbershop quartet.

Niles

Do you mind?

And they go into an overlap fight, then:

Martin

Can I just try singing? I want to be done with this when Daphne gets home. I don't want her knowing anything about this or she'll insist on coming to the pageant and I'm nervous enough as it is.

Niles

Fine. Why don't we just see what we're working with? *(indicates music)* We'll start right here. And I really want to see you attack that note.

Niles *begins to play and* **Martin** *begins to sing.*

Martin

"O NIGHT WHEN CHRIST WAS BORN . . . O NIGHT DIVI-I-I-I –"

On the syllable "–vine," **Martin** *misses badly and his voice trails off.*

Niles

Sometimes the note sees the attack coming and retreats.

They then hear a banging coming from above.

Martin *(looking up)*

Hey, shut up! This bozo upstairs bangs his broom handle against the floor whenever I sing.

Frasier

Ignore him, Dad. You know, there is another voice exercise that helped me immensely when I sang the role of Colonel Fairfax in *The Yeoman of the Guard*. The principle is to distract yourself with a physical exercise, thus freeing your voice. You hit a note, then slide up the octave as you descend slowly to a crouch position. Observe.

Frasier *demonstrates the exercise.*

Frasier *(cont'd)*

It works.

Niles

That's interesting. I wonder if the reverse is true.

Niles *squats down and rises up as he sings a descending octave.* **Frasier** *and* **Niles** *continue squatting and standing, going up and down the octaves.*

Frasier

Come on, Dad.

Martin

No, I'm afraid with three people doing it it might look stupid.

Frasier

We're just trying to help.

Niles

I'm starting to think your problem is all psychological. You've convinced yourself you can't hit that note.

Martin

I've convinced the guy upstairs, too.

Frasier

Niles may be right. You may just need some positive reinforcement. Let's try it again, but this time concentrate on eliminating any negative thoughts. All right?

Martin

Okay.

Niles *begins to play, and* **Martin** *to sing.*

Martin *(cont'd)*

"FALL ON YOUR KNEES."

Frasier

You've got it, Dad.

Martin

"OH, HEAR . . ."

Frasier

I hear sweet music.

Martin

". . . THE ANGELS' VOICES . . ."

Niles

I hear one angel . . .

Martin

"O NIGHT . . ."

Frasier

It's a good night!

Martin

"DIVINE . . ."

Frasier

Something's divine!

Martin

"O NIGHT . . ."

Niles

Yeah, Dad!

Martin

"WHEN CHRIST WAS BORN . . ."

Frasier

A star is born!

Martin

"O NIGHT . . ."

Frasier

Bring it on home.

Martin

"DIVI-I-I-I –"

He tries for the note, misses again, **Niles** *and* **Frasier** *cringe, and soon* **Martin's** *bellowed note trails off.* **Eddie** *buries his head under a cushion.*

Frasier

Well, that was better.

From above we again hear the broom banging.

Niles/Frasier/Martin

Oh, shut up!!

CUT TO:

Scene D

INT. MASSAGE ROOM – NIGHT – NIGHT/2
Masseur, Martin
Martin *is being massaged.*

Masseur

So, how'd you end up doing? Whoa – your neck tensed up again, didn't it?

Martin

That answer your question?

FADE OUT.

Scene E

FADE IN:

INT. MASSAGE ROOM – NIGHT – NIGHT/2

Masseur, Daphne

WE'RE CLOSE ON THE **Masseur**.

Masseur
These shoulders are awfully tight.

WE WIDEN TO REVEAL IT'S **Daphne** HE'S MASSAGING.

Daphne
It's been a stressful few days.

Masseur
I'd be happy to listen.

Daphne
Oh, no . . . Well, it started yesterday. I had something on my mind . . .

CUT TO:

Scene H

INT. FRASIER'S LIVING ROOM – DAY – DAY/1 (**Daphne's** VERSION)

Daphne, Niles, Frasier, Martin, Eddie

It's the same scene as before. **Martin** *is decorating the tree.* **Frasier** *and* **Niles** *are nearby.* **Niles** *has an eggnog. There's mistletoe over the door.* **Daphne** *enters with* **Eddie** *on a leash.*

Daphne (V.O.)
Lucky for me, Dr. Crane's brother was over. He's always such a good friend to me.

Daphne
Afternoon, all.

They all ad-lib hellos, then:

Niles
You know, Daphne, that's awfully dangerous standing under that mistletoe – a piece could fall into your eye.

Frasier
Let me freshen that.

Frasier *takes* **Niles's** *eggnog.*

Daphne
Oh, thank you, Dr. Crane. *(then)* The oddest thing just happened. I

was walking Eddie past that church on Chestnut and he turned to go inside – as though that's where he thought we were going.

Frasier

That's strange. He did the same thing yesterday when I was walking him.

Daphne

Any idea why he'd do that, Mr. Crane?

Martin

Nope. Dogs are weird.

Martin *exits to the kitchen, followed by* **Frasier**.

Daphne

You know, that worries me a bit.

Niles

What does?

Daphne

Well, I think your father's been going to that church. I had an uncle who did the same thing. Had no interest in church his whole life, then he started going every day. Turns out he'd gotten some bad news from his doctor. He didn't even last the year.

Niles

Well, first of all, I can see you're upset, so come here.

He opens his arms to her and she hugs him.

Daphne

Thank you, Dr. Crane. You're always so supportive.

Niles

Second of all, I think you're worrying over nothing. I've never known my father to have so much as a hangnail without letting everyone know about it.

Daphne

That's true. Maybe I just got myself worked up remembering my Uncle John.

Niles

Look at you – just saying his name gets you upset. Come here.

He reaches out to hug her.

Daphne

I'm fine.

Niles

No, you need a hug.

Daphne

Well, all right.

Niles *hugs her again. From off-stage we hear the same scary-sounding, nutmeg-induced cough from* **Martin** *in the kitchen.*

Daphne *(cont'd)*

Mr. Crane, are you all right?

Frasier (O.C.)

We're fine, Daphne.

Niles

You see, nothing to worry about. Well, I've got to run. Now, what did I do with my keys?

Daphne *starts looking around, then:*

Daphne

Oh, here they are.

They are on the floor about a foot away, but in order for **Daphne** *to get them she has to bend over directly in front of* **Niles**. *She does so, and* **Niles** *does not look at her butt. She hands them to him.*

Niles

Thank you, Daphne.

Daphne

Honestly, Dr. Crane, I've never known anyone who lost his keys the way you do . . .

Niles *starts out as* **Frasier** *and* **Martin** *enter from the kitchen.*

Frasier

Hold the elevator, Niles. Dad, don't worry. Niles and I will be there for you.

Daphne

What's that about?

Martin

Never mind.

Frasier *and* **Niles** *exit.*

Daphne

Well, I know it's time for your exercises, but what if we played a game of cribbage instead? We could even have a beer.

Martin

Thanks anyway, Daph, but I'm not in the mood. I'm just going to go lie down.

Daphne

Mr. Crane, did you ever call Dr. Stewart for the results of your physical?

Martin

Oh, yeah, couple of days ago. I'm fine. Come on, Eddie.

Eddie *runs to join* **Martin** *as he heads for the hall.* **Martin** *stops in front of the Christmas tree, staring at it.*

Daphne

Is everything all right?

Martin

Oh, yeah. It's just all over so fast.

Martin *heads off, and over* **Daphne's** *very concerned look, we hear:*

Daphne (V.O.)

Well, that was enough to convince me I was right. And the next twenty-four hours were a living hell.

CUT TO:

Scene J

INT. FRASIER'S LIVING ROOM – NEXT DAY – DAY/2 (**Daphne's** VERSION)
Daphne, Martin, Niles, Eddie
Martin *is there, on the phone.*

Daphne (V.O.)

. . . The worst came the next day.

Daphne *enters the front door, unseen by* **Martin.** *She wear a long red dress and carries several bags.*

Martin *(into phone)*

I'm just terrified about this, Father. It all came about so suddenly. I'm not prepared . . . Tell me again what I'm supposed to say when I see Jesus the first time . . .

Daphne's *horror-stricken.*

Martin *(cont'd) (into phone)*

All right . . . Yeah, I'll see you in a little while. Good-bye.

He hangs up. **Daphne** *tries to put a good face on things.*

Daphne

Hello.

Martin

Oh, hi.

Daphne

You know, Mr. Crane, I'm so excited about the gift I just got for you – why don't you open it now?

Martin

Well, we usually wait till Christmas, but to tell you the truth, I could use a little cheering up.

Martin *takes the box and begins opening it.*

Daphne

You know, if there's something on your mind, I'm always here to talk about it . . .

Martin

You're nice to offer, but no thanks. This is one of those things a man's gotta do alone.

He removes a sweater. It's a red, green, and gold pullover – a little garish, yes, but very **Martin**.

Martin *(cont'd)*

Wow, look at this!

Daphne

You like it?

Martin

Are you kidding? I love it. I'm never taking this sweater off – they'll have to bury me in it.

Daphne *starts to tear up.*

Martin *(cont'd)*

Daph, are you all right? It looks like you're crying.

Daphne

Oh, Mr. Crane, I know why you've been going down to that church.

Martin

You do?

Daphne

Yes. I'm just so worried for you.

Martin

Well, it'll all be over soon enough. What're you getting so upset for?

Daphne

Because I care about you and I can't believe you were going to let this whole thing happen without ever telling a soul.

Martin

Well, it's embarrassing.

Daphne

Embarrassing?

Martin

You think I want a bunch of people looking at me up there, stiff as a board, a lot of stupid makeup on my face? . . .

Daphne

So how much time have you got?

Martin *(checks watch)*

About twenty minutes.

Daphne

Twenty minutes?

Martin

And I can't wait till it's over. This is the last Christmas pageant I'm ever signing up for.

Daphne

You're in a Christmas pageant? I thought you were dying.

Martin

Why'd you think that?

Daphne

Well, you just got your test results, you're down at the church all the time . . .

Martin *starts laughing.*

Daphne *(cont'd)*

Why are you laughing?

Martin

Because it's funny.

Daphne

Well, I don't think it's so bloody funny.

Martin

Are you kidding? It's hysterical. Ooh – I'm dying.

Daphne

You will be.

Daphne *picks up the box the sweater came in and hurls it at* **Martin**.

Martin

Hey, watch it.

Daphne

Don't you tell me what to do!

And they go into an overlapping fight: "I was worried sick," "Well it's not my fault," "It bloody well is," etc. Meanwhile, the front door opens and a stricken-looking **Niles** *enters, his jacket ripped and covered in grease stains and pine needles, and his hair mussed. He makes his way across the room then bends over to tie his shoe. Finally* **Martin** *notices him.*

Martin

Niles – you okay?

CUT TO:

Scene K

INT. MASSAGE ROOM – NIGHT – NIGHT/2
Masseur, Niles
Niles *is on the table.*

Masseur

You can talk about it if you like.

We see **Niles's** *squished face through the face hole.*

Niles

I'm not ready just yet.

FADE OUT.

End of Act One

ACT TWO
Scene L

FADE IN:
INT. MASSAGE ROOM – NIGHT – NIGHT/2
Niles, Daphne
WE ARE CLOSE ON **Niles**.

Niles

I can't tell you how good that feels. I don't think I've ever had a massage like this.

WE WIDEN TO REVEAL IT'S DAPHNE WHO'S MASSAGING HIM.

Daphne
Well, I'm glad. *(then)* As long as you're so relaxed, maybe I ought to just give you my Christmas present right now.

She starts to lie down on top of **Niles**.

Niles
Umm. Oooh.

Niles (V.O.)
Yeow!

CUT TO:

Scene N

INT. MASSAGE ROOM – CONTINUOUS – NIGHT/2
Niles, Masseur
Niles's *shoulders are being massaged by the* **Masseur**.

Niles
Ow. You woke me up!

Masseur
Sorry. I guess this ankle is a bit tender.

Niles
Yours would be too if you'd had the day I'd had . . .

CUT TO:

Scene R

INT. FRASIER'S ELEVATOR/HALLWAY – LATE AFTERNOON – DAY/2
Niles, Albert, Jane, Doris, Vern (V.O.), **Woman, Man**

Niles (V.O.)
I went out to do some shopping, then I arrived at Frasier's building . . .

Niles *stands before an elevator. Its doors open and we reveal a middle-aged woman,* **Doris**, *and a couple in their seventies,* **Albert** *and* **Jane**. **Albert** *is a dour-faced man, who finds the worst in everything. There is also a very large Christmas tree.* **Niles** *steps in and moves near* **Doris**, *away from the tree.*

Niles
Excuse me, I don't want to crowd you, but this is a brand new hand-tailored Italian suit. You know how hard it is to get sap out of virgin wool.

Albert

Another reason we didn't need this tree.

Jane

Oh, Albert.

Albert

Well, we're leaving for Florida in three days. Besides, this thing's a fire hazard.

Jane

Mr. Doom and Gloom.

Niles

You know, they make a chemical now that you can use to fireproof a tree.

Albert

Causes cancer.

Niles

Happy holidays, then.

The elevator stops.

Jane

What just happened?

Doris

I think the elevator stopped.

Niles *pushes some buttons.*

Niles

Not to worry – I'm sure we can get it going again.

Albert

We've probably got about twenty minutes of oxygen.

Niles

Sir – you're only going to alarm everyone.

Doris

I work in an E.R.

Niles

Ah, then maybe you can instruct these people on how to stay cool in a crisis.

Doris

I was on duty that night the elevator cable snapped in the Bing building. They brought these people in on cookie sheets.

Niles *pushes the intercom button.*

Niles

Hello? Is someone there?

Vern (v.o.)

Yeah, who is it?

Niles

There's a group of us stuck in one of your elevators. We've pushed all the buttons, but the doors won't open and we can't seem to move off the eighth floor.

Vern (v.o.)

All right, where are you calling from, Sir?

Niles

The Elliott Bay Towers.

Vern (v.o.)

Well, both my crews are out – they're on the other side of town. Could be a good hour and a half before I can get anybody there.

Doris

Well, I can't wait that long – my children are upstairs alone in the apartment.

Albert

Haven't got a gas stove up there, have you?

Niles

Shut up, Albert.

Vern (v.o.)

Well, there is another way. If somebody felt like climbing through the trapdoor on top of your car, there's a manual release switch up there that would open up your doors.

Doris

Well, that's what we have to do then. Someone's got to go up there.

Albert

That's a pretty small opening.

Niles

Well, obviously I have more confidence in your wife than you do. There you go, ma'am. Alley-oop.

Niles *forms a basket with his hands, and offers* **Jane** *a leg up.*

Doris *(to Niles)*

It's got to be you.

Niles

Did I mention this is virgin wool?

Doris

My children are alone.

Niles

Exactly how do you expect me to get up there?

Doris

You could climb up the tree.

Niles

What?

Doris

Surely you climbed plenty of trees when you were a boy?

Jane

That's Dr. Crane's brother.

Doris/Albert *(knowingly)*

Oh.

Niles

Fine.

Niles *removes his coat and hands it to* **Doris**. *He starts climbing up the tree.*

Niles *(cont'd)*

I suppose in times of crisis, someone has to step forward and be a
hero. Today, that man is Niles Crane. Ow! Dammit. Tomorrow it will
be Mr. Li, my dry cleaner.

Albert

All right. Grab his feet and we'll push him through.

They do so.

Niles

Not so fast, not so fast!

Niles *vanishes through the opening and we hear a thud.*

Niles (V.O.)

Yow! Not to worry. I landed in a nice, soft puddle of grease. I'm
looking for the release switch, just bear with me . . . This might be it.

The doors open.

Doris

Quick!

They all run out, **Doris** *still carrying* **Niles's** *coat.*

Niles (V.O.)

Did that do anything? Hello? People? Lady with my coat?

Niles *sticks his head back inside the elevator, upside down.*

Niles *(cont'd)*

Where did you all go?

The doors close again, and we hear the elevator start to move upward.

Niles *(cont'd)*

Oh my God! We're going up. Someone stop this thing!

RESET TO:

INT. HALLWAY – SECONDS LATER

A **Man** *and a* **Woman** *are rounding the corner, as the elevator doors open and* **Niles** *crawls out. His suit is torn and covered with grease, and he has pine needles all over him.*

Woman

Why is that man crawling?

Man

That's Dr. Crane's brother.

Woman *(knowingly)*

Oh.

Niles (V.O.)

I was slightly shaken by what I had done . . .

CUT TO:

Scene S

INT. FRASIER'S LIVING ROOM – MOMENTS LATER – DAY/2 (**Niles's** VERSION)

Niles, Daphne, Martin, Eddie

Niles (V.O.)

But I'd completely composed myself as I arrived at Frasier's.

Niles *calmly enters to find* **Daphne** *and* **Martin** *in mid-fight,* **Daphne** *hurling a box at* **Martin. Daphne** *wears a shorter, sexier version of the red dress we saw her in earlier.* **Martin's** *sweater is red, blue, gold, yellow, orange, green, white, magenta, turquoise, and fuchsia.*

Niles (V.O.) *(cont'd)*

But before I could tell my story, my father was out the door to his Christmas pageant and it was some time later, after Frasier returned home, that I finally brought them up to speed.

CUT TO:

Scene T

INT. FRASIER'S LIVING ROOM – LATER – DAY/2 (**Niles's** VERSION)
Niles, Frasier, Roz, Daphne, Eddie
Niles *is on the couch, with* **Daphne** *at his side.* **Frasier** *is there.*

Niles
Of course, I don't know what you use to get elevator grease out of virgin wool.

Frasier
Well, brown suede seems to be leeching it out nicely.

Niles *begins tending to the couch with his handkerchief.*

SFX: doorbell rings.

Frasier *crosses to it.*

Frasier *(cont'd)*
Anyway, no Christmas is complete without a bit of tumult. But now we can all relax and enjoy this beautiful holiday evening together.

Frasier *opens the door to* **Roz***, who stands there scowling at him, holding a present.*

Roz
Merry Christmas.

She throws the present into the room and stalks back out.

CUT TO:

Scene V

INT. MASSAGE ROOM – NIGHT – NIGHT/2
Roz, Masseur
Roz *is on the table.*

Roz
You sure you want to hear about this?

Masseur
Why not?

Roz
Okay. Well, I've been a little depressed because of all the weight I've been putting on.

Masseur
Oh, everyone gains weight around the holidays. You'll drop it all in January.

Roz

Actually, I'm pregnant. I'm not dropping this weight until the middle of May. Anyway, I was getting a cup of coffee . . .

CUT TO:

Scene W

INT. CAFE NERVOSA – DAY – DAY/2 (**Roz's** VERSION)
Roz, Niles, Martin, Frasier, Daphne, Eddie
Frasier *is at a table with* **Niles** *and* **Martin**. *There's a piece of cheesecake on the table.* **Roz** *enters.*

Roz

Hey, guys.

They ad-lib hellos.

Roz *(cont'd) (to Niles)*

That's a nice suit.

Niles

Yes, and it's brand new. So since you're probably going to be ordering some food, I'd rather not risk getting it stained.

Roz

What do you mean I'll probably be ordering some food? Is that a crack about my weight? I'm pregnant. Pregnant people gain weight.

Niles

Well, I see our little hormone cocktail was mixed extra-strong today.

Niles *exits.*

Martin

Well, I should get going too. I've still got a couple of hours before my pageant and I need the time to rehearse.

Frasier

Look on the bright side, Dad. Tomorrow morning it'll all be a memory.

Daphne *enters and crosses toward them. She overhears the following:*

Martin

Yeah, but even when it's all over, I still have to make peace with the man upstairs.

Daphne *whimpers into her hand and heads to the ladies' room as* **Martin** *heads to the door and out.*

Roz

Frasier, are you sure we have to do this thing this afternoon?

Frasier

Come on Roz, it's an hour out of your life to a good cause. There's no better feeling than that of giving to others.

Roz

Then you're about to feel great. Give me that.

She slides over his cheesecake and begins eating it.

SFX: Frasier's cell phone rings

He answers it.

Frasier *(into phone)*

Hello . . . Well, yes, Mrs. Doyle, she is. Hold on. *(covers phone; to Roz)* It's your mom. They forwarded her from the office.

Roz *takes the phone.*

Roz *(into phone)*

Hello . . . No, it's no bother, Mom. *(rolls her eyes)* I'll pick you up at the airport . . . yup, ten A.M. . . . . I'm looking forward to it, too. Bye.

Frasier

Oh, wait. Let me wish her a merry Christmas.

Roz *(into phone)*

Hang on, Mom.

Roz *hands him the phone and moves to the counter.*

Frasier *(into phone)*

Mrs. Doyle, it's Frasier again. I just wanted to say happy holidays. And also, just a word to the wise – Roz has put on quite a few pregnancy pounds of late and she's rather sensitive about it, so you might want to be careful about what you say. *(sees Roz coming)* Anyway, looking forward to seeing you. Bye-bye.

Frasier *hangs up as* **Roz** *rejoins him.*

Roz

You know, Frasier, I think I'm going to meet you over there. I still have some gifts to get.

Frasier

I still have all of mine to get. I don't know what it is this year – nothing I see seems to be quite right.

Roz

It's really sweet that you're trying to make your gifts so special. You know, I'm sorry if I've seemed irritable lately. I'm just nervous about my mom coming. I just can't figure out how I'm going to tell her I'm pregnant.

Frasier

You mean you haven't told her?

Roz

No. And I just know she's going to go insane. I've wanted to talk to her, it's just . . . well, you know how it is when you've got something to tell someone but you're not quite sure how to put it?

Frasier

Yes, I do.

SFX: Frasier's cel phone rings again.

Roz

Well, I'll let you get that. See you in a bit.

She starts out as **Frasier** *answers the phone.*

Frasier *(into phone)*

Hello . . . Yes, I had a feeling you might call back . . .

CUT TO:

Scene X

INT. SHOPPING MALL – AFTERNOON – DAY/2
Frasier, Roz, Sally, Billy, Vic
A small area decorated as "Santa's Village." There's a large chair for Santa, a bag of toys, etc. **Frasier**, *dressed as Santa, is there, as* **Roz**, *dressed as Mrs. Claus, arrives.*

Frasier

Hey – I was beginning to worry about you.

Roz

Well, you should have. I'm on the verge of a complete breakdown. Shopping was a disaster – then, when I went to slip into this darling little costume, the pants split.

Frasier

I'm sorry. Did you try to put too much padding in? *(off her look)* You didn't put any padding in, did you?

Roz

Of course, on top of all that, I keep thinking about my mom – how am I going to tell her?

Frasier

Well, that may be easier than you think.

Roz

Ha! You don't know my mom.

Frasier

If you like, I could tell her for you.

Roz

Are you kidding? She'll be mad enough knowing that I didn't tell her for a full three months. The only worse thing would be hearing it from someone else.

Frasier

Maybe we should discuss this later.

Roz

Discuss what?

Frasier

Oh, nothing.

Roz

Oh my God! When you talked to her in the cafe you told her, didn't you? Frasier!

Frasier

Hello, children. Ho, ho, ho! Who's first?

Roz

I'm gonna kill you.

A little girl, **Sally***, steps up.* **Frasier** *quickly seats* **Sally** *in his lap.*

Sally

You're gonna kill Santa?

Frasier

No, little girl. Mrs. Claus said she wanted to kiss me.

Roz

Yeah, I'll kiss you. Come here, I'll kiss you good.

Frasier

No, not yet Mrs. Santa – we have to give out some toys. *(to Sally)* Were you a good girl this year?

Roz

Don't tell him if you weren't. He'll blab it to everyone. *(handing her a gift)* Here, run along.

Sally *goes.*

Roz *(cont'd)*

Frasier . . .

Frasier

Well, you talk to your mom about everything, how was I supposed to know?

A little boy, **Billy**, *comes up.*

Billy

Hi, Santa. I'm Billy. I want a pony for Christmas.

Roz

You got it. Now beat it.

Billy

Mommy – Mommy – I'm gonna get a pony!

Billy *runs to his* **Mother**, *who glares at* **Roz**.

Frasier

Roz, can't we talk about this later?

Roz

No, we can't.

A big kid, **Vic**, *steps up.*

Vic

Hi, Santa.

Roz

Oh my God, what are you, twenty? Get out of here.

Frasier

Will you try to stay calm?

Roz

No, I will not, because I'm not calm. I am completely freaked. I'm pregnant, and you told my crazy mother, and my Christmas is ruined, and I'm too fat to even be Mrs. Santa! I hate this holiday!

She kicks the big sack of presents, knocking it over, and strides off. A group of parents and children look on in horror.

Frasier

Mrs. Claus was up very late helping me make all these toys . . .

CUT TO:

Scene Y

INT. FRASIER'S LIVING ROOM/HALLWAY – NIGHT – NIGHT/2 (**Roz's** VERSION)

Roz, Frasier, Martin, Daphne, Niles, Eddie

Roz (V.O.)

Of course, I still had to stop by Frasier's. I had to give him his champagne glasses . . .

*We see **Frasier** open the door to **Roz**, who throws his present into the room. She turns to go, **Frasier** goes after her.*

RESET TO:

INT. HALLWAY – CONTINUOUS

Frasier

Roz, please stop. I'm sorry about what happened, but it was a mistake. And I can't let you go. How would it look if I turned a pregnant woman away on Christmas Eve when there's so much room here at the inn?

Roz

Just give me my present and I'll get out of here.

Frasier

Fair enough.

He steers her into the apartment.

RESET TO:

INT. FRASIER'S LIVING ROOM – CONTINUOUS

Frasier *(cont'd)*

Niles, Daphne – Roz is here.

They murmur lackluster hellos.

Frasier *(cont'd)*

Oh, come on, people. Let's liven things up in here – it's Christmas Eve. For heaven's sake, what are the Cranes known for, if not their legendary holiday spirit?

*The front door opens and **Martin** enters, dressed as a wise man. **Eddie** is with him.*

Martin

I hate singing, and I hate Christmas, and I'm going to bed.

Martin *starts to the hall.*

Frasier

Dad, I take it you didn't quite hit that high note?

Martin

No. And as usual, Eddie buried his head. Only this time he buried it in the Christ child's cradle. Then I guess he mistook the Christ child for one of his chew toys 'cause he picked it up in his mouth and started shaking it. Mary and Joseph went ballistic, Eddie took off with it still in his mouth, and half the population of Bethlehem went chasing off after him. I never should have agreed to be in that pageant.

Daphne

You would have saved me a lot of grief.

Martin

Hey, don't start that again.

Frasier

Now, now, let's not say anything we're going to regret.

Roz

You're one to talk.

Frasier

Oh, now, Roz.

Daphne *and* **Martin** *begin fighting,* **Roz** *and* **Frasier** *continue fighting.* **Niles** *lies low on the couch with his washcloth. Finally:*

Frasier *(cont'd)*

Oh, now that is enough! This is the night we celebrate peace and togetherness, and I will not let that be ruined. I intend to get us all in the right frame of mind by giving you all my gift. I was determined this year to do something a little more meaningful, and after a great deal of effort, I have. My gift doesn't come from some fancy store, all wrapped in glittery paper – my gift comes from my heart. Tonight, I intend to sit each one of you down and tell you, in my own words, just how much you mean to me.

They all stare at him in horror – this is the worst idea they've ever heard.

Frasier *(cont'd)*

Or, I could get someone over to give us all massages.

As the group mumbles "That's a better idea," "More like it," etc., we:
FADE OUT.

End of Act Two

Room Service

Episode #40570-113

Written by
Ken Levine & David Issacs

Created by
David Angell/Peter Casey/David Lee

Directed by
David Lee

A surprise visit from Frasier's past.

Frasier discovers his brother and breakfast for two in his ex-wife's hotel bathroom.

ACT ONE

Scene A

FADE IN:

INT. RADIO STUDIO/HALLWAY – DAY – DAY/1

Frasier, Betsy (V.O.), **Lilith, Roz**

Frasier *is on the air.* **Roz** *is in her booth, scrawling a note on a piece of paper.*

Frasier

Good morning, Betsy. I'm listening.

Roz *holds up her sign that says "bathroom" and taps on the glass.* **Frasier** *sees her and gestures for her to wait for a minute.*

Betsy (V.O.)

Hi, Dr. Crane. My problem is, my husband wants to take me on a cruise for our anniversary.

Frasier

Sounds enchanting.

Roz *continues waving.*

Betsy (V.O.)

Yes, except I keep having this dream where I'm in our cabin and all of a sudden I see a few drops of water leaking in. At first it's just a trickle, then it's a stream, then it's gushing, pouring, water everywhere, and nothing in the world can stop the flow.

No longer able to stand it, **Roz** *exits her booth.*

Frasier

That's a very powerful image, wouldn't you say, Roz?

Frasier *turns and sees Roz is gone from her chair.*

Frasier *(cont'd)*

Roz agrees.

RESET TO:

INT. RADIO STUDIO HALLWAY – CONTINUOUS

As **Roz** *exits her booth, she encounters* **Lilith.**

Lilith

Excuse me, I'm looking for Frasier Crane. They said he'd be in here.

Roz

Lilith, it's me, Roz Doyle.

Lilith

Oh, yes – Frasier's fun-loving producer. *(noticing her stomach)* Who, apparently, has been having a bit too much fun . . . loving.

Roz

I'd love to send one back your way but I've got to pee.

Roz *dashes off.* **Lilith** *enters* **Roz's** *booth.*

RESET TO:

INT. FRASIER'S BOOTH – CONTINUOUS

During the following **Lilith** *will drift over to the console.* **Frasier** *relaxes in his chair with his back to* **Roz's** *booth.*

Frasier

Betsy, perhaps this exercise will help. Visualize being on that boat. You're in your cabin – no cracks, no leaks, it's dry as a bone. You go to your door, open it, and –

Frasier *nonchalantly turns his chair toward the glass and sees* **Lilith**.

Frasier *(cont'd)*

Aaah!!

Betsy (V.O.)

What is it? The water's coming in through the door?

Frasier

No, Betsy. Someone just walked in and frightened me. It's my ex-wife so if you're a regular listener you know what I'm talking about.

Betsy (V.O.)

That's it. We're going to Vegas.

Frasier

Thanks for your call. Stay tuned for the news.

Exasperated, **Frasier** *turns off the mike and strides into* **Roz's** *booth.*

Frasier *(cont'd)*

Hello, Lilith.

Lilith

Surprise.

Frasier

I think we're a little past that now, aren't we? What brings you to Seattle?

Lilith

I'm attending the National Conference on Self Psychology.

Frasier

Really? Are you sure you want to hold up that mirror, Lilith? *(off her look)* Well, whatever. You're in town and I'm glad you're here. How's Freddie?

Lilith

Fine. We have an amazing child.

Frasier

Yes, we do. And Brian?

Lilith

Fine. I have an amazing husband.

Frasier

Yes. Did you two get the gift basket I sent for the holidays?

Lilith *puts her hands to her face and begins to break down.* **Roz** *enters.*

Roz

Frasier, what did you do?

Frasier

Nothing, I sent her a gift basket. Fruits and festive nuts.

Lilith

It's not the basket, you nit. It's Brian. He left me.

Frasier

He left you?

Roz

Maybe I should go.

Lilith

No, everyone else knows it, you might as well know it too. How can I put this succinctly? . . . Brian was looking for someone more . . . feminine. And he found him.

Frasier/Roz

"Him"?

Lilith

Stan Jablonsky, that little hussy.

Frasier *crosses to* **Lilith**.

Frasier

Oh Lilith. I'm genuinely sorry.

Lilith

I didn't know where to turn but I knew that you would somehow be here for me.

Frasier

So you didn't just come for the conference?

Lilith

No.

Frasier

Well, you shouldn't be alone tonight. Niles and I are attending a reception at the Union Club. Why don't you join us?

Lilith

Thank you, Frasier, I'd love to. *(taking Frasier's hands)* I don't know if I deserve your compassion but I already feel better just holding your strong, comforting hands.

It's an awkward moment for **Frasier**. *He's not quite sure how to react.*

Frasier

Yes, well, it's good to hold you, Lilith, but if you'll excuse me, I have an appointment. Station manager. Very important. Can't break it. See you tonight. Bye.

Lilith *squeezes his hands.* **Frasier** *smiles and quickly exits.*

Roz

Boy, that's rough, leaving you for a man. You really had no idea?

Lilith

None at all. Stan was a contractor we hired to expand our master bedroom. Ironic, isn't it? No sooner do I get the closet of my dreams, than my husband comes out of it.

DISSOLVE TO:

Scene B

INT. CAFE NERVOSA – LATER THAT DAY – DAY/1
Frasier, Niles
Niles *is at a table, eating pastries.* **Frasier** *enters.*

Frasier

Hello, Niles. *(re: pastry)* That bun looks good.

Niles

Now, now. Remember your diet.

Frasier

Of course. Thank you. *(he sits)* Speaking of buns I could do without, Lilith is back.

Niles

Oh, that explains why blood was pouring from my faucets all morning.

Frasier

Go easy on her, Niles. Her husband has left her. And get this . . . for a
man.

Niles

Damn. I owe Dad five dollars.

Frasier

The poor thing. She's obviously devastated. Her whole world's been
turned upside down. Of course, look who I'm telling – no one knows
better than you how a messy divorce can leave a person . . .

Frasier *notices that* **Niles** *has nodded off to sleep.*

Frasier *(cont'd)*

. . . Strangely relaxed.

Frasier *shakes* **Niles**.

Frasier *(cont'd)*

Niles? Niles?

Niles

Huh? What? Yes?

Frasier

Am I boring you?

Niles

Damn – did I do it again? I'm sorry, Frasier. Seems I'm suffering
from a bout of narcolepsy.

Frasier

Good Lord. When did this start?

Niles

After the divorce. I checked with my doctor. I'm fine, it's just a
reaction to stress – my way of escaping the frustration of the whole
ugly mess. But please, go on with what you were saying.

Frasier

Well, Lilith is deeply distressed and she's come to me to help her
make some sense of all this. I must say I find it all a bit disconcerting.

Niles

How so?

Frasier

We have a destructive pattern. Whenever Lilith comes to me in need,
I find her vulnerability highly desirable. Against my better judgment,
we wind up in bed and I always have terrible regrets.

Niles

And you felt this way about her today?

Frasier

Ohh, baby!

Niles

Well, do your best to avoid her.

Frasier

I can't. She's joining us at the reception tonight.

Niles

What? She's going to be there?

Niles's *cell phone rings.*

Frasier

Niles. It's nothing but a bunch of stuffed shirts talking about their portfolios and prostates.

Niles

Exactly. And you've ruined it. *(then)* Excuse me. *(into phone)* Hello . . . *(to Frasier)* Damn, it's one of Maris's cadre of lawyers. *(into phone)* Yes, we've been over that . . . No, I can't . . . How dare you. She already has the house. I'm not even allowed to visit the koi pond . . . uh-huh . . . uh-huh . . .

Niles *falls asleep again.*

Frasier

Niles . . . Niles . . .

Niles *(waking up, on phone)*
I'm not even allowed to visit the koi pond.

Frasier *snatches the phone away.*

Frasier *(into phone)*

He'll call you back. *(folds up phone)* Well look at us. A narcoleptic and a weak-willed sexual obsessive. Don't we look like a couple of brothers in an O'Neill play? *(then)* Niles, help me. I need the power to resist her.

Niles

You know you can. And if I sense any wavering I'll be by your side, ever vigilant.

Frasier

Thank you.

Niles *picks up a pastry.*

Niles

Think of Lilith as this pastry. It may satisfy a momentary craving, but
in the end you'll regret it. Much like my situation with Maris – it
wasn't easy, but I did find the courage to stand up to her and say . . .
I'm trying to remember my exact words. I think it was . . . uh . . .

Niles *nods off to sleep.* **Frasier** *takes the pastry from his hand and bites into
it. It is as delicious as he hoped. He addresses a passing waitress.*

Frasier *(re: pastry)*

Two more of these.

D<small>ISSOLVE TO</small>:

Scene C

INT. FRASIER'S LIVING ROOM – THAT NIGHT – NIGHT/1
Martin, Daphne, Niles, Frasier, Lilith, Eddie
Martin *is trying to get* **Eddie** *to do a trick, holding out a treat, as* **Daphne**
enters.

Martin

Hey Daph, look. I've taught Eddie a trick.

Daphne

Oh, I love animal tricks. I was reading in a movie magazine that
there's a stunt dog they taught to ride a motorcycle into a burning
building, pick up a baby in his teeth, and then jump out a window to
safety. What did you teach Eddie?

Martin

To roll over.

Daphne

You must be very proud.

S<small>FX</small>*: the doorbell rings.* **Daphne** *moves to answer it.*

Martin

Oh forget it, Eddie.

Daphne *opens the door to* **Niles** *as* **Frasier** *enters the living room.*

Niles

Good evening, Daphne . . . Dad.

Frasier

Oh hello, Niles. Sherry? It'll give you a chance to relax while we wait for Lilith.

Martin *(panicked)*

You never said she was coming up here.

Daphne

You just said you were going to dinner.

Martin

You never said she was coming up here.

Frasier

It's just to rendezvous. She'll be here for two minutes.

Martin

But you never told me. You were home an hour. You never told me. Not a word. *(to Daphne)* Did he say anything to you?

Daphne

No, nothing. *(to Frasier)* You could have told us, you know. We could have made plans to be elsewhere.

Frasier *(he's had enough)*

She's coming. Both of you suck it up! She's been through a devastating week. Her husband left her. I'd like you both to show a little compassion. Unless, of course, you have to go hide in your rooms because two minutes of polite conversation with a woman who needs you is too much to ask.

SFX: *the doorbell rings.* **Martin** *and* **Daphne** *start hurriedly exiting.*

Martin

Out of my way!

Daphne

Me too!

In his haste, **Martin** *drops his cane.* **Daphne** *starts to go back to retrieve it.*

Martin

Leave it!

Martin *and* **Daphne** *exit.*

Niles

Now remember, Frasier. I'm here for you if you feel yourself starting to weaken.

Frasier

Fear not. I'm completely in control.

Frasier *opens the door. It's* **Lilith** *as we've never quite seen her before. She's a knockout. Her look is soft and seductive. Her hair is out of its customary bun. Her figure is revealed. Note: she wears a fashionable wrap around her shoulders.*

Frasier *(cont'd) (immediately)*

Ohh, baby.

Lilith

Thank you, Frasier. I needed that. I treated myself to a little makeover this afternoon. Probably just an attempt to compensate for the battering my ego's taken recently. Pretty transparent, huh?

Frasier

No, but if you stand in front of the light –

Niles

Frasier!

Lilith

Niles, sorry to hear your marriage ended in a shambles.

Niles

Ditto.

Frasier

Well, now that the pleasantries are out of the way – let me take your wrap.

Lilith *takes off her wrap, revealing her bare shoulders. The look is not lost on* **Frasier**.

Frasier *(cont'd)*

Yowsa. Lilith, what is that intoxicating fragrance you're wearing?

Niles

Frasier, can I see you in the kitchen?

Frasier

No!

Lilith

It's something new, called "Encore."

Frasier

Bravo. I can almost feel the curtain rising.

Niles

Frasier! *(to Lilith)* Excuse us. We'll be right back . . . Eddie will keep you company.

Niles *hustles* **Frasier** *into the kitchen.*

Lilith *(to Eddie)*

Hello, Eddie. Remember me?

Eddie *sees* **Lilith** *and runs out of the room.*
RESET TO:
INT. KITCHEN – CONTINUOUS

Frasier

Thank you, Niles. This is going to be tougher than I thought.

Niles

Just calm down. Let me get you a bottle of water.

Niles *opens the refrigerator and leans in. We can't see his face.*

Frasier

Damn her lily-white hide. She knows what she's doing, dressing like that. The woman plays me like a lute. Look at me – I have all the resistance of a horny stag. Niles, what am I going to do? Niles? . . . Niles? . . .

Niles *has fallen asleep in the refrigerator.* **Frasier** *shakes him awake.*

Niles

I did it again?

Frasier

You fell asleep with your cheek right against the ice tray.

Niles

That's strange. I dreamt I was tangoing with Maris.

Frasier

I need your help resisting Lilith.

Niles

All right, I think I've got the answer. When you feel yourself yielding to her, summon an image so repellent you're incapable of any sexual desire. Do you remember that summer at Uncle Henry's farm, when we found that dead horse lying in the hot sun, crawling with maggots?

Frasier

Of course I do.

Niles

Well hold on to that picture. You can ride that horse to safety.

Frasier

Thank you, Niles, that might do the trick. When it comes to an ugly image, you can't beat a dead horse. Lilith can bat her eyes and push her breasts up to Canada and I won't budge.

Frasier *and* **Niles** *exit to the living room.*

CUT TO:

Scene D

INT. LILITH'S HOTEL ROOM – NEXT MORNING – DAY/2
Lilith, Niles
Two people are in bed sleeping. We can't make out who they are. The woman turns over. It's **Lilith**. *Her arm falls over her companion.*

> **Lilith** *(eyes still closed; murmuring)*
Morning.

Her bedmate turns over. It's **Niles**.

> **Niles** *(eyes still closed; sleepily)*
Morning.

As the realization hits, their eyes pop open – and if that's not an act break we don't know what is.

FADE OUT.

End of Act One

ACT TWO

Scene E

FADE IN:
INT. LILITH'S HOTEL ROOM/BATHROOM – CONTINUOUS – DAY/2
Lilith, Niles, Waiter, Frasier
Niles *and* **Lilith** *in bed.*

> **Lilith**
My God. What did we do? What did we do?

> **Niles**
Well, first we –

> **Lilith**
I know what we did. What do we do now?

> **Niles**
Let's just try to stay calm. These things happen. They happen every day. *(losing it)* Every day in France and people die for it! Frasier's going to kill us. *(then)* Why did you have to look so damned bewitching all evening?

Lilith

Oh, so it was my fault, Mr. Sweet-and-Attentive? Why'd you have to drive me home and walk me to my door?

Niles

The way the moonlight bathed your alabaster shoulders –

Lilith

Your sensitive and manly touch –

Niles

Yours too.

Lilith

Take me.

They dive for each other but then pull up short.

Niles/Lilith

No!!

Lilith *(cont'd)*

We've got to resist this. It's wrong.

Niles

Of course it is. Last night was simply two wounded people acting out of loneliness and confusion.

Lilith

Not to mention four bottles of wine. But for whatever reasons we're here, we must never let this happen again.

Niles

Yes, of course. *(beat)* But just to clarify . . . because of the ramifications of our indiscretion or, because, you know . . .?

Lilith

You were fine. My God, you Crane men.

There's a knock at the door.

Niles *(panicking)*

Who's that?

Lilith

Don't panic. No one knows we're here.

Niles

I told Frasier I was driving you home.

Lilith *(now panicking)*

Why did you do a stupid thing like that?

Niles

It wasn't stupid at the time. How did I know the minute we got inside this room you'd be on me like a hawk on a titmouse?

There's another knock at the door.

Lilith *(sotto)*

Just be quiet.

Lilith *gets up, throws on her robe and crosses to the door.*

Lilith *(cont'd) (tentatively)*

Who is it?

Waiter (O.C.)

Room service, Ma'am.

Lilith *(to Niles, relieved)*

Oh that's right. We ordered breakfast last night.

Lilith *opens the door and lets in the room service* **Waiter.** *He enters, rolling a breakfast cart into the room. He's a chipper fellow.*

Waiter

Good morning, Ma'am, Sir.

The **Waiter** *starts to set up breakfast at the table.*

Waiter *(cont'd)*

I have eggs Benedict and eggs Florentine.

Lilith

Did you bring ketchup?

Waiter

Oh, No, I'm sorry. Let me go get that for you right now.

Niles

Ketchup on eggs Florentine?

Waiter *(joking)*

Oh, your first breakfast together?

Lilith

Just get it!

The **Waiter** *exits.* **Niles** *gets out of bed and slips on a bathrobe.*

Niles

Now I remember ordering this. It's the breakfast I always order after a night of passion.

Lilith

Eggs Benedict . . . very rich.

Niles

Well I only have it once a year. *(then)* Let's dig in.

They sit at the table. There's a knock at the door.

Lilith

Well, that was quick.

Lilith *crosses to the door and is just about to open it when they hear:*

Frasier (O.C.)

Lilith, are you awake?

A startled **Lilith** *and* **Niles** *speak in hushed tones.*

Lilith

It's Frasier!

Niles

What do we do?

Niles *nearly knocks the tray over getting up.*

Frasier (O.C.)

Lilith?

Lilith

Just a second.

Niles

Why did you answer?!

Lilith

I don't know. I'm not very good at this. Hide in the bathroom.

They both dart for the bathroom.

Niles

No, not you!

Lilith

Here, take the cart with you.

Niles *starts to push the cart into the bathroom. Then:*

Niles

Food in the bathroom?

Lilith

Go!

Lilith *shoves* **Niles** *and the cart into the bathroom, knocking* **Niles** *down.*

Frasier (O.C.)

Lilith? Lilith?

Lilith

Coming.

Lilith *runs to the door, feigns complete insouciance and opens the door.*

Lilith *(cont'd)*

Hello, Frasier. What are you doing here?

Frasier

Surrendering, Lilith.

Frasier *enters. He heads toward* **Lilith** *and tries to kiss her.*

Lilith

But Frasier –

Frasier

Oh, don't punish me because I played hard to get last night. It took everything I had to resist you.

Lilith

But Frasier, this is wrong.

Frasier

Who cares? Can you honestly say when you were lying in bed last night you weren't thinking about me?

Lilith *(considers a moment)*

Yes.

Frasier

Oh, drop the mask, Lilith. We both know why you came to Seattle. We both know why you dressed so enticingly last night.

Frasier *hears the toilet flush.*

Frasier *(cont'd)*

Is someone in your bathroom?

Lilith

No, it's a . . . defective toilet. Did that all night long. I'd better check it.

Lilith *dashes into the bathroom.*

RESET TO:

INT. LILITH'S BATHROOM – CONTINUOUS

Lilith *enters.* **Niles** *is sitting on the toilet, asleep. They talk in whispers.*

Lilith *(cont'd)*

Niles!

Niles *(startled awake)*

Yes?

Lilith

You fell asleep and flushed the toilet.

Niles

Damn. Is he still here?

Lilith

Yes.

Niles

What does he want?

Lilith

He wants to make love to me.

Niles

Does the man have no scruples? He specifically asked me last night to keep him away from you and then the minute my back is turned he sneaks over here and yes, I'm aware of the irony.

Lilith

I'll just ask him to leave.

RESET TO:

INT. LILITH'S HOTEL ROOM – CONTINUOUS

Lilith *returns to the hotel room.* **Frasier** *has removed his clothes and is now in a bathrobe.*

Lilith *(cont'd)*

Oh dear God.

Frasier

Oh, drop this charade, Lilith – you're not even convincing.

Lilith

I think I'm going to be sick.

Frasier

Well, that had a ring of truth to it . . .

There's a knock at the door.

Waiter (O.C.)

Room service.

Lilith

Go away.

Waiter (O.C.)

I have your ketchup, Ma'am.

Lilith

Not necessary.

Waiter (o.c.)

Okay, but I need the bill.

Lilith

Later.

Frasier

Let's just take care of this.

Frasier *opens the door. The* **Waiter** *enters with a bottle of ketchup. During the following the* **Waiter** *notices there's a different man in a bathrobe.*

Waiter

Sorry to disturb you. Here's your ketchup . . . Sorry it took so long.

Lilith, *who's standing behind* **Frasier**, *signals the* **Waiter** *not to say anything.*

Waiter *(cont'd)*

I'll still need the bill. Where's the cart?

Lilith

In the bathroom.

Frasier

Why is the breakfast cart in the bathroom?

Lilith

Uh . . . I was going to take a hot bath while I ate.

Frasier

Still, Lilith . . . food in the bathroom?

Lilith

Be back in a second.

Lilith *goes into the bathroom.*

Frasier

This is a little embarrassing. My ex-wife. We're sort of reconnecting.

Waiter

Yes Sir. That's wonderful.

Frasier

And who knows? It might work out this time.

Waiter

Ohh-kay.

Lilith *comes back with the bill.*

Lilith

There you go. There's a generous, generous tip there for you.

Waiter

Thank you, Ma'am.

Frasier

Listen, while you're here, would you please bring me up some Eggs Benedict? Silly for her to eat alone.

Waiter

Ohh-kay.

The **Waiter** *nods and exits.*

Frasier

Now where were we?

Lilith

Look, I don't think it's a good time for this.

Frasier *takes* **Lilith's** *hands.*

Frasier

Why not, my darling? We're here. We're finally alone. You need your Frasier.

From the bathroom we hear a loud crash as the breakfast cart goes over.

Frasier *(cont'd) (crossing to the bathroom)*
What the hell was that?

Lilith

Frasier, stop. Don't go in –

Frasier *opens the bathroom door.* **Niles** *is lying sprawled on the toppled breakfast cart.*

Frasier

Niles!

Niles *(sitting up)*

Yes?

Frasier

Oh my God!

Lilith

I'm so sorry. We didn't mean for this to happen.

Frasier

Oh my God!

Niles

She's telling the truth. It was a mistake. A stupid, misguided –

Frasier

Stop it, Niles. I don't want to hear how or why or – I just want to get out of here.

Frasier *exits the hotel room.*

Lilith

Frasier, Frasier!

But he's out the door.

Niles

This is my worst nightmare.

Lilith

You have egg on your face.

Niles

That's an understatement. I'm mortified. I –

Lilith

No. Actual egg. It's in your hair, too.

There's a knock at the door. **Lilith** *opens it and* **Frasier** *comes back into the hotel room.*

Niles

I knew you couldn't stay mad at us.

Frasier

I'm in a bathrobe, you jackass.

Frasier *begins collecting his clothes as something dawns on* **Lilith**.

Lilith

I can understand your shock and – believe me, if I could erase everything that happened last night I would. But if you look at this rationally for a moment, we didn't technically do anything wrong.

Frasier

What?! You didn't do anything wrong?

Niles

I'm a little unclear on that myself but I'm willing to go along with it.

Lilith

You and I are no longer married. Neither is Niles. I won't say this is my shining hour but we're not responsible to you or anyone else for our actions.

Niles *(jumping on the bandwagon)*

Right! And I'm frankly a little insulted by your outburst.

Frasier

I can't believe this! You're actually defending what you did?

Lilith

Just listen. The past few days have been the worst of my life. I've never felt less self-assured, more in need of validation, both as a person and as a woman. And Niles was feeling the same thing.

Niles

Exactly. *(realizing)* Wait a minute.

Lilith *(to Frasier)*

Our physical reaction to each other was nothing more than a desperate attempt to reaffirm our own worth.

Frasier

Very impressive, Lilith. But I happen to be a psychiatrist too. Let me tell you what really transpired. This is a passive-aggressive manifestation of the deep resentments that you both have toward me. You were punishing me for my notoriety. My successful adjustment after our marriage. It is this shared bond that brought you two to your palace of sweet revenge.

Lilith

Allow me to rebut: What a crock.

Frasier

It is not!

Lilith

This is yet another example of your complete self-absorption and the reason we could not stay together in the first place.

Frasier

I think I have a right to – why am I defending myself?

Niles

If you ask me, you're both off the mark. Last night was all about two people ruled by very strong superegos, tortured by them, who had a chance, however misguided, to break through and rediscover their ids together. Call me an old softy, but that's how I see it.

Frasier *(a beat; then)*

Okay then . . . the three of us have certainly analyzed the crap out of this.

Lilith

Where does that leave us?

Niles

Yes. Where do we all go from here?

Frasier *(after a beat)*

I don't know.

There's an awkward silence. A cell phone rings in the closet.

Niles

Oh, that's mine.

Niles *goes to the closet to search for his cell phone.*

Lilith

You realize if you had simply given in to me last night instead of this morning, the three of us wouldn't be in this hell?

Frasier

No, it would be the two of us in a whole different hell. Well, we're young – our best hells are still ahead of us.

Niles *(into phone)*

Niles Crane . . . Absolutely not. We agreed on a figure . . . Well that's too damned bad. I've been manipulated enough by you jackals. I'll see you in court. *(hangs up)* The very idea that Maris would still think – *(realizes)* Hey, wait a minute . . . I'm not sleeping. By all rights the strain of that conversation should have caused me to go out like a light. And instead I feel alert. Almost invigorated.

Lilith

It's not surprising. Your experience with Maris over the past few months has been emasculating. Last night may have gone a long way toward restoring your self-confidence.

Niles

Yes. And by the same token, you can give up the neurotic assumption that Brian left you because you're not attractive. You've had ample evidence to the contrary.

Lilith

Yes, I have. To hell with Brian. If he wants a doting little wife he can keep Stan.

Frasier

Well, this just worked out great for everyone, didn't it? You two solved your problems. The waiter got a handsome tip. Come on, everyone, on my cue . . . a rousing chorus of "Oh Happy Day."

Lilith

Please try to understand.

Niles

Yes, what happened was nothing more than –

Frasier

Oh, stop it, both of you. Enough. It happened, and I'm going to have to deal with it . . . *(then)* I suppose in a twisted way there is one positive in this for me. You see, Lilith, I have never stopped desiring you, even though we are completely wrong for each other. But now, from this day forward, whenever I look at your face, I'll see the back of my brother's head, and that's better than a dead horse any day.

Lilith

Well I'm glad to hear that . . . I suppose. You know, Frasier –

Frasier

Enough, Lilith.

Lilith

All right. Maybe I'll just go have some breakfast.

Lilith *goes into the bathroom. There's an awkward silence.* **Frasier** *and* **Niles** *don't know what to say to each other. Finally:*

Niles

Are we okay?

Frasier

No, we're not. *(beat)* But we will be.

Niles

Well that's enough for now. *(then)* We're an odd little family, aren't we?

Frasier

Yeah, like the one in *Deliverance.*

There's a knock at the door.

Waiter (O.C.)

Room service.

Frasier *opens the door. The* **Waiter** *enters with another breakfast cart.*

Waiter *(cont'd)*

Here's the eggs Benedict, and –

The **Waiter** *looks around and notices there's no* **Lilith**, *just two men in bathrobes.*

Waiter *(cont'd)*

Ohh-kay.

And as he turns and exits, we:

FADE OUT.

End of Act Two

Two men, two women, and a lot of confusion.

A lust triangle.

The Ski Lodge

Episode #40570-114

Written by
Joe Keenan

Created by
David Angell/Peter Casey/David Lee

Directed by
David Lee

ACT ONE
Scene A

FADE IN:
INT. RADIO STUDIO – DAY – DAY/1
Frasier, Roz, Connie
Frasier *is in his booth after the show.* **Roz** *enters from her booth.*

Frasier
Good show today, Roz. I particularly thought –

Roz *notices a woman,* **Connie**, *talking to an employee in the hall.*

Roz
Oh God, it's Connie from promotions. She drives me up the wall. Every time I see her she hits me up for another charity.

Frasier
Well, Roz, maybe it's time you set some limits. How hard can it be to say no just once? *(then)* Well, look who I'm talking to.

Roz *shoots* **Frasier** *a look as* **Connie** *enters.*

Connie
Hi, Frasier. Roz, I was looking for you.

Roz
Listen Connie, before you say anything, I've got to get this off my chest. I've bought Girl Scout cookies from you, helped pay for your kid's band uniforms, and bought tickets for every raffle your church ever had . . . I'm tapped out. So whatever you came for, I'm not interested.

Connie
Well then, I'll just go. By the way, my church had its raffle drawing yesterday. You won the grand prize. *(placing envelope on table)* Sorry to bother you.

Connie *exits.*

Roz *(calling after)*
Oh Connie, Connie don't – Oh, forget it. What did I win?

Roz *runs to the envelope and opens it.*

Roz *(cont'd)*
Oh my God, this is incredible. It's a one-weekend rental of a deluxe private ski lodge on Mt. Baker, complete with lessons from a former Olympic champ.

Frasier

That is a grand prize, indeed. I must admit, I'm a bit envious. Well, I hope you have a wonderful weekend.

Roz

Thank you, Frasier.

Frasier

Though I don't suppose you'll have much use for those ski lessons.

Roz

There'll be other stuff to do.

Frasier

Oh, tons. Just because you can't ski – or for that matter hike, sled, or snowboard – doesn't mean you can't relax by the fire with a nice warm snifter of . . . Oh, sorry.

Roz

Well, the scenery will be nice.

Frasier

Breathtaking . . . though I hope you can enjoy it after that four-hour drive, and you so carsick these days –

Roz

Frasier, I know what you're hinting at here. But this is the first thing I've ever won in my life. It means something to me. I'm not about to give it away, or sell it, or trade it for a . . .

Frasier

Big-screen TV?

Roz *hands* **Frasier** *the envelope.*

Roz

The key's in the mailbox.

FADE OUT.

Scene B

FADE IN:

INT. FRASIER'S LIVING ROOM – EVENING – NIGHT/1

Daphne, Martin, Niles, Frasier, Eddie

Martin *sits watching a game on TV.* **Eddie** *sits nearby. The sound is up very loud.*

SFX: *The doorbell rings.* **Daphne** *enters from the kitchen and crosses to the door.*

Daphne

What do you need that so loud for? I swear you've gone deaf as a post.

Martin

It's just a cold stopping up my ears. I'm fine.

Daphne *opens the door to* **Niles***, who's on his cell phone.*

Niles *(into phone)*

Good God, man, whose lawyer are you, anyway? No, I will not calm down. *(to Daphne, calmly)* Hello, Daphne. *(on phone)* They call that a settlement? Call them and turn it down. *(louder, over TV)* I said turn it down, you ninny!

Martin *(turning down the TV)*

Okay! Geez, you could ask a person nicely.

Niles *(hanging up)*

I have got to find a new divorce lawyer. Claude is clearly no match for Maris's team.

Daphne

Real sharks, are they?

Niles

When I was courting Maris I sent her a valentine that read "You're the girl my heart adores. Everything I have is yours." Now they insist it's a pre-nup.

Daphne

That's terrible. *(to Martin)* Can you imagine using that as a weapon – a valentine?

Martin

Sure, I'd love a Ballantine.

Daphne

That does it. You're getting a hearing aid whether you like it or not.

Martin

I don't need a hearing aid. My ears will be back to normal in no time.

Daphne

You said that two days ago. Soon you won't be able to hear a word I say.

Martin

Gee, we wouldn't want that. There'd be no reason to keep living.

Daphne *scowls and turns away.*

Martin *(cont'd) (taking a shot)*

I heard that.

Daphne

I didn't say anything!

Frasier *enters.*

Frasier

Well, what's everyone standing around for when you should all be packing?

Daphne

Packing for what?

Frasier

For the fabulous ski trip I'm taking us on this weekend.

Niles

You're kidding. You won the raffle?

Frasier

In a manner of speaking. We have a gorgeous ski lodge with an Olympic champ in residence to give us lessons.

Daphne

It sounds like heaven. Skiing all day, then warming up with a nice hot rum drink, curled up under blankets in front of a roaring fire.

Niles

Yes, I feel the steam rising from my toddy already.

Daphne

Oh, damn . . . I can't go.

Niles *(stricken)*

Why not?

Daphne

My friend Annie. It's her birthday Saturday and I promised I'd spend it with her.

Niles

Well, bring her along.

Daphne *(to Frasier)*

Could I? I know she'd love it. She's very gung ho for sports. She was captain of my girls' rugby team at school.

Frasier *(leery)*

Well, I'm not sure how many bedrooms there are.

Niles

If we're short she can have mine.

Daphne

Where will you sleep?

Niles

Oh, I'll find someplace.

Daphne *(to Frasier)*

You're sure you don't mind?

Frasier

Not at all. What could be more fun than a gung ho girls' rugby captain?

Daphne *exits to her room.*

Frasier *(cont'd) (to Niles)*

I'll kill you for this.

Niles

I'm sorry, it's the only way Daphne will come. And if you think I'm letting a moonlit ski lodge go to waste, think again.

Frasier

Niles, you just filed for divorce last week. Can't you wait a while?

Niles

Wait? I've waited five long years for this. *(to Martin)* Dad, wouldn't you say it's time?

Martin *(checks his watch)*

I've got ten past twelve. That can't be right. Oh, wait, I put it on upside down again.

Frasier *(a beat, then)*

If you want to make a fool of yourself with Daphne, that's your affair. But you're not ruining this ski trip by asking along a girl who sounds to me like a serious avalanche risk. I'm telling Daphne forget it – no guests.

Daphne *reenters.*

Daphne

I called Annie and she's all excited. Turns out she just bought new skis with the money she made from her last swimsuit calendar.

Daphne *exits to the kitchen.*

Frasier *(to Niles)*

Well, I hope you're happy. We're stuck with her now.

FADE OUT.

Scene C

FADE IN:

INT. SKI LODGE LIVING ROOM – DAY – DAY/2

Niles, Martin, Frasier, Daphne, Annie, Guy

The lodge has a living and dining room area with a fireplace. Off this is a small kitchen. Another downstage door leads to a bedroom. Doors leading to two more bedrooms face each other upstage. Stairs beyond this lead to a second floor landing with doors to three more bedrooms.

Martin *and* **Niles** *enter carrying luggage.*

> **Niles**
>
> Wow, look at this place.

> **Martin**
>
> Nothing like a change of scenery. *(then)* Where do you suppose the TV is?

> **Niles**
>
> At this altitude I'm surprised my ears haven't stopped up. How's it affecting your ears, Dad?

No response.

> **Niles** *(cont'd)*
>
> Dad?

> **Martin**
>
> What?

> **Niles**
>
> How are your ears?

> **Martin** *(covering badly)*
> Great. Never been better. No hearing aid for me.

Behind **Niles's** *back* **Martin** *madly flexes his jaw to make his ears unpop. He has no luck.* **Frasier** *enters carrying bags.*

> **Frasier** *(calling back over his shoulder)*
> No need to struggle with that, Annie. I'll be back to help you in a moment. *(reacts to lodge)* This is some place, isn't it?

> **Niles**
>
> I'm just glad we made it all right, the way you kept taking those curves so sharply. Poor Annie kept being thrown up against you.

> **Frasier** *(naughtily)*
> What can I say? I'm a bad driver.

Niles
I'll grant you she's comely, but don't you find her a tad – what would a polite euphemism be? – stupid?

Frasier
She's just unschooled, like Eliza Doolittle. Give her the right Henry Higgins and she'll be ready for a ball in no time.

Niles
Leave it to you to put the "Pig" back in "Pygmalion."

Daphne *and* **Annie** *enter with their bags. They all ad-lib hellos.*

Daphne
Goodness. This place is just lovely.

Niles
And lovelier still now that you're in it.

Frasier *(to Annie)*
Stunning vista. Makes one think of the Matterhorn, doesn't it?

Annie
I wouldn't know, I'm not very musical.

Martin *opens one of his bags and removes two large bottles of rum.*

Martin
There's a relief. With all that swerving you did on the drive up, I was afraid these might break. I'm going to make us all a batch of my special hot buttered rum.

Frasier
You're actually going to put butter in the rum?

Martin
It's cold in these mountains – you need a little fat in your booze.

Martin *crosses into the kitchen.*

Frasier
Good thinking, Dad. When we're done with the buttered rum I'll whip us up a nice hearty batch of pork nog.

Annie *(earnestly)*
None for me, thanks, I'm a vegetarian.

Niles
Daphne, let me help with your luggage. Which room do you want?

Daphne *(points)*
That one on the left upstairs should have a nice view.

Niles

What a coincidence. That's right next to my room.

Annie

I'll take the one next to that.

Frasier

Allow me.

Niles and **Frasier** *take the bags and exit into the bedrooms.* **Annie** *watches* **Niles** *go.*

Annie

That Niles is quite a cutie. Now he's the one getting divorced?

Daphne

Poor thing's been just miserable.

Annie

Well, I may just have to cheer him up.

Daphne

You just leave Dr. Crane alone. No offense, but I've seen the way you go through men. The last thing he needs is for someone else to break his heart.

Annie

But it's my birthday. Besides, you're not his nanny.

Unseen by them, **Guy** *enters carrying groceries. He's in his mid-thirties, French, and very good-looking.*

Daphne

Can't we just have a nice relaxing ski trip? Does the whole weekend have to be about sex?

Guy

Hello.

Daphne and **Annie** *turn and see* **Guy.** **Daphne** *is very impressed.*

Daphne

Hello.

Guy

I am Guy.

Daphne

Daphne.

Annie

Annie.

Guy

I hope you're ready to ski tomorrow. I'm going to work you very hard.

Guy *exits to the kitchen with the groceries.*

Daphne

Dibs on the Frenchman.

Annie

You can have him. He's not half as cute as Dr. Crane.

Frasier *has emerged from his room just in time to overhear this.*

Frasier

Enough! My ears are burning.

Niles *emerges from his room just as* **Guy** *reenters from the kitchen, followed by* **Martin**.

Daphne

Everyone, did you meet Guy, our ski instructor?

Guy

I will also be your chef. Tonight, Entrecôte à la Guy.

Niles

A ski champion and a gourmet – *vous êtes formidable.*

Guy

Parlez français?

Niles

Oui. J'ai habité six mois à Paris quand j'étais un étudiant.

Guy

You speak very well.

Annie

Oui.

Frasier

Oh, you speak French as well?

Annie

No, all I know how to say is *"oui."*

Frasier

Well, I'm sure that'll be enough to get you through the weekend.

Martin *glances out the window.*

Martin

Well, ain't that a postcard. Look – two deer in the snow, just kinda nuzzling each other.

They all look out and see it and say "Awww," "How cute," etc.

Daphne

How romantic.

Frasier

Enough to put ideas in one's head.

Frasier *steals an appraising glance at* **Annie**.

Annie

Isn't it?

Annie *glances at* **Niles**.

Niles

Yes.

Niles *glances at* **Daphne**.

Daphne

I should say so.

Daphne *glances at* **Guy**.

Guy

Absolument.

Guy *steals a glance at* **Niles**. *They all stare out the window.*

Martin

Well, I better start that rum cooking.

FADE OUT.

End of Act One

ACT TWO

Scene D

FADE IN:

INT. SKI LODGE LIVING ROOM/KITCHEN – EVENING – NIGHT/2

Daphne, Guy, Niles, Annie, Frasier, Martin

Dinner is over. **Daphne** *and* **Annie** *sit in the living room area finishing their rum drinks while watching* **Guy** *skillfully stoking the fire.*

Daphne

Look at you – you're handy, a chef, a ski champ . . . is there anything you don't do?

Guy

There are a few things. *(turning)* Niles – you look *très élégant.*

Niles *has emerged from his room, wearing silk pajamas and a dressing robe, and comes downstairs.*

Niles

I simply had to change. After that meal I felt I was going to burst out of my trousers.

Annie *(saucily)*

Ooh my!

Daphne

Annie.

Frasier *comes out of his room having also changed into a handsome dressing gown and pajamas.*

Daphne *(cont'd)*

Dr. Crane, what a smashing robe. *(to Annie)* Doesn't he look handsome?

Annie

Oh, yes, quite. Well, look at this – I've finished my buttered rum.

Frasier

Never let it be said that Frasier Crane would permit a lady to go thirsty. *(to Daphne)* Daphne, go see if Dad's finished with that second batch.

RESET TO:

INT. KITCHEN – CONTINUOUS

Martin *stands at the stove where a large pot of rum sits, steam rising from it. He's still trying to unpop his ears.* **Daphne** *enters. He hurriedly turns and stirs the rum.*

Martin

Almost there. I just need to replace the rum that's boiled off.

Martin *adds more rum to the pot.*

Daphne

Just what Annie needs. *(peering back through the door)* She's all over poor Dr. Crane as it is, and after I begged her to leave him be. *(turns to Martin)* Why couldn't she be hot for Frasier?

Martin
Who?

Daphne *(loudly, annoyed)*
Annie. Oh, I should just forget about those two and concentrate on Guy. I could sure go for that tall drink of water.

Martin
That what?

Daphne
Tall drink of water.

Martin *obligingly gets* **Daphne** *a tall drink of water.* **Daphne**, *not noticing this, exits.* **Frasier** *enters.* **Martin** *turns around with the drink of water and* **Frasier** *takes it.*

Frasier
Thanks, Dad, but it's the rum I really need. I'm hoping it'll help clinch things with Annie.

Martin
Annie?

Frasier
Yeah.

Martin
Well, I know a little something about her – she's hot for you.

Frasier
Says who?

Martin
Daphne. She said, "Annie's hot for Frasier."

Frasier
I knew my charm would win her over. I really should register this dressing gown with the love police.

RESET TO:

INT. SKI LODGE LIVING ROOM – CONTINUOUS
Annie *has seated herself next to* **Niles**, *a sympathetic hand on his knee.* **Niles** *is uncomfortable.* **Daphne** *hovers disapprovingly.*

Annie
I know the pain you're going through. I mean, I've never been divorced myself, but my last boyfriend was . . . eventually.

Niles
Well, you know, *c'est la vie.*

Annie

What you need is something to take your mind off it. I'll tell you
what always works for me –

Daphne *(grabbing Annie)*

Time to go upstairs.

Annie

What for?

Daphne *drags* **Annie** *up the stairs.*

Daphne

I need to give you your birthday present. It's in my room.

Annie *(calling to Niles)*

See you in a bit.

They disappear into **Daphne's** *room.* **Guy** *sits closer to* **Niles**.

Guy

Your friend Daphne – she did not like the way Annie was flirting with
you.

Niles

You're right, Guy. She didn't like it, did she?

Guy

No. In fact, she dragged Annie right off to her bedroom.

Niles

Well, I think I know what that means.

We hear **Annie's** *girlish shriek of laughter from* **Daphne's** *room.* **Guy** *gazes
up at the bedroom with Gallic suavity.*

Guy

I think we both know. Daphne was jealous.

Niles

She was jealous, wasn't she? *(delighted)* Well who would have
thought it?

Guy

I am surprised by nothing. You know, I think you did not like Annie's
flirting either.

Niles

I certainly didn't. It made my skin crawl.

Guy

Annie is not your . . . cup of tea?

Niles *(leans in; confidentially)*
Just between us, my interests lie elsewhere this weekend.

Guy *(smiles)*
Really?

Frasier *enters from the kitchen.*

Frasier
Rum's ready.

Niles *(to get rid of him)*
Guy, perhaps you can give my dad a hand with the drinks.

Guy
I am at your service.

Guy *exits to the kitchen.* **Niles** *turns excitedly to* **Frasier**.

Niles
Daphne wants me!

Frasier
She told you that?

Niles
No. But Annie was flirting with me and Daphne dragged her away in a jealous rage.

Frasier
You're imagining things. Annie was not flirting with you – I'm the one she's hot for.

Niles
I think I know when I'm being flirted with.

Frasier
It's sheer vanity. Next thing you'll be thinking Guy's after you.

RESET TO:
INT. KITCHEN – CONTINUOUS
Martin *stands ladling the rum into cups and handing them to* **Guy**. **Martin** *takes a sip from one.*

Guy
How do you like your rum?

Martin
It's kinda small, but the view's nice.

Guy
No, your rum.

Martin

Oh. Yeah. Could you speak up a little?

Guy

I like your rum too. But I wonder if it's clouded my judgment about something. Your son Niles – is it just me, or is he attracted to –?

Martin

Stop right there. It's not just you. He's got it bad.

Guy

Really? This is not a delicate subject for you?

Martin

Nah. I've known Niles has had those feelings for years. I didn't encourage it during that so-called marriage of his, but now that he's free, whatever makes him happy – I say go for it.

Guy

You are a wonderful father.

RESET TO:

INT. SKI LODGE LIVING ROOM – CONTINUOUS

Guy *and* **Martin** *enter from the kitchen,* **Guy** *carrying a tray with six steaming cups of* **Martin's** *hot buttered rum and a jug with the leftovers.* **Daphne** *and* **Annie** *reenter from* **Daphne's** *room. Both wear nightgowns.* **Frasier** *and* **Niles** *fetch them drinks.*

Martin

Okay, everybody, come and get it.

Niles

Daphne, just in time.

Frasier

Annie, what a lovely gown.

Annie

Daphne just gave it to me.

Guy *gives* **Niles** *a "There, see?" look as he takes two drinks.*

Frasier *(tasting his drink)*

Whoa! That's even stronger than the last batch.

Martin

You might want to go easy – it can have some pretty powerful effects. First time I made it was for your mom. I'd been wanting to pop the question but I was afraid she'd say no. This gave me the nerve to ask her and I got myself a great big yes – and it wasn't the last yes I got from her that night either. Scares me to think how close I came to chickening out that night. You know, as you get older it's not your failures you regret, or the times you make an ass of yourself. It's the times you didn't even try, when you just lost your nerve.

Frasier
Wise words, Dad. Faint heart never won fair lady.

Annie
I'd certainly hope that if a man fancied me, he wouldn't be afraid to take a chance, go for a bold gesture.

Niles
Yes. We must never be too timid to pursue our heart's desire.

Guy
And not give a damn what the world thinks . . . right Miss Moon?

Daphne
Indeed.

Martin
This is my best batch ever. It takes an hour to make each one, but it's worth it just to sit and savor every sip.

General agreement. Then **Daphne** *downs hers. They all follow suit.*

Daphne
Well, I'm done.

Niles
Time for bed.

Guy
I'm ready.

Annie
Me too.

Frasier
'Night, Dad.

Martin
What, already? You sure? You're young people. What do you wanna go to bed for? *(realizing)* Oh. Good night.

Martin *heads for his room as* **Frasier, Niles, Daphne, Guy,** *and* **Annie** *reach their respective doors. Note:* **Daphne** *and* **Annie,** *slightly in their cups, switch rooms.* **Annie, Daphne,** *and* **Guy** *exit into their rooms.* **Niles** *and* **Frasier** *stop.*

Niles

I thought Daphne's room was –

Frasier

I guess they switched.

Frasier *and* **Niles** *exit to their rooms. A moment.* **Daphne** *and* **Annie** *both emerge into the hall and cross to their correct rooms.*

Annie

Sorry, I took the wrong room.

Daphne

Yes – I thought we'd gotten that backwards.

Annie

Oh well, no harm done.

Annie *and* **Daphne** *go into their correct rooms.* **Frasier**, *having heard* **Annie's** *voice, peers out of his door.*

Frasier *(whispers)*

Annie?

Niles, *having heard* **Daphne**, *opens his door.*

Niles *(whispering)*

Daphne?

Frasier *and* **Niles**, *seeing there's no one there but each other, wave limp good nights.*

Frasier

'Night, Niles.

Niles

Good night.

They close their doors. **Guy**, *hearing* **Niles's** *voice, opens his door.*

Guy

Allo!

Daphne, *hearing* **Guy's** *voice, opens her door.*

Daphne

Oh, hello.

Guy *(whispers)*

I know what you want. Don't be timid – go for it!

He disappears back into his room. **Daphne**, *atwitter, disappears behind her door.*

CUT TO:

Scene E

INT. NILES'S BEDROOM/ANNIE'S BEDROOM – CONTINUOUS – NIGHT/2
Niles, Annie, Guy
A small bedroom. **Niles** *notices that there are connecting doors to the bedrooms on either side of him. He knocks gently on the door into what he thinks is* **Daphne's** *room but is now* **Annie's** *room. Hearing no reply, he opens the door and peers in.*

RESET TO:

INT. ANNIE'S BEDROOM – CONTINUOUS
Niles *enters. There's no one in the bedroom, but a half-open door leads to the bathroom from which we can hear water running and the sound of someone gargling.*

>   **Niles** *(calls to the bathroom)*
> Hello? It's me, Niles.

>   **Annie** (O.C.) *(gargling)*
> Wait.

>   **Niles**
> I can't wait. I may lose my nerve and not say what I came to say. I need you. I've wanted you since the moment I laid eyes on you.

Annie *emerges from the bathroom.*

>   **Annie**
> I feel the exact same way.

>   **Niles**
> Annie!

>   **Annie**
> I see you're surprised. I've tried to send you signals tonight, but as usual I was too damned subtle. Just promise you won't mention this to Daphne.

>   **Niles**
> My lips are sealed.

>   **Annie** *(advancing)*
> Not for long I hope.

SFX: knock on Annie's door. **Niles,** *thrilled at any interruption, turns to the door.*

>   **Niles**
> Come in!

Guy *enters.*

Niles *(cont'd) (saved)*

Guy!

Guy

Niles. I thought I heard your voice in here.

Annie

What do you want?

Guy

Niles – you told me you wanted to see that thing. You know – in my room.

Niles

Oh yes! Thank you . . . for reminding me.

Annie

What thing?

Niles

Won't take long. We'll catch up later.

Niles *and* **Guy** *exit* **Annie's** *bedroom.*

CUT TO:

Scene H

INT. SKI LODGE LIVING ROOM – CONTINUOUS – NIGHT/2
Niles, Guy
Niles *and* **Guy** *speak in whispers.*

Niles

Boy, that was close. I owe you a big one.

Guy *starts for his room,* **Niles** *crosses to his own bedroom door.*

Guy

Your room?

Niles

You're right – of course. My room's out. She's bound to hear me in there.

Guy

Oh, you are the type who makes noise. We could still go to my room.

Niles

It's as good a place as any.

They hurry to **Guy's** *room.* **Guy** *opens the door.*

Guy

Entrez.

Niles *and* **Guy** *exit into* **Guy's** *bedroom.*

CUT TO:

Scene J

INT. GUY'S BEDROOM – CONTINUOUS – NIGHT/2
Niles, Daphne, Guy
Niles *and* **Guy** *enter to find* **Daphne** *there waiting on* **Guy's** *bed.*

> #### Niles
> Daphne!

> #### Daphne
> Dr. Crane!

> #### Guy
> Miss Moon. Is your room not satisfactory?

> #### Daphne *(mortified)*
> Oh, dear. I seem to have made a dreadful mistake.

> #### Niles
> What are you doing in Guy's room?

> #### Daphne *(a way out)*
> Is this Guy's room then? I was looking for Annie's room.

> #### Guy
> Ah, now it makes sense.

> #### Daphne
> I'll just go.

> #### Niles
> Wait for me! That hall is horribly dark. I'll show you the way. *(to Guy)* My room should be safe now.

> #### Guy
> Ah, very well. I'll see you later.

> #### Niles
> Excellent. Come along, Daphne.

Niles *and* **Daphne** *exit* **Guy's** *room.*

CUT TO:

Scene K

INT. SKI LODGE LIVING ROOM – CONTINUOUS – NIGHT/2
Daphne, Frasier, Niles
Niles *and* **Daphne** *exit* **Guy's** *room just as* **Frasier** *emerges from his room.*
He is now naked under his bathrobe and carries a bottle of Dom Perignon.

Daphne
Dr. Crane?

Frasier *(embarrassed; suddenly nonchalant)*
Oh. Hello.

Niles
Frasier!

Frasier
Was that Guy's room you were both in?

Niles
Yes. You see Daphne was just –

Daphne
Looking for Annie. I need to talk to her.

Frasier
To Annie? For how long?

Daphne
Two minutes.

Frasier
Right.

Daphne *(to Frasier)*
Is that champagne?

Frasier
Yes. I was just – bringing it . . . to . . . Dad. *(then)* Carry on.

Frasier *crosses down toward* **Martin's** *room.* **Niles** *hustles* **Daphne** *up the few stairs to his door.*

Niles
Before you see Annie could you come to my room?

Daphne
What for?

Niles
There's something I need to tell you.

They go into **Niles's** *room.*

CUT TO:

Scene L

INT. NILES'S BEDROOM/DAPHNE'S BEDROOM – CONTINUOUS – NIGHT/2
Niles, Daphne, Annie, Frasier, Guy, Martin

The room is dark. **Niles** *and* **Daphne** *enter.*

Niles
This may come as a surprise to you –

Niles *turns on the light.* **Annie** *is waiting in* **Niles's** *bed.*

Daphne
Annie!

Annie
Daphne!

Daphne
Didn't I tell you to leave Dr. Crane alone?

Annie
And now I see why. You wanted him all to yourself!

Daphne
I do not want him all to myself!

Annie
Oh, I see! It's a threesome you're after. Well, I don't do those any more.

Niles
Annie, I think there's been a misunderstanding here.

Annie
I don't see how. You barged into my room not five minutes ago and told me how much you wanted me.

Daphne *(to Niles)*
You did?

Niles
Well, technically, yes –

Annie
Then as soon as this one bats her eyes it's shove off, Annie. *(to Daphne)* This is the worst birthday I've ever had!

Annie *runs into her room through the connecting door.*

Daphne
I'm sorry, Dr. Crane. I've ruined everything for you.

Niles
No, you haven't. Those things I said to Annie, I can explain –

Daphne
No, it's none of my business. I've had enough embarrassment for one evening.

Daphne *hurries back into her own bedroom followed by* **Niles**.

RESET TO:

INT. DAPHNE'S BEDROOM – CONTINUOUS

Daphne *and* **Niles** *enter. She turns on the light.* **Frasier** *lolls on her bed, naked under a sheet, a glass of champagne in his hand.*

Daphne *(cont'd)*

Dr. Crane!!

Frasier *(aghast; covering himself)*

Daphne!

Niles

Frasier! You snake!

Frasier

Sorry! Wrong room!

Daphne

Get out of here! Right now!

Frasier

Right. Just give me a second and off I go. Is it next door I want then?

Daphne

Just go!

Frasier

Right. Sorry again!

RESET TO:

INT. NILES'S BEDROOM – CONTINUOUS

The room's now dark. **Frasier**, *a towel around him, races in from* **Daphne's** *room and closes the door behind him. In the darkness we hear:*

Guy

Bonsoir, chéri.

Guy *turns on the light. He is naked in* **Niles's** *bed.*

Frasier

Guy!

Guy

You are not the Crane I want!

Frasier

You're not even the sex I want!

Guy

Where is Niles?

Frasier *opens the door to* **Daphne's** *room.*

Frasier

Oh, Niles! Company!

Niles *enters.*

Niles *(spotting Guy; to Frasier)*
My God, what are you doing in here with Guy?

Guy
Don't be jealous, Niles. It's not how it looks.

Niles

Excuse me!?

Frasier

Well, much as I'd love to stay and help you two sort this out, there happens to be a beautiful woman on the other side of this door who wants me desperately.

He flings open the connecting door to **Annie's** *room.*

Frasier *(cont'd)*

Hello, Annie.

Annie (O.C.) *(shrieks, then)*
Go away! Get out! Get out! Get out!

Frasier

Sorry!

He closes the door as **Daphne,** *alarmed, enters from her room.*

Daphne
What's going on? *(sees him)* Guy!

Annie *enters from her room clad only in a towel.*

Annie *(to Frasier)*
How dare you barge in on me when I'm naked!

Frasier
I'm sorry. I was misled. My father told me you wanted me.

Annie

Your father did?

Frasier
Blame Daphne. She told him.

Daphne
I did not. I said she wanted your brother.

Guy

Could Niles and I please have some privacy?

Annie *(to Niles)*

You're just putting the moves on everyone, aren't you?!

Niles *(to Guy)*

Would you kindly get out of my bed. I am not gay, Guy.

Guy

Oh, please! Acknowledge your true nature and stop chasing these lesbians!

Daphne

Lesbians!

Guy

Your father himself said you were gay.

Niles *(incredulous)*

My father?!

Pandemonium. There's a five-way overlap. "My father said that?" "Who are you calling lesbians?" "You're the most horrible family I've ever met," "Would everyone please just go to bed," "I've never been so humiliated in my life!" etc., etc.

Finally **Martin** *enters.*

Martin

Hey you want to keep it down in here? Some of us are trying to sleep! . . . *(realizes)* Hey, my ears must've popped. I can hear again! Well, good night all.

Martin *exits.*

Niles

All right. We could discuss this till we've figured out every detail of what went on here tonight, but if you ask me, breakfast will be embarrassing enough as it is. I say we go to bed and forget any of this ever happened.

They all mumble their assent and head for the various doors. Just before they go:

Frasier

Wait. Let me make sure I have this straight . . . All the lust coursing through this lodge tonight . . . all the hormones virtually ricocheting off these walls . . . and no one was chasing me?

Daphne

Good night, Dr. Crane.

Frasier

Good night.

Guy, **Annie**,*and* **Daphne** *exit to their rooms.* **Frasier** *wearily follows, as we:*
FADE OUT.

End of Act Two

Season Six

Three Valentines

A Valentine's date for Frasier, or just a business meeting?

Frasier is confused about the dress code in Cassandra's hotel room.

Three Valentines

Episode #40570-136

Written by
Rob Hanning

Created by
David Angell/Peter Casey/David Lee

Directed by
Kelsey Grammer

ACT ONE
Scene A

FADE IN:

INT. FRASIER'S LIVING ROOM – VALENTINE'S DAY – DAY/1

Niles, Delivery Guy, Eddie

Niles, *dressed impeccably in a suit and tie, enters from the kitchen carrying a bottle of champagne and two champagne flutes. He is alone in the apartment. He places the flutes on the dining table next to a spread of gourmet hors d'oeuvres and an ice bucket, but in the process of nestling the champagne bottle into the ice, he notices something on the label that greatly displeases him. Exasperated, he marches over to the phone and dials.*

(During the following phone call, he tidies an already tidy living room, repositioning a few couch pillows, moving a beautiful floral arrangement a few inches to the left, snatching a near-invisible piece of lint off the floor, and adjusting the large, decorative quilt that is draped over **Martin's** *chair.)*

> **Niles** *(into phone)*
> Hello, François, this is Niles Crane. You delivered some Champagne earlier for Valentine's Day – only you brought me the 1990 and I asked for an '88 rosé . . . I'm glad you're sorry but I will be needing the '88 . . . My date will know the difference. She happens to be president of our wine club . . . Remember, I'm not at home, I would never entertain at the Shangri-La. My brother was kind enough to let me use his place . . . *(looking at Martin's chair)* What could I do? I threw a quilt over it. Now hurry – that bottle is all that stands between this night and perfection!

Niles *hangs up, goes to the stereo and turns on some music. He surveys the apartment and, content with what he sees, sits on the couch. As he settles in, he notices that the crease in one trouser leg isn't quite right. He tries adjusting it. He stands up, shakes his leg out, sits down again – still no good. Checking his watch, he hesitates for a second, then gets up and disappears into the kitchen . . .*

. . . Returning a moment later with an iron and an ironing board. He plugs in the iron and sets it down and then, with difficulty, sets up the ironing board. As he finishes and begins to take his trousers off, he notices **Eddie**, *who has run in from* **Martin's** *room. He perches somewhere and stares at* **Niles**.

> **Niles** *(cont'd) (to Eddie)*
> What are you staring at?

He finishes taking his trousers off and starts to iron the crease. He checks his watch, and irons more quickly.

As he irons, he notices a loose thread on one of the trouser cuffs. He pulls gently on the thread, but it just gets longer, so he puts down the iron, crosses to the desk by the kitchen door, gets a pair of scissors out of a drawer, and crosses back to the ironing board. As he bends over the pants leg to trim the thread he looks at **Eddie** *again.*

> **Niles** *(cont'd) (to Eddie)*
> Don't get too comfortable there. The minute she comes you're going to have to – Ow!

He's cut the tip of his finger with the scissors.

> **Niles** *(cont'd) (to Eddie)*
> Now look what you made me do. I'm bleeding.

Niles *looks at the cut and the sight of the blood makes him woozy. He starts to swoon, but he catches himself. He quickly looks away, steadies himself on the ironing board, and holds his cut finger in the air above his head.*

> **Niles** *(cont'd) (to Eddie)*
> Will you just get out of here?

Niles *attempts to shoo* **Eddie** *out of the room by snapping his fingers and pointing to the hall, but this causes him to notice his bloody finger. He gets woozy again and falls over onto the couch and passes out.* **Eddie** *jumps onto the couch and licks* **Niles's** *face. After a few seconds,* **Niles** *comes to. He remembers about his finger and holds it over his head, out of sight.*

Niles *notices that while he was passed out, his finger bled onto the arm of the couch, leaving a small stain. Horrified, he tries to clean the stain with his handkerchief, but it won't come out. He gets up, shoos* **Eddie** *out of the room, and as* **Eddie** *exits to the hallway,* **Niles** *wraps his handkerchief around his cut finger, careful to look away while doing so. He then exits to the kitchen.*

Immediately, **Eddie** *runs back into the room, jumps up on* **Martin's** *chair and watches everything that follows.* **Niles** *returns from the kitchen carrying a rag and a tin of cleaning fluid. He sits and scans the directions on the side of the can. After doing so, he cautiously moves a nearby lit candle away from the stain and the cleaning fluid. Then, he pours some of the cleaner onto the rag and rubs the stain.*

Niles *stands to look at the sofa and smiles – satisfied. Then, as he goes to put the lid back on the cleaning fluid, his handkerchief falls off the cut finger. Seeing the blood, he again becomes woozy and faints, falling onto* *the couch while still holding the open can of cleaning fluid. It empties out onto the sofa next to him.*

After a few seconds **Niles** *comes to, puts the cleaning fluid down on the coffee table, again remembers his finger and quickly puts it in the air. While still holding it above his head and out of sight, he wraps the handkerchief around it and hastily crosses . . .*

Into the kitchen. As he puts the cleaner and rag away, he pauses to sniff the air. Concerned by something he smells, he checks the pots on the stove – they're okay. He checks the oven – fine. He shrugs, then wanders back . . .

Into the living room, where he finds his pants are now on fire on the ironing board. Panicked, he runs over and tries to smother the flames with one pant leg – succeeding only to spread the fire to the other pant leg. He instinctively flings the trousers away from him, causing them to land . . .

. . . On the section of the couch soaked with cleaning fluid, which immediately ignites. An alarmed **Eddie** *barks as* **Niles** *quickly exits to the hallway, returning with a large fire extinguisher. He aims it at the couch and squeezes the handle, but nothing happens. Realizing that the safety pin must be removed,* **Niles** *tries to pull it out, but can't get it to budge. Finally, the pin comes free, causing the fire extinguisher to start discharging with such force that* **Niles** *is unable to control it. Foam sprays in every direction covering the walls and every piece of furniture – but the couch – as* **Niles** *battles to get the thing under control. He finally manages to aim it at the couch, but by then the nozzle just sputters a little and the last of the foam dribbles out and onto the rug.*

Tossing aside the empty canister, he exits to the kitchen again, returning after a moment wearing oven mitts on each hand and carrying two of the pots that were on the stove. He gets as close as he can to the couch and dumps the contents of the two pots onto the flames, dousing them with a lot of boiling water, some spaghetti and a big pile of shrimp. This does the trick – the flames are extinguished.

Coughing a little from the smoke, **Niles** *crosses to the front door and opens it to air out the apartment. He fans the door back and forth to get some air circulating. Not satisfied with the result, he opens the door wide and tries to push out the smoke by waving his arms. He waves them so wildly, however, that the handkerchief flies off his finger. When he goes to retrieve it, it is now sufficiently bloody that it causes him to faint yet again, this time on the floor. As soon as* **Niles** *faints,* **Eddie** *jumps up onto the still-smoking couch and starts eating the shrimp.*

A beat later, a **Delivery Man** *carrying the champagne, appears at the door and stops to take in the tableau: foam everywhere, the charred couch covered in shrimp and spaghetti, and a passed-out, pantless* **Niles** *sprawled on the floor.*

AND WE . . .

FADE OUT.

End of Act One

ACT TWO

Scene B

FADE IN:

INT. RADIO STUDIO – VALENTINE'S DAY – DAY/1

Frasier, Cassandra Stone, Roz

Frasier *is on the air.* **Roz** *is in her booth.*

Frasier

That's all for today, listeners. Good-bye and good mental health.

Cassandra Stone *enters* **Frasier's** *booth.*

Cassandra

Hello, Frasier.

Frasier

Ah, Cassandra.

Cassandra

I just had to say how much I loved your show today. Well, okay, every day.

Frasier *(modest)*

Thank you. You're too kind, as I tell you every day. How's that new publicity campaign going?

Cassandra

Oh, great. It'd be a lot easier if I had a few more like you to promote. Cultured, charming, photogenic . . .

Frasier

I'm also a wizard with a crêpe pan if you want to work that in somehow.

As they share a laugh, **Cassandra** *fixes* **Frasier's** *jacket collar, smoothing his lapels while she's at it. Their moment is interrupted when someone waves to* **Cassandra** *from the hallway.*

Cassandra

Oh, I've got to speak to my copywriter. I'll stop by again sometime, okay?

Cassandra *quickly exits.*

Frasier

My jacket and I look forward to it.

He begins to hum as **Roz** *crosses into* **Frasier's** *booth.*

Roz

All right, what happened?

Frasier

What do you mean?

Roz

You're doing your humming. The happy humming – not to be confused with the sad humming, or that aria you sing after you get lucky.

Frasier

What aria?

Roz

I didn't catch the title. I'd need to hear it a second time.

Frasier

Very amusing, Roz. It happens there's someone new at the station who's quite taken with me, and it's none other than that lovely little peach in publicity, Cassandra.

Roz

Oh, poor Frasier.

Frasier

What?

Roz

I hate to be the one to tell you this, but . . . that woman's just, well . . . a flirt.

Frasier

Obviously you haven't seen how she virtually accosts me in the hallway every day.

Roz

She's been treating everyone that way. She even flirted with me her first day until I took off my baseball cap and parka.

Roz *moves back into her booth as* **Cassandra** *reenters* **Frasier's** *booth.*

Cassandra
Frasier, you have a second?

Frasier
Oh. Certainly, Cassandra.

Cassandra
I was just wondering if you might want to have dinner with me.

Frasier
Dinner? Really?

Cassandra
Yeah, I thought it'd be nice to get to know each other a little. *(realizing)* Oh, gosh, tonight's Valentine's Day, isn't it? You probably have other plans.

Frasier
As it happens, I don't. Dinner would be lovely.

Cassandra
Great.

She gives him a big smile, squeezes his arm, and goes. **Frasier,** *watching her walk away, starts humming and crosses into* **Roz's** *booth.*

Frasier
Well, I certainly didn't misread the signals that time. She just asked me out to dinner.

Roz
Really?

Frasier
Yes. She coquettishly pretended to forget it was Valentine's Day, but I saw right through that.

Roz
You're sure this is a date-date, right, and not a business dinner?

Frasier
Reasonably sure.

Roz
Then, good for you.

Frasier
Then again . . . she has mentioned wanting to talk about her new marketing campaign. I suppose it is possible she really did forget it

was Valentine's Day. I guess I'll just have to ask her if she's viewing me in, you know, a romantic way.

Roz

Are you crazy? What if the answer is no? Then it's awkward all through dinner, and it'll be weird every time you see her at the office – not to mention how embarrassing it'll be when everyone else around here finds out.

Frasier

You're right, I can't just ask her. I guess I should just go to dinner and see how the evening plays out. I'll know what she has in mind by the way she acts, how she dresses, the way she treats me.

Roz

Much better.

Frasier

So, I'm sure you have plans tonight.

Roz

I'm going out with Bob – y'know, the tax accountant.

Frasier

Oh, Roz – isn't he the one who drones on so incessantly you call him "the cricket"?

Roz

No. *(then)* I call him "the cricket" because he rubs his hands together really fast during sex. *(off his look)* Hey, it beats being alone.

OFF FRASIER'S REACTION, WE:
FADE OUT.

Scene C

FADE IN:
INT. RESTAURANT – THAT EVENING – NIGHT/1
Frasier, Cassandra, Violinist, Mario
Frasier *sits alone at a table.* **Cassandra** *enters and approaches* **Frasier**.

Frasier

Ah, Cassandra. Our plans were so last minute, I thought maybe I'd misunderstood somehow.

Cassandra *plants a big kiss hello right on* **Frasier's** *mouth.*

Frasier *(cont'd)*

But your arrival certainly has cleared things up . . .

Cassandra *slips off her coat – she looks stunning.*

Cassandra

You don't think I'd pass up dinner with the sexiest man in radio, do you?

Nearby, a tuxedoed **Violinist** *finishes serenading a couple and presents a red rose to the woman.*

Violinist

Compliments of the gentleman.

The woman is delighted, and gives her date a big kiss.

Cassandra

Oh, that is so romantic. Will you excuse me for a second?

Cassandra *moves off to the coat check.* **Frasier** *makes sure* **Cassandra** *isn't watching, then signals the* **Violinist**.

Frasier

Excuse me – you see that woman over there by the coat check? We're on a first date, and I want to make sure she knows I'm interested.

Violinist

Then you should have offered to check her coat.

Frasier

Just come over and play something romantic when she gets back.

Frasier *gives him money, and the* **Violinist** *moves off.* **Cassandra** *returns to the table. The maître d', Mario, approaches her.*

Mario

Miss Cassandra, so nice to see you again.

Cassandra

You too, Mario. How's the sexiest maître d' in Seattle?

She gives **Mario** *the same big kiss on the mouth that she gave* **Frasier**. **Frasier** *reacts to this. The* **Maître d'** *hands them the wine list and moves off. The* **Violinist** *starts to approach them. As* **Cassandra** *looks down at the wine list,* **Frasier** *waves away the* **Violinist**. *The* **Violinist** *shrugs and moves off.*

Cassandra

Oh, they have the best wine list here. You feel like sharing a bottle?

Frasier

If you like.

Cassandra

Good thing I took a cab here – I'm a real lightweight. Then again, I'm sure a gentleman like you won't mind escorting me back to my room after dinner, will you?

Frasier

I think that can be arranged.

As **Cassandra** *opens the menu,* **Frasier** *signals confidently for the* **Violinist** *to come back to the table.*

Cassandra

They have a great menu here.

Frasier

What do you recommend?

Cassandra *(off menu)*

Oh, I don't know. I think I'll start with the tomato and onion salad and then have the garlic chicken with scallions.

Frasier

Really? Interesting choice.

Frasier *waves off the* **Violinist** *again.*

Cassandra

And for you, let's see . . . are you in the mood for oysters?

Frasier

Actually, I'm not sure.

AND WE:

FADE OUT.

Scene D

FADE IN:

INT. HOTEL ROOM – LATER THAT EVENING – NIGHT/1

Frasier, Cassandra

Cassandra *opens the hotel room door.* **Frasier** *just stands out in the hallway.*

Frasier

Well, here we are. Last stop. Your hotel.

Cassandra

I can't wait until I find an apartment. Come on in.

Cassandra *pulls him in and closes the door.*

Cassandra *(cont'd)*

God, I can't believe we got caught in the rain like that – I'm freezing. Of course, there is a way we can warm up fast.

Frasier

Yes, all we have to do is . . .?

Cassandra

Have a brandy.

Frasier

Yes, have a brandy.

Cassandra

The mini-bar's over there. I'll be right out.

She squeezes his shoulder as she exits into the bathroom. **Frasier** *goes to the minibar and takes out his cell phone and dials. And we:*

CUT TO:

INT. ROZ'S APARTMENT – CONTINUOUS

Roz

SFX: phone ringing

The room is dark. A bedside lamp goes on and **Roz** *reaches for the phone.*

Roz

Hello?

DURING THE FOLLOWING WE INTERCUT BETWEEN **Frasier** AND **Roz**:

Frasier

Roz, I'm in Cassandra's hotel room.

Roz

Well, I guess things are going well.

Frasier

I think they are, but I'm not sure. She does keep bringing the conversation back to business. I'm just waiting for a totally clear, unambiguous sign.

Roz

Oh for God's sake, Frasier, the woman invited you back to her hotel room. The only sign you're going to need is "Do Not Disturb."

Cassandra *reenters wearing a bathrobe.* **Frasier** *conceals his phone.*

Cassandra

I just had to get out of that dress.

Frasier

Here's your brandy.

He hands her a glass of brandy.

Cassandra

I'll just go dry my hair.

She exits back into the bathroom.

Frasier *(into phone)*
All right, I'm back. What should I do?

Roz
Let's see, she ditched her dress and she's hitting the sauce – what do
you need, runway lights on the mattress?

Frasier
It's not as clear cut as it seems.

Roz
Frasier, she's way out on a limb here. You know how rejected she'll
feel if you don't make a move? You're going to blow it forever.

Frasier
You're right. I probably should take off my jacket and tie.

Roz
Yeah, go get her, cowboy.

Roz *hangs up.* **Frasier** *puts his phone away.* **Cassandra** *opens the bathroom
door a crack and calls to him.*

Cassandra (O.S.)
Frasier, are you making yourself comfortable?

Frasier *tentatively removes his jacket and hangs it on the back of a chair,
then loosens his tie a tiny bit.*

Frasier
Yes.

Cassandra (O.S.)
If it's okay, I still have a few questions about the ad campaign I'd like
to ask you.

Frasier
Of course. That's what I'm here for.

Frasier *grabs his jacket and starts to put it back on.*

Cassandra (O.S.)
Or, if you prefer, we could just talk about it over breakfast tomorrow.

Frasier
Breakfast you say?

Frasier *smiles, takes off his jacket, and removes his tie.*

Cassandra (O.S.)
I hope I wasn't being presumptuous. We will be having breakfast
together, won't we?

Frasier

Absolutely.

He pulls his sweater halfway over his head, when . . .

Cassandra (O.S.)

Great. So, who else is supposed to be there?

Frasier

Where?

Cassandra (O.S.)

At the breakfast meeting. The one for the sponsors here at the hotel tomorrow. You just said you were going, right?

Frasier

The meeting, of course.

Frasier *quickly pulls his sweater back on and is still straightening himself as* **Cassandra** *reenters.*

Cassandra

Frasier, what are you doing?

Frasier

Well, I . . .

Cassandra

I thought you were going to make yourself comfortable? Check the closet, I think you'll find something in there you can slip on.

Frasier

All right.

Cassandra

I'm just going to take my lenses out.

Cassandra *exits to the bathroom again.* **Frasier** *goes to the closet and finds a bathrobe hanging inside the door. Chuckling to himself, he starts getting undressed, now including his pants.*

Cassandra (O.S.) *(cont'd)*

Y'know, I'm really glad I asked you to dinner.

Frasier

Oh, so am I.

Cassandra (O.S.)

You may not believe this, but I almost chickened out at the last minute. It just goes to show, it's always better to take the risk. I mean, so you say no. I'm an adult, what's a little embarrassment.

Frasier

I couldn't agree more.

Frasier *is just stepping out of his trousers, when . . .*

Cassandra (O.S.)

Did you find the slippers?

Frasier

What?

Cassandra (O.S.)

In the closet. You stepped in that puddle after dinner, I figured you might want to get out of those wet socks. I mean, it's up to you – I know some people feel funny about taking their shoes off in someone else's room.

Frasier *scrambles frantically to put his clothes back on.*

Cassandra (O.S.) *(cont'd)*

My gosh, it's really starting to come down out there. You know what I'm thinking?

Frasier

No, I truly don't.

Cassandra (O.S.)

You are coming back for breakfast anyway. Why don't you stay the night?

Frasier

Well, ah . . . All right.

Cassandra *enters.*

Cassandra

It's funny, when I got up this morning, I never imagined you and I would end up doing this tonight.

Frasier

You know, when you say "doing this," you of course mean . . .

She gets into bed.

Cassandra

Spending the night together. Oh, you're going to love this bed. It's so comfortable.

Frasier

Oh, good.

Frasier *quickly disrobes.*

Cassandra

Would you mind turning off the lights?

Frasier

No, not at all.

Frasier *clicks off the lights and gets into bed. It is very dark.*

Frasier *(cont'd)*

Ah, this is nice. *(then)* You know, Cassandra, I have to make a confession. I'm sure you'll find this amusing – especially seeing where we've ended up. All night, I've been desperately trying to figure out if we were on a romantic date or a business date. Isn't that silly? But I guess all's well that ends well. So, let the games begin.

There is the unmistakable sound of snoring.

Frasier *(cont'd)*

Cassandra . . . Cassandra?

But **Frasier's** *only reply is more snoring. And we:*
FADE OUT.

End of Act Two

ACT THREE

Scene E

FADE IN:
INT. RESTAURANT – VALENTINE'S DAY – NIGHT/1
Martin, Daphne, Maître d', Waiter
Martin *and* **Daphne** *are waiting to be seated at a restaurant.*

Daphne

You know, there was really no need to do this. I would've been perfectly happy going to the movies by myself.

Martin

Come on, I couldn't have you sitting alone in some dusty old theater on Valentine's Day. Now, I want you to know that tonight's on me. You order anything you like. Cost is no object. This night only comes around once a year.

Daphne

This is all very nice, but Valentine's Day really doesn't mean that much to me.

Martin

In that case, they got a nice chicken cordon bleu for $8.95. But you gotta order it in the next seven minutes.

The hostess signals that their table is ready and leads them to it. As they cross through the crowded room . . .

Martin *(cont'd)*

Y'know, I'm impressed with you, Daph. A lot of women get to the point where they can't stand being alone on any night, let alone Valentine's Day. But you got a good head on your shoulders. Here let me take your coat.

They get to their table. **Martin** *takes* **Daphne's** *coat.*

Daphne

No, no, I'll keep it.

Martin

It's better to hang it up. I noticed a rack over there.

Daphne

So did I, and it's on the coat check girl.

Martin *grabs their coats and heads off to the coat check as the* **Maître d'** *comes over.*

Maître d'

Happy Valentine's Day, and welcome to Russano's.

Daphne

Thank you.

Maître d'

The waiter will be by to take your drink order when your husband gets back.

Daphne

Oh, he's not my husband. I don't have a –

But the **Maître d'** *is gone.* **Daphne** *looks around the restaurant. The mood is intimate. Couples talk softly, some holding hands.* **Daphne** *takes on a reflective look.* **Martin** *returns.*

Martin

I wish there was something else I could check. Besides my blood pressure. *(laughs at his joke, then)* Hey, I noticed a couple over there splitting a real beaut of a steak. *(off menu)* Here it is – "T for Two. A thirty-ounce T-bone. Perfect for lovers or just plain steak lovers." What do you think, Daph?

Daphne *begins to cry.*

Martin *(cont'd)*
Look if you'd rather have the lamb chops . . .

Daphne
Oh, it's not the food, it's my whole life.

Martin
What happened?

Daphne
Look around you, nothing but couples in love. It's never going to be me. I'm just going to wind up a dried-up old maid in a quilted robe with a smelly, deaf cat on my lap.

Martin
I thought you said you were okay with that.

Daphne *cries a little louder.* **Martin** *looks around nervously.*

Martin *(cont'd)*
Now, Daph, come on. There's no need to get all upset.

Daphne *tries to pull herself together.*

Daphne
I'm sorry. I don't know what came over me.

Martin
That's all right. It's all over now.

Daphne
I haven't cried like that since, well . . . New Year's Eve.

She starts crying again.

Martin
Aw, Daph, you'll find someone. You have a lot of great qualities, and don't you ever doubt that.

Daphne
Thank you, Mr. Crane. I know it's not easy for you to say these sorts of things.

Martin
That's okay. *(then)* So, ready to order?

Daphne
What kind of qualities?

Martin
Uh, you know . . . you're smart . . . nice looking . . . fun to be with.

(then) So, you going with the soup or the salad?

Daphne

You really think I'm nice looking?

Martin

Well, sure.

Daphne *(tearing up)*

That's so sweet of you. I'm getting emotional again.

Martin

Ah, jeez.

Daphne

Oh, don't worry. I'm fine. Let's change the subject.

Martin

Fine. Now take a sip of water and we'll start this evening all over again.

Daphne

Nice looking how?

Martin

Well, pretty, and tall, and you take care of your hair . . . You know, attractive. What do you want from me?

Daphne

Sorry, I just don't hear this sort of thing much these days.

Martin

Well, you're just in a slump. That's all.

The **Waiter** *approaches.*

Martin *(cont'd)*

If you ask me, you're a pretty great catch.

Waiter

It's not my place to say so, Miss, but I think your father's right. You're a very attractive woman.

The **Waiter** *moves off.*

Daphne

Well, how about that? That's a nice little ego boost.

Martin

Yeah.

Daphne

I feel so silly all of a sudden, getting upset out of nowhere like that.

Well, I feel better now. *(then)* Ready to share a nice steak?

Martin

What the hell made him say that – "your father"?

Daphne

What?

Martin

Why'd he assume that I was your father? There are plenty of guys my age who go out with women like you. What's he saying, I could never attract someone young and pretty?

Daphne

Oh, thank you, Mr. Crane.

Martin

Does this all have to be about you?

Daphne

Oh for heaven's sake, you're a very attractive man with many wonderful qualities.

Martin

Yeah, I know, I know. Let's just order.

They both start looking at their menus. After a beat:

Martin *(cont'd)*

Like what?

Daphne

Oh, I don't know. The veal piccata or –

Martin

Not that.

Daphne

I know. Well, let's see, you're honest, gentle, kind, you have a good sense of humor. Still have all your hair and I believe all your teeth. *(off Martin's look)* Now, come on, where's that sense of humor? *(then)* And most of all, you're good company. I enjoy living with you.

Martin

Thank you, Daphne. I like living with you too.

Daphne

Thank you.

They again start reading their menus. After a beat.

Daphne *(cont'd)*

So, why do you like living with me?

Martin

Oh for God's sake, let's just both agree to cut this out.

Daphne

All right, I'm wonderful, you're wonderful. *(then)* You know, it's funny when I think about the two of us. Sure, we have our little fights, but for the most part we get along so well together. And when I think about how I enjoy looking after you and how you always cheer me up when I'm blue, it's sorta like you're my –

Martin

What?

Daphne

No, it might sound funny to say it.

Martin

Go on, you can say it.

Daphne

All right. It's sort of like you're my pet.

Martin

What?

Daphne

In a good sense. Like you and Eddie.

Martin

I'm not crazy about this comparison.

Daphne

Well, I take you for walks. I give you your dinner.

Martin

I only wish I ate as well as Eddie.

As the bickering continues, "Are you complaining about my cooking?" "Why'd you really think I wanted to go out tonight?" "I'm going to feed you real dog food one of these days, and we'll see how you like it," "It'll probably be a nice change of pace," "You don't think I'd really do it, but I will," etc. We . . .
FADE OUT.

End of Act Three

About *Frasier*'s Creators/Executive Producers

DAVID ANGELL, PETER CASEY, and DAVID LEE are the creators/executive producers of the hit comedy series *Frasier*, a Grub Street Production in association with Paramount Network Television for NBC-TV. The team joined forces as *Cheers* supervising producers/writers in 1985. Among them, they have amassed thirty-four Emmy Award nominations and received twenty-one Emmy Awards for *Frasier* and for *Cheers*.

DAVID ANGELL, a native of West Barrington, Rhode Island, and a graduate of Providence College, moved to Los Angeles in 1977 to pursue his career as a scriptwriter. He joined the *Cheers* staff in 1983 as a staff writer.

PETER CASEY, a San Francisco native, graduated from San Francisco State University in 1975. Shortly thereafter, he moved to Los Angeles, met David Lee, and they began writing as a team, finally joining the staff of *The Jeffersons* in 1979. During their six-year tenure, they served as writers, story editors, and finally, producers.

DAVID LEE, a native of Claremont, California, is a 1972 graduate of the University of the Redlands, majoring in music theory and theatre. He and Casey met while working as proofreaders and typists at a script-mimeo company.

CHRISTOPHER LLOYD is the executive producer/showrunner of *Frasier*. For fourteen years a comedy writer/producer, he previously worked on *The Golden Girls* for which he received two Emmy Awards in the category of Best Comedy Series. Afterward, he produced two seasons of *Down Home* before joining *Wings* as a producer. From there he moved to *Frasier*, for which he has served as a writer/executive producer since its inception. He is the recipient of five Emmy Awards in this capacity. Lloyd is a native of New York and a 1982 graduate of Yale University.